THE
ANCESTORS WITHIN

REVEAL AND HEAL THE ANCIENT MEMORIES YOU CARRY

AMY GILLESPIE DOUGHERTY

FEATURING: REV. ASHERAH ALLEN, ARIELLE, DR. ALLISON BROWN, DEENA CHESTER,
TANYA L. COLUCCI, CAROL DUTTON, M.J. GRAVES, ROBIN IVY HAYWOOD, JONIANNE JEANNETTE,
JACQUELINE M KANE, JAMES KEALIIPIILANI KAWAINUI, ELIZABETH R KIPP, SONDRA LAMBERT,
RIKA RIVKA MARKEL, LISA A. NEWTON, JEN PICENO, DR. AHRIANA PLATTEN,
CRYSTAL RASMUSSEN, MARCIA COLVER REICHERT, JEANNE RUCZHAK-ECKMAN,
NOAH SMITH, MYRNA Y. TRIANO, MICHELLE TROUPE, PHOENIX TRUEBLOOD

WAKANDA

Wakanda is an expression of the powers of the Great Spirit that moves through all life. The center circle is like the Sun and Moon seed that flowers in every aspect of life. The blue is the masculine or Sky Father, the red is the feminine or Mother Earth. The blue curving out from the center is life giving water and the red angular lines from the center are life taking fire. Together they are transformative powers to help blossom the Spirit in the physical. The spiral is the enlightenment journey that all souls take in life. The green is the growing knowledge, and the gold is the harvest of wisdom. The purple body with hands up is the soul surrendering to Creator and becoming balanced and in harmony. The three parts inside the body are the Native trinity: Mother, Father and all physical life birthed from the two. The deep purple around the edges, like the Earth and her atmosphere, are the womb of the spirit giving birth to all life on her back.

I have been creating art all of my life. But it wasn't until I began seeking spiritually that I found inspiration to share my journey of life through painting. I believe that artists of all kinds are scouts of the human spirit. I feel that it is our responsibility to delve deep within ourselves into the greater potential of who we are and then share that with whatever talents we are gifted with. Once, at a gathering of Native elders and youth, a spiritual leader of the Northern Cheyenne people sitting across from me stated in a very powerful way that, "To be a true Indian, you have to know who you are and then give that back to the people."

Kevin Chasing Wolf Hutchins
https://chasingwolfcreations.com/

TABLE OF CONTENTS

INTRODUCTION | I

CHAPTER 1

THE ADOPTEE'S DREAM | 1

Recognizing Your Ancestors in a "Whole" New Way

By Amy Gillespie Dougherty,
Founder of Irigenics™ Ancestral Eye Reading

CHAPTER 2

THE SECRETS OF THE STONES | 11

How to Channel Your Ancestors Through Crystals

By Melissa Jolly Graves

CHAPTER 3

BRIDGING THE WORLDS | 20

Chakra Weaving for Healing Ancestral Ties

By Asherah Allen, SC-C, Lic., Ac., L.M.T.

CHAPTER 4

ANCESTORS AND AUTISM | 29
Real Thoughts From Your Past

By Noah Smith

CHAPTER 5

PLANTING A FAMILY TREE
FROM THE LAND OF MY FATHERS | 36
Digging Through the Past
and Preserving it for the Future

By Sondra Lambert, CHT

CHAPTER 6

HEARING MY GRANDMOTHER | 46
How to Use Affirmations to
Bridge Communication to Your Ancestors

By Lisa A. Newton, M.Ed.

CHAPTER 7

CUTTING THE CORD | 54
Release Ancestral Karma through Spiritual Hypnosis

By Allison Brown, EdD

CHAPTER 8

UNLOCK YOUR ANCESTRAL STORY | 63
Take Charge of YOUR Life

By Jacqueline Kane, R.T., LMT, EFT, BP

CHAPTER 9

HEAR THE WHISPERS OF YOUR ANCESTORS | 73
Connect and Embrace the Power of Your Gifts and Talents

By Deena Chester, A.S., B.A., M.C.S, C.Ht

CHAPTER 10

RAPTURE JOURNALING | 81
Surviving Your Ancestral Story:
Recognizing the Opportunity for Change

By Carol Dutton,
Subtle Energy Medicine Specialist, and Reiki Master

CHAPTER 11

SHAMANIC JOURNEYING | 90
Breaking Limiting Patterns
by Connecting With Our Ancestral Guides

By Tanya L. Colucci, M.S., LMT

CHAPTER 12

THE WOVEN WEB | 100
Discovering and Removing Energy Strings

By Marcia Colver Reichert, CHT, LMT, NMT, Shaman

CHAPTER 13

THE HEART SPACE | 108
The Portal to Ancestral Healing

By Michelle Troupe

CHAPTER 14

RECONNECTING THE BROKEN BONDS AND HONORING OUR ANCESTORS | 115
Life-Changing Healing Practices

By Phoenix Trueblood,
Shamanic Practitioner, Granddaughter of Native Elder

CHAPTER 15

BECOMING A TRANSITIONAL CHARACTER | 124
Leverage Your Ancestral Gifts to Heal Transgenerational Trauma

By Elizabeth R Kipp,
Ancestral Clearing® Practitioner

CHAPTER 16

WHEN THE HOMELAND CALLS | 133
Traveling to Your Ancestral Roots

By Dr. Ahriana Platten, Ph.D.

CHAPTER 17

FINDING YOUR WAY THROUGH ANCESTRAL FIRE | 141
How Love Heals

By Robin Ivy Haywood

CHAPTER 18

BUILDING A RELATIONSHIP
WITH YOUR ANCESTORS | 147

Connecting with the Power of your
Ancient Bloodline to Heal Generational Trauma

By Crystal Rasmussen
Generational Healing® Teacher & Spiritual Guide

CHAPTER 19

LETTING GO | 157

The Collective Consultation Approach
to Communicating with Ancestors

By Arielle,
Spiritual Medium

CHAPTER 20

ANCESTRAL HEALING THROUGH GENEALOGY | 165

Find and Recognize Repetitive Familial Patterns

By Jeanne Ruczhak-Eckman

CHAPTER 21

TURNING CURSES INTO BLESSINGS | 174

Discovering and Embracing the
Gems Our Ancestors Are Giving Us

By Rika Rivka Markel

CHAPTER 22

CLEARING ANCESTRAL TRAUMA | 182

Letting go of the Cycle of Pain and Suffering

By James Kealiipiilani Kawainui,
Native Hawaiian Healer, Spiritual Counselor, Kahu

CHAPTER 23

ANCESTRAL POWER: | 191

Claim Your Sacred Wisdom and Magic

By Jen Piceno, Shamanic Priestess, Energy Medicine Practitioner,
ORDM, RMT, LMT, THP

CHAPTER 24

CONNECTING THROUGH HEART | 201

Use Universal Love to Travel Time/Space,
Access Ancestors, and Shift Perspective

By Jonianne Jeannette, CMT

CHAPTER 25

OUR ANCESTORS THE WAYSHOWERS | 210

Creating Flow by Making Life-Changing Decisions with Ease

By Myrna Y. Triano,
LMT, CST, Integrated Energy Therapy ®Master/Teacher

OUR CAST OF AUTHORS, ARTISTS, AND ONLINE TOOLS | 218

25 online tools and access points to reveal
and heal the ancient memories you carry

CLOSING CHAPTER | 222

MY PERSONAL ACKNOWLEDGEMENTS | 224

AN OVERFLOW OF GRATITUDE AND GRACE | 226

ABOUT THE AUTHOR | 229

In every moment of your life
Forever the world is changed
Because you are here

Your ancestors have waited your whole life for THIS moment!

DEDICATION

This book is dedicated to all people who seek their origin. It's for those who have wondered: *Who am I? Where do I come from? Why does this pattern keep repeating itself in my life?* It's for those who have poured over records, maps, newspapers, and microfiche, traveled the world, tested their DNA, watched documentaries, read books, and stared into the mirror in search of themselves.

Today's your day, and—perhaps more importantly—today is the day your ancestors have waited for your whole life. Today's the day you discover your ancestors are alive within you: their memories, unresolved traumas, outcries, interests, skills, and abilities.

Today's the day you hold in your hands the work of twenty-five author-experts who have come together to share ancestry-related experiences, studies, and tools, clearing the mist between you and your lost family members.

We hope you find in this book a whole new way to unravel the mystery of you, and we believe your ancestors are rejoicing today, the day they've been waiting for.

INTRODUCTION

As I penned yet another title for this book, I felt a rising dread. *I don't even want to send this. She won't like it. It won't be good enough.*

My eyes grew wide in realization. *There it is! An ancestral touch-point.* I was caught in an ancestral pattern in my current experience that was really the reflection of trauma in the life of my ancestors—much more trauma than I was currently experiencing.

I chuckled. *I know this one—3:30, right eye.* The ancestral pattern I was repeating revealed itself in my eyes—*No matter what I do, it won't be good enough for that woman!*

I evaluated my options and reached for my cell phone as my inner voice cautioned, *don't engage the beast, Amy.* I'd said it so many times to my clients, and now I was saying it to myself, recognizing that any emotional response was about my inner beast and not the current situation or my publisher.

I took my own advice, drew a deep breath, and texted, "Can we let the title go for today? I want to sleep on it."

In barely a minute, my phone pinged my publisher's response, "Sure."

Yes! I had found another 2021 workaround to escape my ancestor's age-old pattern.

Though it was simple, I knew the weight and value of what I'd just done. I'd informed my cells, my mind, and my spirit that I was evolving. My personal, genetic evolution was well underway, as was the evolution of my soul. *This pattern is NOT a threat anymore. The technology of 2021 has fixed it.*

Shrugging my shoulders, I released the tension I'd been feeling about my title. My mind drifted back to the book's beginning, just ten days earlier.

A colleague in my mastermind group had thrown down the gauntlet. "What is your vision? Imagine what you love to do, which is the thing the world wants to see you succeed at."

My morning meditation took on a new stroke as I decided to rise to the challenge, this time drawing my vision.

I've created many vision boards and engaged in many visual meditations over the years. I've even written an entire (unpublished) book about how to determine your life's purpose. Now I needed a breakthrough, and I felt like automatic drawing might bring it about.

On January 6, at 6:30 a.m., I pulled out my sketchbook and created a heart map, a tool I learned a few years earlier. Pulling out my colored pencils, heart by heart, my vision evolved:

Discover your ancestors

Engage your ancestors

Embrace your ancestors

Honor your ancestors

Understand your ancestors

Connect your ancestral clues

Recognize your ancestors

The pattern I played out (or, more accurately, short-circuited) that morning was an ancestral touch-point, with the unknowing participation of my publisher. It was a repeat pattern in which I encounter a matriarch-type figure who I just couldn't please. This time, I not only recognized that I stumbled into this pattern many times in my life, but I also followed my entire journey to the present moment and transformed my response.

I know from experience that knowing your ancestors—and understanding just how deeply their experiences show up in your current life—is paramount to resolving them. They are also a tool for your evolution.

I continued my heart-map, all the while tamping down the inner voice of self-doubt.

How will my vision reach people? I drew the hearts as the answers came to me: books, meditations, summits, and podcasts.

Who will my vision serve? I drew a heart: Those seeking themselves, especially youth, at-risk teens, foster children, adoptees, and those who feel unloved, misunderstood, unwanted, labeled, or weird.

How will my vision reach them? A big red double heart: Through those who work with underserved families and children, teachers, those who counsel and do family placements, and those who bring self-discovery tools to their clients.

The inner voice of self-doubt crept in, despite my efforts. *Who are you to do this? There are so many who have worked with ancestral patterns, epigenetics, and dynamics so much longer than you.*

I argued my qualifications to myself. *I'm adopted! I came to this life unable to know, with a burning* need *to know—and I found my answers! I connected ancestral clues and found answers that have been confirmed beyond a doubt.*

It was true. My ancestral studies had unlocked a treasure trove of inexplicable synchronicities related to my genetic family and even my adopted family. I was amazed many times before these occurrences became normal, almost expected.

I continued to argue my point. *The story of my journey for inner truth will help people who don't know their origin. It will help those who think they will never know who they are.*

A wave of emotion came over me as my body recalled that feeling, *I don't belong here! I don't fit in! Where did I come from?!* My eyes filled with tears, but I pursed my lips and persisted in my vision. At the bottom of my heart map, I wrote:

People of the world will seek connection with, and come to understand, their ancestral gifts, talents, wisdom, and unresolved traumas so that they may reveal and unleash their own inner power and potential.

That's it! The first book must be about epigenetics and repeat patterns, so people can understand why it's so important to recognize your ancestors in your current life. I made a note in the margin.

From there, things happened very quickly. Just six hours later, I was under contract for this book, and four days after that, we started discussing a second edition. In the same timeframe, there was a discussion of an ancestral summit and bringing together 101 voices and perspectives of recognizing, engaging, and embracing your ancestors with 101 tools of discovery, connection, and celebration. The vision had taken on a life of its own, propelled forward by the Divine embrace of our universe.

Then, over just three weeks, twenty-four amazing authors, healers, genealogists, and teachers came together to create this first book for you. As things moved quickly and smoothly forward, I felt I landed on "the thing the world wants to see me succeed at."

Now is the time to bring our ancestral connections to the forefront.

Your ancestors have waited your whole life for THIS moment.

Turn the page.

SPECIAL NOTE
TO THE READER
About the Healing Crisis

Before you dive into the following pages, there's something I'd like you to understand. In the healing world, we call this "the healing crisis."

The healing crisis happens when an old pattern, injury, pain, or trauma comes back into our awareness to be healed, released, or resolved. The arrival of such energy can cause a temporary worsening of symptoms—the healing crisis.

The healing crisis can be worsened when met with resistance (in the form of thoughts, sensations, feelings, and emotions). This resistance is a survival mechanism. Our deep brains love the status quo because it has kept us alive so far, and that's the brain's number one concern: keeping us alive. Even if we completely understand that the status quo *must* be threatened for our evolution, our brains present resistance to this change.

I encourage you to reflect on your past, habitual reactions to healing opportunities. Sometimes the thing that causes the greatest resistance also presents the biggest opportunity for healing. Often the past words, ideas, practices, and conversations that trouble us and repel us the most are the very things we should consider.

The healing crisis and our resistance to it present an opportunity to go a layer deeper. They are doors to release and relief, but sometimes in the middle, it feels so bad you think you might die. Please know that we (author-healer-experts) *get it*. And we're here for you.

Skilled healers recognize a healing crisis and assist their clients with tools such as dialoguing, energy work, hands-on practices and modalities, and mindset and awareness coaching. Many of those services can't be offered from here. Still, by purchasing this book, you can gain access to a very special Facebook group called The Ancestors Within Community (https://Facebook.com/groups/ancestorswithin). Many of our author experts are hanging out to answer questions and provide live training.

We hope you'll take advantage of this incredible benefit—especially if you're stuck or have questions about what you're feeling. You're not alone. We're here to help you. We welcome your questions and promise to honor your concerns. This group will become a safe space to do the work of healing.

See you there!

DISCLAIMERS:

This book offers self-discovery and health information that is intended for educational purposes only. You should not rely on this information as a substitute for, nor does it replace professional medical advice, diagnosis, or physical or mental health treatment. If you have any concerns or questions about your health, you should always consult with a physician or other healthcare professional. Do not disregard, avoid, or delay obtaining medical or health-related treatment or advice from your healthcare professional because of anything you read here. The use of any information provided in this book is solely at your own risk.

Ongoing medical, epigenetic, and DNA research and development are sure to shed additional light on the subjects discussed in this book. We cannot guarantee that this information will remain forever current, and we encourage you to reach out to us with questions or to perform your own research.

Because this book is about ancestry, and sometimes DNA and epigenetics, it contains numerous uses of gender-related pronouns and words related to familial roles, such as *he, she, mother,* and *father.* Furthermore, the use of these words generally assumes a connection to biological gender.

However, despite this historical use of these words, we do not intend to imply that we believe one's self-identified gender always aligns with the Xs and Ys of DNA or socially defined roles. We understand that it does not. Furthermore, we recognize that terms related to gender are evolving even as we write. Perhaps, adjustments will be made to our use of traditionally gender-related vocabulary in the future, and we'll address that in subsequent books.

In the meantime, we want you to know that all people are welcome to read and embrace *The Ancestors Within*. Indeed, we hope that it will help you and every reader to (as we say in the subtitle) *Reveal and Heal the Ancient Memories You Carry*.

Would you like to meet the authors and learn more about their amazing perspectives? Would you like to be first to know about the next *The Ancestors Within* book and new ways to discover more amazing ancestral connections?

Please join The Ancestors Within Community on Facebook today:

https://www.facebook.com/groups/ancestorswithin

IRIGENICS
ANCESTRAL EYE READING

If you'd like to train in how to do Irigenics™ Ancestral Eye Reading, to help your clients discover and engage their ancestors and their ancestral patterns, please visit:

http://www.irigenics.com/training

CHAPTER 1

THE ADOPTEE'S DREAM

Recognizing Your Ancestors
in a "Whole" New Way

AMY GILLESPIE DOUGHERTY, FOUNDER OF
IRIGENICS™ ANCESTRAL EYE READING

MY STORY

If you've ever doubted your personal power, consider for a moment the unbroken line of ancestors who came before you. If there were any break in your line of DNA—any ancestor who died before creating another life—you wouldn't be here.

That line goes back for *thousands* of years. Even if you're an identical twin, you are the only person connected to your specific ancestors. You are their hope for greatness!

Your ancestors have waited your whole life for THIS moment! This is even more true if you were adopted or felt blocked from your ancestral information. The true essence of your ancestry lives safe and secure inside of you. You are the treasure chest.

Ancestral gifts, education, training, oaths, intentions, physical attributes, and traumatic experiences that were your ancestors' are woven in your epigenetics. You can take a DNA test to get a pretty clear image of your family's geographic and ethnic background (six to eight generations back).

As an adoptee growing up in rural America, I coveted the lives of my cousins who came from big families of nine and ten children. It was easy to see their similarities in voice, mannerisms, looks, talents, and how they did things. After years of working with ancestral clues, I know the ones who didn't seem to *fit in* were simply threaded back to earlier ancestors, and their birth order explained those discrepancies.

I wondered what it would be like to sit down to dinner, surrounded by those who looked like me, laughed like me, felt insecure like me.

At the same time, I contemplated, *how in the world does anyone think they would get away with placing a child for adoption? They look just like their siblings and cousins; they talk like them, they move like them. I think it's just a matter of crossing paths with those that share your lineage.*

I could never have imagined how true my thoughts as a nine-year-old girl actually were.

As soon as my birthmother discovered she was pregnant, she decided to place me for adoption. When I was born, I was quickly placed in a permanent home of wonderful people who didn't look anything like me.

I met my birthmother when I was 19, long before I knew anything about ancestral eye reading. We quickly identified our many shared traits and interests, including that my first corporate job had been for the same company, in the same office that she'd worked at, and that we'd even sat at the same desk. Crazy, right?

Imagine this sort of thing has happened to you (even if you weren't adopted, this incident could have been with a cousin, a great-grandparent, etc.). You just haven't connected the information yet.

Things were very different with my birthfather. We didn't meet until I was 54, long after I'd identified ancestral patterns that were distinctly validated once we started sharing notes about our lives.

I knew he was the son of a doctor and a librarian, so when he accepted my invitation to meet for the first time at the International New Age Trade Show, I was a bit nervous. I had finally achieved my little-girl-dream-come-true of being an exhibitor at INATS and was receiving an International COVR (Coalition Of Visionary Resources) award the next night.

As we sat in the hotel café, face-to-face for the first time, he held up his hands with a grin, "Give me fingerprints!" I pointed to my eyes, "Give me eyeballs!" We laughed and settled into comfortable banter.

Huh! I got HIS "carrying" radio voice.

Soon, we discovered similarities way beyond the physical, including interests, talents, travels, careers, traumas, and early-life visions. Believe it or not, my husband and I bought a farm in Virginia that had the same name (according to county plot books) as my paternal ancestor's castle in Scotland.

By the time I met him, I had developed a system of profiling ancestral information and impressions from the eyes. I believe this experience can be impactful for any of us, and I *know* it can be life-changing for adoptees. It allows them to find genetic clues inside themselves.

My birthfather was involved in developing fingerprint software to profile identity information. Our shared affinity for connection and patterns was likely something his father had used as a doctor, and my maternal grandfather had used designing stained glass windows.

I was blown away when he asked to see my Irigenics™ Ancestral Eye Reading exhibit! My fears were released when we walked past the U.S. Games display, and he asked, "Is Tarot coming back in?"

What?! I got my metaphysical interests from my FATHER!?"

But, of course. Metaphysics is just another aspect of clues, connections, mysteries, and patterns, my inherent gift.

There was no mistake that my birthfather and I played some kind of magnetic board game of life since my birth. He drove past my homes in Minnesota, Colorado, and Virginia. He attended college in the town where we went to do our "shopping," and we may even have thrown our pennies into the same wishing well at Musicland in the mall.

My jaw was left hanging at Christmas when my new mother-in-law had Mr. and Mrs. Santa Claus set out, wearing the "Gordon plaid" of my paternal birth family.

Who even owns a green-plaid Santa?

The clues of my genetic inheritance were always within me. They were playing themselves out in my adopted home and my life from the time of my birth. I'm exactly who I was born to become. I had only to look at my own life experiences to find validation.

Now let's dig into yours.

THE TOOL

(YOUR ANCESTRAL CONNECTIONS)
www.amygillespie.com/resources

Whether we look at those "beyond chance" clues as a board game or a treasure map, they're a series of clues that may not appear to tally up to the origin of you.

Yet, my experience over the past eleven years (and meeting my genetic family as an adult) has shown me time and again that our life experiences offer several clues to our ancestral origin, like a great treasure map that leads us back to ourselves.

EPIGENETICS REVEALED THROUGH REPEAT RESPONSES TO SITUATIONS

Our ancestors' repeat thoughts and words come through us via generations of epigenetic imprinting. Often, we experience this imprinting as *intuition*. These are our responses to a trigger. While one person screams, "You Never Listen to ME!" another says, "Oh, they never listen to me anyway." Same situation—totally different response.

Epigenetics has been researched in animals for decades; the DNA and instinctual response to a situation or threat. It's a magnificent evolutionary system that evaluates whether specific variables continue to pose a threat to our genetic line (creating drama or trauma).

In people, however, it's more difficult to study because it isn't always an action. The response can be thoughts, words, and feelings, which don't fit clearly into a study but make great puzzle pieces for our tool.

In Irigenics™ Ancestral Eye Reading, I use your eye photographs as your treasure map. While the map doesn't tell me your ancestors' nationality or names, it does tell me which triggers are going to come up in your life for resolving (escape, identity, religious oppression, gift for expression, affinity for athletics, and more).

Still, I can't read the eyes of the entire world, so let's take a look at how your ancestors show up in your life.

Like a jigsaw puzzle, you can enjoy this activity over many evenings. You can also do it as a "deep dive" weekend retreat. Read through this entire exercise before beginning.

You will find detailed instructions, PDFs, Treasure Maps, Ancestral Labyrinths, and timeline links at www.amygillespie.com/resources

If you don't have online access and want to do this on your own, you may take a long roll of paper and create a timeline of the experiences of your life.

DNA TESTING

DNA testing is widely available and affordable. You can learn which regions of the world your ancestors came from, and some aspects of your health. With certain DNA companies, you can even input your personal information for those who have matching DNA to contact you by email.

- Write down any DNA or genealogy clues you have about who your ancestors were, their careers, locations, talents, quirks, or unique information.

Note: for some of you, this list may be long, in which case, you may want to leave it for last after filling in "your information."

For those who are adopted, you might not know your DNA clues or may just have your test results. You can write your bullets now or leave your DNA clues for the last part of this exercise. Remember, not knowing is also a clue.

YOUR BIRTH STORY

Birth stories are hugely important to an understanding of oneself and one's ancestry. For adoptees like me, birth stories can be a blank void starting and ending with, "Well, I'm adopted! I don't know anything." That isn't true. You know what you were *told* about your birth, and that's a clue.

Most people will find an ancestor (usually within two to four generations) who had a similar experience of their birth story. You can read more about the ancestral echo, which repeats in pregnancy in the chapter I wrote for *The Ultimate Guide to Self-Healing, Volume 4. Chapter 6: Resolving Cellular Memories.* If your birth story lacks detail, consider using this pre-birth and in-utero visualization: https://irigenics.com/guidedexercise/

- Write down any birth story clues of you.

(e.g., "I was adopted through a church, and the records were sealed." "I was raised by my grandmother." Or, "I was sent to boarding school.")

Just so you know, many times, the pattern of abandonment and adoption originated generations ago, when a child had to be placed in hiding for their safety. Sometimes, the parent swore an oath that the child would know the greatness from which they came one day. Thus, that pattern of *"a deep desire to know their origin"* would repeat every couple of generations, waiting for technology to catch up in a way that would reunite the individual with the knowing and pride of "their people."

That day could be today.

EARLY TRAUMAS

The next thing to list is any traumas you endured before age two or three. You won't remember those traumas, as they're stored in your preconscious memory, but they do impact your personality and approach to life. Ask someone older than you who would remember your early life if you experienced any traumas, accidents, or bizarre experiences before you reached age two or three.

You can bet these early traumas reflect similar experiences of your ancestors and are one of the few experiences that create a permanent change in your eyes.

- Write down any early traumas (as they were told to you by adults).

CHILDHOOD GIFTS AND INTERESTS

Next, consider any significant interests, awards, and events from your childhood, up to about age eight.

Did you have a natural love for dancing, music, writing, or animals? Did you excel in sports, sandcastles, tree-forts, or crafting?

In my story, I was proficient at embroidery, crewel, and crochet. My birthmother was a professional knitter and needle pointer. I later discovered our ancestors had been seamstresses and embroiderers. On my paternal side, I dreamed of becoming a zoologist, as my paternal grandfather had.

What did you want to be when you grew up? Did you play doctor, nurse, soldier, or teacher? On my birthfather's side, my biological cousins, who knew nothing of me, had jobs and interests that mirrored my own: pharmaceutical sales, working with eyes, music therapy, genetics, and zoology.

Childhood interests and aspirations reveal inherent gifts (usually around age seven), even if we turned away from those careers for something "more practical"—*especially* if we turned away for something more practical.

- List your childhood interests, talents, games, etc. Note your age for each.

YOUR PHYSICAL BUILD

The way your body is built—your stature—offers clues to your birth order from your genetic father (whether he knows you exist or not: genetics are funny like that).

This connection between birth order and body build was validated for me in 2019 at the Greater Philly Expo Center.

I was walking past a family with three daughters. The oldest was obviously (to me) a second-born daughter who followed a first-born son.

Sensing that the son's absence represented a traumatic experience, I whispered, "Did you lose a son?"

The hint of panic in the mother's voice was unmistakable. "How'd you know that?"

I pointed to the oldest daughter. "It's her body build. She's a perfect second-born daughter after a first-born son. You see, she has that kind of boxy build: square shoulders, narrow hips, and a big rib cage without being busty. Often, these children are all about sports but a bit socially awkward."

The mom laughed, shaking her head, confirming I'd nailed it. "She's all that! We lost our first-born son to health problems at six months of age. The girls don't know."

Their birth order was obvious to me in their body build, energies, and even clothing choice. The youngest had a mystical, healing energy about her, along with the entertainer's twinkle in her eyes. She was a fourth born, not a third, even if she didn't know it.

With a sympathetic voice, I nodded to the girls, "Sometimes this pattern happens when the first child has been a late-stage miscarriage. Perhaps one of your daughters is intended to grow up to do something significant, and there needed to be a missing first-born-boy to *set* the birth order, personality, drive, and interest."

Her husband, who'd been listening intently, reached for her hand, giving her a loving look. "We've felt like there was something much more to this story than we could understand."

I explained, "Missing siblings leave clues within the other children. Even if a child doesn't know a sibling is missing, their bodies will reflect it, and so will their intuition."

Let's be clear that there can only be one first-born (even if they're twins), and they are easy to recognize. First-born boys are slim (bean poles), with their heads in the clouds of engineering, stars, ideas, and innovations. First-born girls are built strong, with significant hips, and determined to save people (mother bears). They usually stop playing and start role-playing by the time they are three.

- List your body build and anything you know about your birth-order from your genetic father. Not knowing is also a clue.

CHARACTERISTIC EXCLAMATIONS AND TRAUMAS

Many of us can identify characteristic exclamations in our personal history.

Early childhood is often when "escape" traumas and patterns first show up. If, for example, you had older siblings who teased you, you might have screamed many times, "Let me Up! Let me Go!" Any repeated, characteristic exclamations, especially from early childhood (up to age eight to ten), have ancestral roots.

When it comes to ancestral recognition, details may vary, but the dynamics match.

Imagine, unbeknownst to you, you had an ancestor in 1857 who got locked in the berth of a ship, unable to see out the window, screaming, "Let me out! Can't you hear me?!" Fast-forward to 2011. You're five years old, and you find yourself locked in a bathroom, screaming, "Let me out! Can't you hear me?!"

The screams and the internal chemical responses are identical.

The dynamics of how you both found yourselves "trapped" are what will match. In short, if it happened to you—it happened to them. For example:

> The door malfunctioned.
>
> You both ignored (or couldn't read) a sign on the door indicating there was a problem.
>
> You both had a sibling holding the door shut from outside while laughing.

The same dynamics play out in different generations, with different players and locations. Thus, our ancestors' identity issues at Ellis Island return as online identity issues, 2020.

Each time you declare or exclaim with emotion, it's as if your ancestor's words are coming through you. Each exclamation presents an opportunity to determine whether the situation is still a threat to your specific genetic line.

In 2020, we can short-circuit most "escape" traumas by simply picking up our cell phone and making a call.

- List your significant exclamations first.
- Then note any trauma attached to the exclamations.
- Then note the dynamics of what was happening that led to the trauma and the exclamation. You'll start to see the pattern.

MONEY, CONTRACTS, AND SIGNATURES

Anytime you observe yourself inexplicably repeating financial patterns or prematurely signing contracts *even though you know better*, you're probably repeating an ancestral pattern.

My Aunt Jane and I were packing my birthmother's home. Jane told the story of my birthmother purchasing La Creuset® bake-ware when she was 18—and how she'd struggled through a second job to pay for it.

I did nearly the exact same thing! When I was 18, I signed a contract for dishes I just *had to have*, but couldn't really afford. It was my first adult experience of a repeat ancestral pattern relating to *signature documents.*

The pattern dynamics were always the same:

Doubt (*Should I sign it?*).

Signing the document, knowing I shouldn't (*I can't afford this! I'm going to regret this!*).

Days of regret (*Why did I sign that?! Why did I let HER talk me into this? Why didn't I wait?)!*

This pattern reflected my ancestors' regrets over signing their names to agreements that cost them greatly, including my birthmother signing papers relinquishing me for adoption.

- List your significant issues with papers, contracts, and signatures (including emails and texts that were sent too soon or to the wrong person).

And, "Oh, so many more."

Please visit the resources for this exercise at
www.amygillespie.com/resources

Chapter 2

THE SECRETS OF THE STONES
How to Channel Your Ancestors Through Crystals

MELISSA JOLLY GRAVES

MY STORY

I remember that day clearly, the day I first felt the power and beauty of the ancestor flow through me.

It was crystal cleaning day. My roommate Mikey and I sat at the rectangle table placed in the middle of the dining room. Laying in the middle of the table between us was a bottle of mineral oil, rags, and my wooden box that held my treasures. The box contained many crystals, stones, fossils, rocks, and artifacts collected from all around the world by friends, family, my husband, and myself.

I was obsessed with collecting these items, but I didn't know why. Every time anyone would go on an adventure, I would ask them to bring me back a stone they found along the way. They had to be found, gifted by nature, not paid for. Each time I received an item, I placed it in my "Crystals of the World" box. I had over 300 items in the box.

I opened the box and poured the contents over half of the table. The stones were all different colors, shapes, and sizes. We spread them out and let them breathe for a few minutes. I prayed that we might have the honor of cleansing the energy. When the time felt right, I picked up the rag, poured mineral oil on it, grabbed my first stone, and polished it. As we cleaned each stone, the colors became more vivid and gave us a unique perspective of the properties each one had. We passed them around to each other as we admired the beauty, differences, textures, and even smells each stone offered.

The more I paid attention to them, the more I could see the auras and the energy around crystals, just as I saw it around people. My hands got warm, my head felt woozy, and my ears rang in a way they hadn't before.

I looked at Mikey, "I feel like I am on drugs or something. I can see the energy of these crystals moving and changing."

Mikey said nothing; he just laughed at me.

"No, I'm serious. My vision is changing, and I can see the crystals breathing and pulsing. Like spring waters, I can honestly see the center of this stone and how each layer springs out of the center and moves to the surface."

"Missy, you just get weirder and weirder," he replied.

I looked down at the stones and thought, *what is wrong with me? Why are my visuals changing? Did I eat or drink something without knowing it? Am I sick?*

Noticing my baffled face, Mikey looked at me and in a loud voice said, "Reiki!"

In a loud voice, I replied, "Reiki!" It was a term we used when strange and energetic things happened around us.

I continued to polish the stones while Mikey started picking them up and looking deeply into them to see if he could see any energy. As he picked up each stone, I saw the energy of the stones travel up his fingers to his arm and then become part of his essence. They completely changed the energy and coding around him.

Normally when I look at people, I can see their energy, aura, shapes, symbols, and colors on their faces and bodies. The energy is in continuous motion, changing color, never still, always rotating. It is a compilation of past and future lives, integrating with the person's current biochemical and electromagnetic field. The best representation of how I see energy on people can be seen on Ink Mapping videos by Oskar and Gaspar.

Prior to that moment, I had only seen that kind of energy on people. I did not see moving energy in the stones, nor did I see the energy exchange between two objects. I could, however, see the energy exchange that occurred when I did Reiki and faith healing on people, and this energy was much like that.

Are the crystals doing Reiki on Mikey? I thought.

"Mikey, do you feel that?" I asked.

"Feel what?"

"The energy traveling up your arm from the crystals?"

"No," he replied.

"Oh," I said sadly.

What is going on with me? I didn't know what to think.

Suddenly, my friends the Angels swooped in. Not the stereotypical kind with two wings and a human face, most people would think about. The kind that changes my vision, completely interrupts the space in the room, and causes ringing in my ears. They have faces of light, animals, and images not seen in this world. The wings are not feathering; they are lights, eyeballs, metal, liquids, or lightning storms that come out from around them. When they speak, I feel it through my entire body, and I have a hard time integrating with my earthly environment.

One angel told me, "Have Mikey pick nine stones and place them to the side. Tell him not to ask questions or tell you anything he's thinking and not to speak until I tell him to." So, I did as I was told. Mikey, knowing my connection with the angels, did as he was told.

He picked the stones and placed them to the side. The angels then told me, "Have him put his hands together in a cupping position like he's holding water and place the stones in his hands. Tell him to shake the stones to intertwine the energies, then roll them onto the table, just as he would during a game of dice. He did.

Laying in front of me were nine stones I didn't know what to do with. The angels left, and the room went silent as I looked at the stones. All the colors and textures on the stones started moving, breathing, and swirling energy. I watched flashes of light spur out of the stones and land behind and around Mikey. I looked up from the stones and there stood multiple spirits, enough to fill up the dining room we were sitting in. The sound of ringing in my ears changed from high-pitched to lower-pitched, more concentrated than I was used to with the angels. I looked back down at the stones, and my eyes became fixated. I couldn't look up or away; they just stared further and further into the stones. The stones became more animated as the energy grew. I started hearing voices that were not of the angels, Mikey, or myself. It was many voices talking over each other. I couldn't decipher one voice from another. I didn't know these spirits or why they were there. Then, just as the angels do to me, the voices from the outside came into my head and started speaking through my mouth.

I was speaking, but I didn't know what I was saying. They filled my head with so many words, timelines, realities, and colors. My lips were moving as fast as an auctioneer asking for bids. This went on for about ten minutes. Then, just as they came, they left. I immediately stopped talking; I was no longer entranced by the stones, I could no longer hear voices or ringing, and the energy of the stones disappeared. I looked up at Mikey. He was silent. Still, his eyes were big, his mouth open in a relaxed position. We stared into each other's eyes, both of us in shock, not knowing what just happened.

Mikey laughed in shock. "What just happened?" He asked. "I have never told you any of that." "I've told no one."

"I don't know what happened. I don't know what I said," I replied.

What just happened? I thought.

The angels appeared and responded, "You unlocked the DNA of the ancestors."

Unlocked the ancestors? Is that who was talking? I telepathically asked the angels.

"Yes, you found their voices through the stones. Their energy, although no longer on this earth, is still alive in the land."

But how?

"All that has ever lived has left behind physical and spiritual energy and signatures. The physical energy is utilized by the trees, soil, sun, waters, and superficial earth. Whatever is not used in other ways finds its way down to the foundations of the earth, to the stones and crystals. All history is written in stones. The stones hold the DNA of things that lived and walked on the earth, as well as the particles from other planets and stars that helped mold this crystalline place of living. The rocks carry the stories of all energies that have connected with your land of living. When you truly connect to the crystals, it is like tapping into the book of the dead. All their stories come to life and reawaken their energy so they can soulfully connect to you."

Why have I not encountered them before? I asked through my mind.

"You have encountered them many times in your life. They are always with you. Today is the first time you truly acknowledged the energy of the stones. Today you looked not only at the beauty of the stones, but you took the time to appreciate and try to understand it. That opened the windows to the spirits contained within the stones. When you saw the energy and the souls of the stones, you then recognized the ancestors within those stones. They are the record keepers of the Universe. Many stories and spirits are held within the stones. When people pick up the stones, they are not just picking up a rock. They call on the ancestors, and all energies of the Universal energy encased in that stone. The stones are companions and lessons for people when they need the energy. They hold their spirit guides."

Stones are a lesson?

"The stones aren't the lessons; they are the vessels for the lessons. They hold coordinates and contact points for energy and spirits. They are record keepers of energy, history, life, and times." The angels then disappeared.

Mikey and I were shell-shocked. I was not sure what just happened, but I knew I wanted to try it again! Over the next few weeks, I did free crystal readings on anyone I could. Each person replied with the same words and reaction, "spot on." I became a pro at doing crystal readings. The more crystals I connected to, the more ancestors I saw. Each ancestor had a new story and lesson. The ancestors and I became as close as the angels and I were. They joined me in healing sessions; they led me to become a Minister, then a spiritual counselor, Shaman, a scientist, and so much more. The angels faded more and more as the ancestor energy grew.

In 2017 I was one of thirty "Masterminds" across the USA asked to speak at The National Symposium for Holistic Healers held at Harvard University. The conference changed my life. I had to explain how I do energy work and readings in a way science and doctors could understand. I am a normal person who just sees energy, nothing more. Now, I need to explain energy and the ancestors in ways that made sense to masterminds!

Time to step up my game, I thought. And step up the game I did. I explained it so well the metaphysical scientists were impressed. This led me down a huge rabbit hole of researching and learning how to present the information in my head to the outer world. The more I researched, the more affirmation I got that the ancestors were right, and people really resonated with the things I was saying.

So, I come to you, the reader, to share my wisdom, hoping you too can learn how to connect with your ancestors. I feel it's important for each of us to carry this knowledge to start putting the pieces of the past and present back together for all generations and timelines to heal and hold peace within our hearts.

When I speak of the ancestors, I'm speaking of the spiritual family members or spirit guides you have either chosen or gained in your conscious journeys. They are the elders of the spirit world. They have been here since the beginning of time. Many have reincarnated and recycled energy several times. They have been gifted with knowledge to share for all who ask the right questions.

The wisdom they offer only comes to those who will cherish it and share it with generations to come. They hold all the answers to life, history, the spirit world, and how things work. They come to us with only love and guidance; they never scold; all they do is for the greater good of all. They are mothers, fathers, siblings, and grandparents to all the living humans. They act as an inner council circle to help guide you through life. All willing to listen to the ancestors will learn—all who fully trust will be trusted.

Connecting to them is easy once you know how. They are always around waiting for someone to speak to. In fact, they are waiting to connect with you right now!

I must point out there are several ways to connect with your ancestors; in this chapter, we will utilize stones to make a connection.

THE TOOL

Before you begin, take a moment to analyze your body and how it feels. Examine your emotions and well-being. See your energy through your senses such as taste, smell, touch, hearing, temperature, and pain or pressure on your body. Be hyper-aware of your surroundings and your entire entity. Close your eyes and just feel for at least three minutes. Shut the eyesight off and turn the feelings on. Note everything.

This is crucial when you are first starting your journey in acknowledging your ancestors. They are not seen; they are felt or heard. When you connect with the ancestors, you will notice a shift in your internal energy, which will help you know when they are around.

After you have done an energy check on yourself, grab a stone. Do not handle the crystals before you do your body check, as we do not want any connections to begin before you examine your own energy. One stone is good for your first time. You can advance to more later.

Interacting with the stones in any way allows for a quantum particle exchange. Touching the stones leaves oils and dead skin cells, which create a chemical reaction. The energy and frequency of your aura and DNA will activate and connect with certain DNA frequencies within the stone. The otoliths crystals your ears, quantumly connect to the crystals around you. Add all this to your electromagnetic energy, and you have all the tools you need for a great connection.

Know and trust in this information. Pick up any stone that seems to call to you. Hold it in your hand and acknowledge the colors, shapes, patterns, feeling, weight, smell; literally, pay attention to everything about the crystal you can acknowledge. Become entranced. Connect to it and thank it for all the energy and beauty it shows you.

Find the color, texture, shape, or pattern that you admire most about the stone. Focus on one spot that catches your eye. Hold that stare; try not to blink. Stare hard and long. Imagine your soul going into the crystal. Acknowledge any vision, hearing, emotional, or energetic change within you.

Some physical sensations you may experience are feelings of hot, cold, or tingles throughout the body. You may feel a change in the room's density. Emotional changes may have you overwhelmed with love, joy, or even sorrow when an ancestor enters the room. You may hear a quiet whisper from across the room.

Do not fear; if you fear, the ancestors will back off. They are here to love and be loved. If they sense fear, they will not show themselves.

Once the connection has been made, you need to acknowledge it. Grab that stone and clench your fist around it. Place the fist and stone over your heart chakra in the middle of your chest or on your forehead over your third eye. Radiate love and compassion from your soul to the rest of the world. Ask the Creator for permission to speak to the ancestors. Skipping this step may lead to unwanted guests. If you ask Creator first, you get permission, protection, and the right guides, which helps your spiritual connection.

Then wait, be patient, and be silent. Sometimes a connection takes time. When the connection is made, and the ancestors have entered, your heart and head will guide the conversation through empathy. Take mental notes of what they say and write them down when you are finished with your session. The next step in completing the cycle of healing is affirming their story. You can do this by researching, talking to others about what they said, and sharing the advice of the ancestors with those who ask for it.

Of course, one chapter in a book is not enough information, so I would like to offer you a complimentary tutorial video on the fundamentals of connection with your ancestors. You can find this at https://www.euphoricsource.com/resources

Remember, knowledge is only knowledge if kept to yourself. We can only obtain wisdom when the knowledge is shared.

Melissa Jolly Graves is a one-of-a-kind associative thinker who has the ability to visibly see and feel energy. In 1979 she was born healer, but she didn't start her journey until 2006, when she became an LPN. She practiced several fields to include Behavioral Health, TCU, Alzheimer's, Mental Health, Senior Care, and Chemical Dependency. While working for Hazelden, she was called to do a different type of healing.

Through meditation, prayer, and the guidance of her Angels and teachers, Melissa was taught how to do faith healing. She furthered her training in energy healing with schooling. In 2012 she started the study of Reiki. In 2015 she became a Reiki Master and teacher. From there, she went on to train in the arts of Qigong, Kundalini, Shamanism, DNA healings, genetic modification, source coding, spiritual counseling, and quantum and frequency healing, and has had the privilege to work with native healers. Currently, she practices 24 healing modalities.

In 2015 Melissa opened the doors to her business, Euphoric Source, which has received many awards since opening its doors. In 2016 Melissa was one of the thirty people in the United States asked to speak at the National Symposium for Holistic Arts Practitioners held at Harvard University. From 2016-2018 she hosted her own radio show, called Euphoria Radio, where she learned how to communicate with people about her abilities. Soon after that Melissa was on Local Insider TV for being one of the most effective healers in the state of Minnesota. From 2017-2019 she was busy working in many temples, hosting ceremonies and spiritual events. Currently Melissa is healing, teaching, advising, hosting spiritual events, writing her books, doing a documentary, running her business and research lab, being a mom and wife, and living life to the fullest. www.euphoricsource.com/resources

Chapter 3

BRIDGING THE WORLDS
Chakra Weaving for Healing Ancestral Ties

ASHERAH ALLEN, SC-C, LIC., AC., L.M.T.

MY STORY

I am hurried leaving work when the phone rings. It's my older sister. She never calls in the middle of the day.

My heart begins to race.

"Where are you?" She asks.

"I'm driving, leaving work."

"Pull over and park the car," she says.

Trembling, I park the car.

"Okay, I parked," I say.

There's an excruciating pause.

"Daddy killed himself."

In an instant, I'm tossed into the vast ocean of shock and grief where nothing about my life as I know it is recognizable. I can't feel the ground or gravity.

I come to and hear myself and my sister wailing and screaming as I punch the steering wheel repeatedly.

"NO NO NO! Why, Daddy? Why?!" I'm sobbing so hard I'm having trouble breathing. My throat hurts from screaming. My hand is throbbing with pain from hitting the steering wheel, but the pain brings me back into my body.

"Oh, shit, I'm going to be late!"

I hang up and somehow manage to pick up my daughter and ask her how her music lesson was, hiding my swollen eyes under sunglasses. Halfway home, I pull over, call my husband, and tell them both I have something very hard to tell them. My daughter begins to cry, and I reach for her hand.

My husband says, "It feels like I've been punched in the head."

We talk on the way home about why he might have done it and how much pain he was in. How I manage to drive us both home safely, only my guardians and the power of motherhood know.

I get home, and my husband holds me until I stop shaking. I have no appetite. We talk about how I spoke with my Dad earlier that day and how he said he hurt his neck when he was walking the dog because it yanked him as it leapt at a squirrel.

"Maybe take some arnica and Advil," I'd told him. "And be sure to ice your neck."

"Good idea," he said, "Thanks, I will."

"I love you, Daddy."

"I love you very, very much," he said. It struck me the emphasis he put on repeating 'very,' but I didn't know what to make of it at the time. I will forever be grateful those were our last words to each other that harrowing day.

It was horrible knowing how badly Daddy's neck hurt after surviving being hit twice by drunk drivers and once backing out of a parking lot. There were years of watching him grit his teeth and sweat from the intensity of pain. Acupuncture, tens units, heating pads, physical therapy, and massage all helped him carry on, but it was still an uphill battle, and he refused pain medication because then he couldn't work. He had major low back surgery due to the accidents, but afterward, his neck pain was even worse. His spine looked like the hunch back of Notre Dame, only sideways. His body's pillar was paralysis waiting to happen, and I knew he didn't want to live that way. I didn't know he was planning for over a year to make sure he didn't.

I call my mom, and she insists she will be okay and that my sisters and I don't need to come home immediately. Unable to work or think, or accomplish anything using executive functions, we are all together within days. Once again, driving, ugh! The drive to the airport is harder than childbirth; I can barely operate the car. I should have asked someone to drive me; I was barely in my body.

I was home at last, and we feel like puzzle pieces coming together. For the first time since the news, I can breathe a little deeper and wake up without chest-crushing anxiety screaming, "NO!" and my heart racing. He didn't leave a note. I learn later in a suicide loss survivors' anonymous group that I would still have been left with a million unanswered questions even if he had. The only answer is in the clipboard he left with every last detail meticulously attended to. He didn't want to cause us pain and, in his suffering, had no way of comprehending how much his action would. He thought of every last detail, including the clean-up company contact information for the mess he knew the gun would make in that corner of the yard. He chose a place he knew my mother couldn't see from the window and be reminded of the incident while looking out. He made sure when he died, she was out running errands and wouldn't be there to see it or to hear it.

The neighbor comes over, and a slow trickle of close friends comes in and out. She brings lasagna. Lasaaagggnnnnaaa. My mom begins to heat it up, and I realize I haven't eaten in days. The lasagna feels like it is saving my life. I can feel my life force returning to me and am suddenly aware of my feet. I decide to stay stone-cold sober through my visit home. I don't want to delay the grief or numb out against it. I don't want to delay the inevitable by covering it up or pushing it deeper down. The lasagna is lifeblood, pure love and caring nourishing me back into my bones, and I begin to feel like maybe, just maybe, life will go on.

Late that night, my twin sister texts me from the basement and writes, "I know this sounds strange, but I think Daddy just visited me."

I text back, "I am certain he did."

To the best of her recollection, she recounts the incident. She was sitting on the end of the bed, her hands gently wrapped around her upper shoulders, and was rocking back and forth sobbing when she felt the presence of Daddy. Seeming confused, he asked, "Why are you sobbing like this?" She answered, repeatedly, "Because I love you so much, and I miss you so much!" She spoke to him, letting him know that she understood. "I know you were hurting Daddy." He replied in his sweet reassuring way, "Now you're gettin' it." Then the most beautiful thing happened, he gave her one of his long heart-melting hugs, only it felt like he was reaching his arms almost inside of hers; they merged. For me, this cinches any doubt. It is becoming more and more clear; he quit his body, not us. He hadn't left us; he never could. He would remain devoted to us as our father for the rest of our lives.

I walk upstairs to his den. This is his sanctuary, the place that holds the most of his essence. My fingertips trace his keyboard, his books, his picture frames with us smiling back. I slump down into his massage chair and put my feet up.

"Daddy, Daddy, I am here, and I know you are too." I send an anchoring cord down into the earth and one up through my crown.

Daddy and I had many conversations here about energy work and both being empathic. I breathe out along the aka cord reaching out from my spiritual heart to his. It was only a few months before I was here with him when he handed me his photocopied notes from one of his favorite books. He took each of my sisters and me aside, talked deeply to us, and handed us his notes from his favorite tomes. I knew then he was saying goodbye. I knew. I feel the guilt, the relentless guilt of wondering what more I could have done to stop him or ease his pain. I knew that he didn't want to live in a paralyzed body. He was told his spine was inoperable. Some people could live that way; some would want to, but not him. He would never be able to consider that type of existence as anything less than a burden to those he loved, even if we wouldn't feel that way. He was done. Anything we could have done would have only delayed his action.

Then it came to me: waves and waves of love along the cord.

"This was my decision to make," his spirit said.

Daddy was such a selfless man, always our rock, always uplifting and supporting us, the embodiment of endurance, putting others first no matter how he suffered. He was the victim of the accidents, but in this, he exercised his agency. He set himself free. At once I understood the answer to the why perfectly. He never wanted to hurt us. He chose to love himself enough to honor his NO.

Wanting to know the root of his pain beyond the physical, I travel the cord from our hearts, asking to show me a cord that leads to the core wound of his emotional/spiritual pain and find the cord attached to his father.

When Daddy was young, his father told him routinely he would never amount to anything. I feel the wounds he is carrying from that message. It made it very difficult to believe that his life in a paralyzed body would have any value. There was so much there to heal around worth and value. We matter simply because we are, not because of our incomes or what we do for a living. I wish people asked, "What do you love," instead of, "So what do you do," when they first meet.

This core wound set the stage, along with capitalism and patriarchy, for my father to doubt his intrinsic value. He was by all rights a very successful businessman. However, he would often recount to me that he made very little money compared to his clients in a self-negating way. Daddy loved and cared for his clients and was in service to their security and happiness. His passion was helping others. I believe the idea that he could no longer care for others as he wished and would have to be taken care of was more than he could bear. He died by suicide the day before his retirement, before paralysis had a chance to set in.

In addition to the physical pain, the wound of not feeling worthy was my father's core wound. I believe many people, particularly male-identified, are burdened with this curse relational to their vocation and recognition as providers. Female-identified people are used to making less money than their counterparts for equal work and are socially conditioned to have value placed on their relationship status and capacity to care give more than on their income. Thankfully, we are entering an age where gender norms, polarities, biases, and social conditioning of expectations of performance of those norms is shifting and healing.

Seeing this wound, I send waves of love and acceptance to the place in my father that feels he will have no value as a paralyzed man, to the part of him that perceives he will only be a burden or drain the family coffers. I send love and acceptance to him as a little boy telling him he will become a loving adult, a man with a family that adores him, friends that cherish him, and that he is more than enough, simply for being him, for being alive and sharing love. I feel the cord soften and begin to shimmer, then send waves of healing into my father, his child soul, and into his father. I ask that the healing extend as far back as needed, where any other ancestor carries the wound of 'I am not worthy.'

"I love you," he says, again and again. "I love you."

I speak the words of the Hawaiian forgiveness ritual, Ho'oponopono, and hear him repeat them back. "I'm sorry. Please forgive me. Thank you. I love you." Gently blowing his spirit onto its resting place, the cord stretches out across the ethers, ever strong. Love is all that remains.

Family, friends, and colleagues gather at his celebration of life some months later, waving our white kerchiefs to the sound of his favorite jazz band playing *I'll Fly Away*. As we dance the second line, a breeze blows into the room and lifts my older sister's hair, tears streaming down all of our faces.

"That's Daddy," she says. "That's Daddy."

I knew then as I do now his love lives on in the hearts of those who loved him; his friends, my sisters, my husband, his grandchildren, his wife, and in his legacy. There is no end to love. Love never dies.

THE TOOL

If possible, have someone read this to you or record yourself reading it and play it back for your journey.

Assume a comfortable position for yourself. Begin to deepen your breath. Relax your belly. Extend your energy down into the earth and up into the starry realms and back down to where they merge in your center.

Place your fingers on your carotid artery on your neck or on any other part of your body where you can feel your pulse. Tune into the heartbeat felt through the pulse. There in your pulse resides the river of blood and spirit that connects you in communion with your ancestors. Ride that rhythm as you release your fingers and place one or both hands over your heart.

Become aware of Anahata, your heart chakra. Imagine a green orb glowing there in the center of your chest. Call up into your present conscious awareness any memory or information you have of the sound of your ancestor's voice, their scent, how they felt, what they looked like. Conjure them in this way before you now.

Out from this orb emerges an Aka/Spirit cord reaching out from you to your beloved dead. Feel them in front of you, an Aka cord reaching out from your spiritual heart and merging with their heart cord. If they are a benevolent ancestor, feel the love that flows between you through this cord of connection. If they are a malevolent ancestor you are seeking resolution with, anchor yourself in love and ask for protection from your guides and guardians.

What is in your heart to communicate with them? Take a moment and say it silently or aloud to your loved one now. See, feel, imagine, or know your ancestor to fully receive the gift of your words and emotions. Now take a moment and listen, listen deeply.

What is in the heart of your ancestor that they wish to communicate with you now? Be open to receive this blessing.

Allow your body to feel what is being communicated; words may not be the method your ancestor uses. You may experience an image floating into your mind, a sensation, a smell; just relax and allow the process of discovery to unfold.

Once you have received this transmission, take a moment in gratitude for the information, the forgiveness, and the healing. In your mind's eye, place a gift in their open hands, a token of your love, affection, or forgiveness.

Perhaps you may leave a literal offering for your loved one later, such as their favorite food, playing their favorite song, or leaving a glass of water for them to drink set by a favorite photo of them. See them accepting this offering with thanks and delight. They may wish to offer you something in return; receive it now.

Feel your spirit ally and ancestor slowing moving away from you back into the realm of the bardo, the spirit world. The cord can remain intact if they were a benevolent ancestor, or you may wish to cut the cord if it was a tumultuous connection that would best be served to end. In this case, in your mind's eye, you can cut the cord with scissors, a knife, or your hand very close to your body so nothing of it remains. See the cord dissolving, burning, or disappearing between you. Take a moment to hold your hand over the place where the cord came away and let healing energy flow in to fill that place. If the cord has remained intact and there was no need to cut it, then see it glimmering and shining with green iridescent radiance, the kind of green you can see in a peacock feather, crystalline and radiant. You can travel this cord of connection to your ancestor any time you choose.

Wiggle your toes, wiggle your nose, yawn, and stretch. Slowly come back to the here and now. If you decide to leave a physical offering, be sure to dispose of it outside, do not eat or drink what their spirit has partaken of. May your journeys be a source of strength, connection, power, and healing for you. May the blood of your ancestors, the cords of connection, your chakra wheels, and their legacy of love be a blessed gateway of reunion whenever you have need.

Blessed Be the Ancestors, their legacy,
and our hallowing of their memory.

Asherah Allen is a Certified Spiritual Counselor, Grief Specialist, and Master Healer. Her passion is being of service in helping people to live their most soul-aligned, spiritually infused, radiantly healthy life. Asherah maintains a successful private in-person and online healing arts practice. Her specialties include trauma integration and pain management. She is a Licensed Acupuncturist, Chinese Herbalist, Licensed Massage Therapist, Certified Yoga Instructor, Meditation Teacher, and Reiki Master Teacher Trainer.

As a Reverend, Asherah offers her services in performing marriage ceremonies, burial rites, baby blessings, sacred rituals, and house clearings. A natural intuitive and empath, she is a skilled tarot and oracle card reader.

Her notable institutions of study include a Masters Degree in Acupuncture and Oriental Medicine from New England School of Acupuncture, a Massage Certificate from Bancroft School of Massage Therapy, and a Yoga Teacher Training Certification from Shri Kali Ashram, Goa, India.

Her favorite pastimes include writing poetry, playing music, and belly dancing.

She would like to acknowledge the great inspiration of the many spiritual teachers and healers she has been blessed to be influenced by and who have brought her to authentic expression, specifically regarding her writing contribution in this incredible book. Asherah offers her deepest gratitude and respect to the following mentors, teachers, friends, and colleagues: Karina B. Heart, Orion Foxwood, Sylvia Brallier, Tiana Mirapae, Kathleen and Breighton Dawe, and Anodea Judith.

Asherah would not be who she is today without the tremendous love, support, and courage of her beloved husband and daughter, sisters, parents, and friends. To them, she offers her deepest heartfelt thanks.

Her contribution is dedicated to all suicide loss survivors.

To learn more about Asherah, get a free guided meditation audio link, or to book a service with her, please visit

http://awakenedhearthealingarts.com/resources/

www.awakenedhearthealingarts.com

Chapter 4

ANCESTORS AND AUTISM

Real Thoughts From Your Past

NOAH SMITH

MY STORY

To all those who know an adult with autism who cannot speak or does not appear to be at an ideal age-appropriate conversational level, you will want to meet my mom!

Mom interrupts as we sit on the recliner sofa where I am relaxed, "Should we move to a table or couch, so this is more comfortable?" Mom is facilitating my typing but reaching across an armrest at an awkward position for her. LOL, how does it feel, Mom? Love it! Mom is starting to get this, all of this. Mom keeps asking me questions, but I know her thoughts. Patience is a virtue, Mom, and I am a virtuoso of patience. I couldn't communicate in earth language until I was 18. Hugs Mom. I really thought my echolalia was conversation because people responded to it.

My sister Adriana started typing just a few months before I did. She had less language. She would read books out loud. But she was only saying words, not her own thoughts. Like me, but different. I was not convinced that typing was for me, but Adriana insisted, "Type your thoughts, Noah!" Dear hugs for this, Mom. It's good to see us telling our story! I hope we reach those who need us.

I've always communicated in my head with many voices and in many languages. People often thought Adriana and I were twins, but I'm older by 22 months. They also thought we were telepathic. We are. Boy, Mom is so awkward helping me but is so excited to hear what I have to say that she doesn't find it off-putting! Tears in her eyes as she didn't know this was going to be about her! She is my closest ancestor and the link from me to them and here in this chapter to you!

I found my abilities as a child but didn't tell anyone until 2020 because I had only typed my thoughts since 2016. Would people believe me? Thoughts were confusing Mom, and no one would answer her questions about why facilitated communication was feeling different with me than with Adriana. Typing was easier with Adriana because she didn't have the thoughts as I did. Mom thought it was because she had less verbal language. So many voices coming into my head, I didn't know who was talking. I now realize these are ancestors trying to help and guide us. They were well-meaning but learning through me how to reach others while helping me find myself too. Finally, the voices have a purpose, and I understand what is happening! For now, they're here to help me tell others what they need. And that is for you to trust your thoughts, especially when you know they are not yours. I am typing heavily and purposeful so that Mom gets this! LOL. Just know these thoughts are from good spirits, energy, or ancestors who want to help you; your spirit guides, ancestors, friends' ancestors, or maybe you don't even know where or why these ancestors tune in to your thoughts.

It is very good to tell my story. I feel the world is ready now. I really hope to reach others like Adriana and me. This is only possible by reaching the parents and caregivers of these people. I can help everyone with something. You can help me by sharing my information. I am a man with autism and have limited verbal speech. You may have said I am nonverbal, but I did speak in echolalia as a child. Echolalia means echoing or repeating phrases. I was very good at getting words out by relating stories to real life. Mom likes to use the example of a VeggieTales song about tofu and seafood when we were at Red Lobster. She knew I was trying to communicate that we were at a seafood restaurant, but it was just echolalia stored in my memory for later use! All the dialogues from VeggieTales, Blue's Clues, Big Comfy Couch, Toy Story, and Barney were in my head. But what else was I thinking? There was so much information I couldn't get out.

Each time I wanted dearly to speak but words only repeated. My thoughts wouldn't come out. The voices I heard were trying to help but really overwhelmed me. I ran and paced. I wanted to get away from all of them, whoever they were.

Jump to 2020. Now I know these voices are ancestors. Each with a purpose to share, a voice to be heard, and I am the messenger! Mom is my messenger, and it's that connection we share through facilitated communication that brought all of this to light! Light language is in my head now, and we have been introduced to this recently by a friend.

Boy Mom, I'm finding so much to talk about. How can we fit it all in? Dear Dad helps but doesn't facilitate like Mom. He is a numbers guy. He can help explain what she does, but he can only get yes, no, and food choices. He's doing the word count on this chapter, so we don't get too chatty!

The light language is from ancestors but feels like it is beyond our realm. There are big feelings with this as it's more than a language we are taught. You feel it instead. It's hard to explain, but you understand, Mom. You are feeling a lot of different things when you facilitate. You are picking up on more than the muscle movement at this point. Our friends see the aura that you emit when you connect with people. Good people or energies are speaking to us through a universal language. Just like Mom can do with typing as a facilitator, she overrides the body's slow and awkward movements to find a rhythm and focus on thoughts from the higher self. This doesn't just happen with autism but anyone who can't express his or her thoughts completely. It's a mind-body disconnection.

I feel the energy of all who came before us and know about past issues each had. It's good to learn from the past to build a better future. However, some things never translated from light language have gone unlearned until now. Now we can share our thoughts and discuss solutions.

Know that I feel energy all the time so writing this out helps my body focus a bit better. Concentrating on specifics gives me a purpose to move my body correctly and not be idle or repetitive. Just know I am always working, so this is as much of a break as it is therapy! Exhausting my mind and body but differently.

Understanding how I work is key to reaching others like me. At first, I may appear severe, but then in many ways, I am a genius! Overnight with communication, my sister and I went from life skills classes to general education high school classes with people assisting us. For us, it wasn't about learning but teaching our helpers and the teachers how to relate to us! We hope to find people who want to assist, really cool friends who will take the time to get to know us and learn to support the way we communicate. This is a learning experience different from what people think. A mom or dad will typically learn to facilitate first. It could be a caregiver or teacher, or maybe a sibling. From there, that person could work with another non-speaker and branch out a bit. Mom had Adriana and me, and we are very different from each other. Mom learned twice as fast, and because she does this every day, she has become very good at helping others like us to communicate. The look on their faces and the feeling of good energy are amazing! Just give her five minutes!

Since the announcement of this book, I've connected with so many new friends. Each has his or her own gifts to share. Each can help with communication and ancestors much differently than I can. Their experience has taught them to trust their instincts and voices they hear or even just feel or know. I'm really a beginner here, sharing all I know.

Boy Mom, I'm getting to that! LOL. Old soul! She wants me to talk about being an old soul! I really think this is where ancestors have appeared most in real-life situations—those people, like me, who connect with older people. We love hearing their stories and learning all we can learn from them. In my head, the ancestors do just this; tell their stories and share their experiences. This brings up the idea that autistics do hear the ancestors. We appear to be lost in thought with no voice of our own. We look as though we are playing with angels and fairies as all small children do. This is because we are! Really! Good things are in our view, and we want to share with you, but you need to meet us on our vibrational level, our realm, world, frequency, or dimension. For Mom, she is now relating to TV shows like Sliders and Stargate and even Charmed and Ghost Whisperer and realizing that these are not made up but realities the world doesn't quite understand yet. Now is the time to see this is the future. And the future is now! No time for skeptics to get in the way as we have a purpose. Autism is not a disability but a difference in sensory perception. We have ways to communicate and describe our realities to share with the world.

THE TOOL

Get out of your own head. Thoughts that come from someone else are your spirit guides. Hugs to those having aha moments! You are already in tune with your ancestors! This is the start of understanding what I do. You need to relax and listen to these voices or feelings. Trust your instincts.

Moms of children with nonverbal autism may have a harder time with this because those children attract more spirits and energy than other children. It may appear chaotic and overwhelming. Your energy is often really overpowering to them, and you interrupt the natural flow that these children are used to hearing in their heads. Just know they hear you, and you don't need to raise your voice. Understand they sense your frustration and your fear.

Just be calm and allow others to show you. Words are not always the answer, especially when there are sensory issues. Know that there are people who can sense, feel, and hear things that you do not. I feel the energies of my fellow healers in this book very strongly. The collaborations here will go beyond writing this book. You can learn like my mom did and is continuing to learn as we write this together. My thoughts and her support do really separate the autism from my higher self. I hope that makes sense!

When we found facilitated communication, Mom questioned others about my connection being different from my sister, who is also nonspeaking and communicates by typing with support as I do. No one said anything about reaching the higher self until I channeled my grandfather. Mom felt it wasn't me or my higher self and didn't know who to ask. This was April 23, 2020, the day I became a medium and knew what was happening. Before that, I would hear voices, and my body would be beyond my control, but as an autistic, that was my normal. I can give a real insight to others like me. Mom can physically get a conversation with facilitated communication. But Mom and others like her need touch to feel for productive movement. I call this "fooling autism" by overriding the body. Mom has gone beyond this by feeling who is sending the message. Is it the higher self or another energy? Adriana and I can read thoughts. I can assist in communication for someone else with Mom's support! Not an easy reality to accept but practicing with lots of different people all the time, you learn quickly what is happening! This was a lot of different information for people to grasp on how Mom could do this. But with my help, we found others who understand us and respect our energy skills. OMG, a community who sees us as powerful and good rather than skeptics who believe what they are told rather than experiencing first hand. I love to help people find their way no matter what form of communication is used. I love that this book will be out for Mothers' Day 2021, as this is my gift to my Mom!

I really hope to reach people who want to learn more. I love to travel and hope to receive invitations to meet groups of people once this pandemic allows. I am on Facebook and Instagram and have direct links on my website. Mom features me on her website because no matter how powerful my energy, my body still needs support to communicate!

Sharonsweb Autism Foundation

www.sharonsweb.com

Noah Smith is an adult on the autism spectrum who found his voice in 2016 through facilitated communication, along with his sister Adriana. Both went from life skills classes to general education overnight! The family moved across town to a school that would accept facilitated communication and provide facilitators. They joined Special Olympics powerlifting, unified track, and began a healthy gluten-free diet. Noah went from a size 3X to a medium. Pun intended!

In 2020, Noah participated in a couple of festivals as an energy healer. Other healers saw and felt his abilities. This was very validating for Mom!

We are collaborating with others for events, including workshops for family and caregivers.

Younger sister Adriana participates in festivals and workshops. Older brother Quinn has Asperger's Syndrome and verbally communicates. The logo of Sharonsweb Autism Foundation is of the three siblings.

Noah is available, with Mom Sharon as his facilitator, to meet in person or on video.

Chapter 5

PLANTING A FAMILY TREE FROM THE LAND OF MY FATHERS

Digging Through the Past and Preserving it for the Future

SONDRA LAMBERT, CHT

MY STORY

I love my life. It is a goal of mine to wake each morning with the intention of making it the best day possible. Yesterday is done, tomorrow is yet to come, so it just feels right for today to lead the way.

As I have walked my path into the footsteps of my grandfather's grandfathers, I know they believed in everyone who would follow. They believed in me. Even now, their voices echo all around me with an invitation to get to know them just a little bit better. The path I chose was to visit the land of my fathers. I stood the ground, honoring them with my stories while researching theirs. I want to share their story and mine with you and give you the tools to go on your journey.

Here we go!

When we are born, we partner with all those who have come before us and all those who will follow in our footsteps. *NO pressure, right?*

Some of those partnerships are direct bloodlines; for others, it is community tradition mixed in the cultural pride of the land of our fathers. Who am I? Where did I come from? Where do I fit? But then, in the gentle whispers of history, we begin to recognize the plans, the hopes, the dreams that our grandfathers' grandfathers had for us. Some come in the form of prayers long ago for "my children's children," while others become the legs we stand upon, whether we know where we got our interests, traits, and abilities or not.

I come to you with my story from a lineage that began in the winter of 1708/09. Europe's winter did not shift into spring. The rivers stayed frozen, the orchards and vineyards failed, and the spring seeds never made it into the ground. That winter, combined with years of war raging between Catholics and Protestants, left the Palatinate people crestfallen. And now, of all things, the dirt they depended on failed them.

Enough was finally enough. They needed new ground to stand on.

Years earlier, William Penn visited the Palatinate region and was so impressed with the work ethics and quality of community he invited all who lived there to come to America. He owned land in Pennsylvania and would provide a place to live and plots to build upon if they could find a way there.

They had a destination; they just needed transportation.

England's Queen Anne was the ruler of this vast new world known as America. It was rough, rugged, untamed, and filled with unknowns. She decided to populate it with non-British European immigrants. Queen Anne put out a wide invitation. She was willing to transport people to America aboard her ships.

The people of the Palatinate now had a place to live and the solution to get there. They left in droves. An entire ethnic, regional community packed, traveled to England, and began a new life in William Penn's Pennsylvania.

They became known as the Pennsylvania Deutch (German) as they landed in Philadelphia harbor.

By 1727, William Penn's son inherited his father's estates and made some changes. The free ride was over. Anyone coming into Philadelphia harbor had to be registered and must stake a claim for a parcel of land. They were no longer allowed to just get off the boat and live free.

My Gangwer family history began on Sept 27th, 1727, when the ship James Goodwill pulled into Philadelphia harbor with Jacob and Suzanna Gangwer onboard. Jacob did not bring with him any shared history or traceable ancestry.

The Palatinate people were known for their loving respect for the land. Jacob found his new home among groves of walnut trees and plenty of limestone, confirming to him that the soil was rich and the land would prosper.

My husband, Larry, and I decided to drive from our home in Maryland to my family's homeland to do some onsite research.

We found records about Jacob and Suzanna Gangwer in the attic of the historical society in Allentown, Pennsylvania. One document we found included all the men who signed the Upper Saucon Township creation document in Lehigh County. Luckily for us, it also showed us where we could find their land. It turns out my family had a memorial stone at the seventh hole of the Weyhill Golf course.

When we got there, we were treated as honored guests and asked if we were members of the *actual* Gangwer family. There was obviously a lot of history yet to be revealed. We were given a golf cart and told to take as much time as we wanted. The marker was a composite of several small gravestones with the land beautifully manicured under three giant arching walnut trees. The respect given to the Gangwer family was undeniable. Now, we needed to figure out why.

Workers there asked if we wanted to see the mine. *What mine?* It had not come up in my research so far. Talk about digging deeper. The mine they referenced was on Jacob Gangwer's land. It eventually turned into the inaugural mine for Bethlehem Steel, which became one of the world's largest steel-producing companies. After the mine dried up, the company built a golf course on the land and left the memorial in honor of my ancestors. They even created a coffee table book that included my forefathers.

My father always said, "There's nothing wrong with being a ditch digger, as long as you dig a good ditch." While farming would never be my personal identity, I took those words to heart and grabbed a shovel to dig through the soil so I could plant my own story. We left with a plastic bag full of dirt that day.

Our research continued with family pride, and interest fueled momentum.

Jacob and Suzanna Gangwer lived a good life. They began the American dream for their family and left us a legacy of making reliable decisions and recognizing quality when you see it.

Jacob's grandson became my Grandpa George Gangwer. He was interviewed before he died at the age of 104 as one of the Revolutionary War's last surviving soldiers. The original farm was in Bethlehem; his grave is a few miles away in Egypt.

Grandpa George had a grandson, Thomas. Like so many others of their day, my grandpa Thomas and his wife Hetty looked toward the frontier. They were determined to be a part of it. They were ready to head west with members of their community and follow in their fathers' footsteps, believing that there is more for those who are willing to go looking for it. Hetty had been a mother figure to her younger siblings, so they did not leave until after her sister Clarise's wedding. They loaded their wagons, with all obligations fulfilled, saddled their horses, and headed to their next homeland. That turned out to be Mulberry, Indiana. Again, farmland filled with lots of walnut trees and limestone.

Five generations later, I was born and raised as an Indiana farmer's daughter, fewer than 20 miles from the original homestead.

I began my genealogy research mostly out of curiosity. What I found both surprised and intrigued me. Nine generations of Gangwers waited so patiently for me to find them. One evening as I was enjoying their journey, I decided to continue the search. My mom's ancestry would be my next incredible journey. The Planks were also Pennsylvania Deutch. I did not have to travel any farther to find them, but the trip took me in an altogether different direction.

My quest was to follow my generational line until it intersected within my parents, Bob and Arlene Gangwer, and this fueled my soul.

Who am I, where did I come from? I was about to find out. You have half the story; now I bring you my mother's side, the Plank land.

The Palatinate immigrants spread out and made Pennsylvania their home. Good land, stable community, and a decision that if this is my life to make it a good one.

Let's jump now to the early 1820s.

I found a Grandpa George on my mother's side of the family, as well. He was quite a guy. Grandpa George Plank and Grandma Elizabeth owned 230 acres near the sleepy town of Gettysburg, Pennsylvania. They built their home, stables for the horses, a bank barn, a brick smokehouse, and a vast orchard. They raised their family in appreciation of all that God had provided for them. The farm was sold to a man named Henry Spangler in the summer of 1862.

Why does this matter, you may wonder? Well, let me tell you. The Spangler farm became the center of one of the biggest battles in American history. The Battle of Gettysburg was literally in/on their front yard.

This battle is often considered a pivot point of the war. It shifted the balance of power. Grandpa George's farm was ultimately destroyed, yet the house was the battle hospital, and the barns gave shelter to the weary. Plank land did not fall to the Confederacy.

We are jumping several generations now.

My grandfather's name was Jesse Truman Plank. He hated the name Jesse, and even though it was a family name, he never used it. He was a farmer in Indiana for his entire life. He told us the story of one night when he was waiting at a crossroads to guide a truckload of cattle to his farm. Suddenly, lights blared, and police swarmed with weapons drawn. The cops thought they had just caught John Dillinger. They left disappointed, and he was left terrified.

His health prevented him from serving as a soldier in WW2. He was considered a homeland worker for the war effort.

He also told us of the night during the war when meat was scarce in Chicago. A man showed up at his door, handed him a wad of cash, and told my grandfather he would be selling a load of pigs that night. They pulled the truck up to his barn, loaded it, and drove away. There were men with shotguns pointed at him the entire time.

My grandfather grew up wanting to be an accountant, but his dad told him he had to do something useful, like farming. My Papa Plank never lost his love for numbers. My fondest memories are of him sitting at his desk, working on his books. He was forever calm, unassuming, and quite brilliant in personal business decisions. As I write this chapter, my mom, at 85 years young, has a comfortable life thanks to her father's love for his bookkeeping.

My grandparents traveled across the country in their RV years before it became a trendy thing to do. They made an RV trip thru Mexico when I was a kid. They brought me back Mexican lace, which my Mama Plank helped me sew into my wedding dress.

As I researched my family's history, it took me on my own journey. I traveled across the Pennsylvania countryside following my Palatinate Pennsylvania Deutch family's path and the immigration journey into central Indiana's farmlands. I found the homestead, or farm or gravesite of every ancestor in my direct maternal and paternal lineage, collecting a plastic bag of dirt from each, marking each clearly while learning a bit about their story along the way.

In celebration of my parents' 50th wedding anniversary, I took my collection of family dirt home to them along with a contribution from the land of every current family member. We sat in their front yard one warm April eve, and together we spent time with those who came before us. As my mom and dad poured the soil into a big half barrel with the help of their youngest great-grandchildren, I told the stories. I spoke of Jacob and the two Grandpa Georges. I told them about how both the Planks and Gangwers moved west. The stories were told, the soil was well mixed, then we planted a family tree. This family tree honors, with genuine appreciation, 300 years of family coming together.

I began my story with hope and a prayer that I would find myself in the lives of my grandparents. Now, our lives are combined in a tangible way. Life does not have a beginning nor an end. Thank God, it just keeps gently moving forward, allowing us to look back, and for those who are willing, see inside ourselves. As a woman, I recognize myself in my grandmothers. Their names were changed in the creation of my story.

They were daughters first, then wives, then mothers before becoming my grandmas. I may not carry my maiden name Gangwer or my mother's maiden name, Plank; however, I proudly carry their legacies, gifting my children's children from my heart to theirs. It's tradition.

This is my story. Now go out and create yours.

THE TOOL

Would you like to listen to me share with you my heartfelt love for this project? I invite you to settle in, settle down and relax, dare to dream with me for just a moment. Listen as I tell my story while encouraging you to create your own. I am here for you.

www.galaxyhypnosis.com/sondra

You will be planting a family tree in the land of your fathers by using your family dirt.

It is quite simple, and now, here is how you can do the same thing.

STEP 1: DO YOUR RESEARCH.

Find the home base of your family. Learn something about the stories of the times, the places, or the events of their lives.

STEP 2: PLAN.

Can you travel to the land of your fathers yourself? If so, that is best, but not required. If you have a location, you can contact the local historical society and hire someone to harvest and mail the soil to you. I personally walked the land of each one, nine generations of Gangwers and seven generations of Planks in America.

STEP 3: COLLECT YOUR SOIL.

I suggest large sealable plastic bags, a shovel, permanent markers, and a journal. Walk the ground, say a prayer, leave a dedication stone, something personal. Share gratitude, have a conversation, telling them how you turned out. Tell your story, make the connection. Please share with this place your impressions of their stories. https://rb.gy/vfox78

STEP 4: CURRENT FAMILY MEMBERS' PARTICIPATION.

Request soil contributions from living relatives connected to your family tree project. Get their stories as well. Partnering with family matters. We had family members sending us soil from Germany, where they were stationed with the US Army. Some sent dirt from outside their college dorms. You get the picture: Ask them to drop it off for you or have it shipped if necessary.

STEP 5: PLAN THE EVENT.

What are you celebrating? Are you planning on planting in the ground or a container? If you have enough, you can make bottles of the lands of our fathers for each family member. You do this after the event.

Make it as unique as you desire and as is appropriate.

STEP 6: GET YOUR STORIES TOGETHER.

Who were they? Where did they live? What work did they do? Write it down, practice being the storyteller. Find some fun facts or cultural add-ins, community spirit, research stories that are just fun. I gathered Gettysburg in the winter in the snow, so I have a bag of wet, heavy mud.

STEP 7: IT'S PARTY TIME.

Invite the spirit of your ancestors to join you, respecting the comfort level of all gathered. You do not want anyone running away freaked out.

Find just the right place at just the right time, then gather your friends, family, whomever you choose and make it special. Share a meal of family favorites or food from your cultural beginnings. Tell the stories so that people ask more questions or identify with those who came before them. Create your stories in such a way that your ancestors are right there at the table with you. Get creative.

Invite each family member to write a note on biodegradable paper as a personal message as a family member standing on this sacred holy ground, a prayer or an appreciation or acknowledging a connection to one of the ancestor stories.

I like to use their first names, Grandpa Thomas or Grandma Elizabeth. Allow them to become real in the imaginations of all within the sound of your voice.

STEP 8: PLANT YOUR FAMILY TREE.

If you plant into the ground, have the digging be part of the ceremony. Share the shovel; laugh a lot.

If you plant in a container, call your generations by name. Mix the dirt all together in the hole or the container.

After it is all mixed, gather any you want for separate family dirt bottles.

Add potting mix to the tree soil.

Add the notes into the soil.

Plant the tree.

STEP 9: COMPLETE YOUR DEDICATION.

The powerful presence at this moment is significant. Absorb the love, absorb the light, absorb the moment. It is precious.

Write in your journal, say a prayer, meditate, whatever completes this moment for you, make it so.

Sondra Lambert

When people ask me to describe who I am and what I do, I usually tell them I am a professional encourager and am exceptionally good at my job. Looking people in the eye and telling them heart-to-heart that they are beautiful, and the world is a better place with them in it.

I have been an internationally certified hypnotist for the past decade with my husband, Larry. We are Galaxy Hypnosis of Crofton, MD.

Creating a personal and interactive partnership with the Subconscious mind is my highest thrill.

I also am the owner and operator of Aura Photo US. Aura Photography translates a person's vibrational frequency into color in real-time. You can experience your energetic signature in living color with me.

Within both skills, I channel like breathing; I close my eyes and see the message I share. I see, then I speak, and most of the time, the conversations take on a life of their own. Connections are made, and healing happens at the speed of need.

Our style of hypnosis also offers you the opportunity to connect with your ancestors. All you need to do is relax, open your imagination and join their journey.

Would you like to go back to a moment in time before you were born thru the eyes of your ancestors? It gives visiting Grandma a whole new twist. Take a journey, learn, heal, gain awareness, or have fun keeping it simple while you drift, float, and dare to dream. It really can be just this easy.

Sondra Lambert

www.galaxyhypnosis.com/sondra

Crofton MD 21114

443 292 4279

Chapter 6

HEARING MY GRANDMOTHER
How to Use Affirmations to
Bridge Communication to Your Ancestors

LISA A. NEWTON, M.ED.

"To learn the wisdom of your ancestors,
first build a bridge of communication using mediation
and the positive light of affirmations.
Affirmations have been universally utilized
by spiritually connected people throughout time."

MY STORY

In September of 2006, I entered a plane with seventeen thousand dollars, wrapped in plastic, taped between my shoulder blades. I had a backpack full of possessions and an oversized purse carrying my laptop and adoption paperwork with the picture of a tiny girl with one name, Dinara. The total time for the adoption was to take six to eight weeks. On the twelfth week, my cell phone rang, and the voice on the other end was gritty and the request unreasonable, "Are you coming back?"

My response to the question was just as brief and firm. Had he not read my blog? How could he ask me that question? I was not going to leave Kazakhstan without Dinara. My face went numb, my fingers icy. "No, I am not."

Within a few hours, the board of the school I had co-founded voted to have me removed for job abandonment. I was alone on the other side of the world; all my life accomplishments were stripped from me. Hours before that phone call, I received word that my father was given a terminal health status, and my mother was irrationally pleading with me not to steal this child from her mother. Worst of all, the tiny girl I was in the process of adopting was gravely ill. The orphanage was expecting her to die. Yet, I never had more resolve, nor had I ever been so firmly focused on the goal to become Dinara's mother. I did not know it at the time, but my giving up everything to fight for motherhood set me on a journey to break an ancestral pattern.

I had always known that I was going to adopt a child. When I was four years old, my mother told me that my friend, Simon, was adopted. And I responded, "I don't see his dot." I had assumed that adopted people had dots. My mother was adopted, and to my four-year-old brain, that meant all adopted people had a mole on their face, like her. I remember thinking that Simon must have had his dot under his shirt sleeve. Another childhood memory was when my mother told me that there is a special love bond between natural-born children and their mothers that is different from that of adopted children and their adopted mothers. I protested, and she pleaded her case with examples from her childhood. I have always known I had the capacity to love any child as my own. I know others do not.

In Kazakhstan, I drew my fortitude from my affirmational chant, a source outside of my upbringing, outside of my mother's anxiety about adopting, and outside my own experiences. The affirmation was "*do whatever it takes*" to get Dinara out of the orphanage and legally my child. I prayed those words over and over until I choked the breath out of my tears. Those weeks depleted my reserve of everything. My money was gone. My parental support was gone. My career was gone. I lived each moment, breathing in and out my chant.

The orphanage thought Dinara was going to die and offered me another child. I spoke through my interpreter to the head doctor. I pleaded with both the words I spoke and the earnestness I felt in my soul, "I am here for Dinara. I know how ill she is. I have everything lined up for her. I have been sending my notes to her pediatric specialist at Texas Children's Hospital. I have her physical and fine motor therapist set up. I see it in her eyes. She is a fighter." The doctor cleared Dinara to come to my apartment for five days to see if I could turn her health around. It worked.

Four full months after I arrived, the courts of Kazakhstan made me her legal mother. The affirmation chant changed to "*Keep her safe, help her grow.*" The US Embassy drew up her naturalization papers, and we began our twenty-eight-hour travel back to my home in transition.

My mother did not want her adopted mother, Blanche, to influence my life or my brother's. She told me unkind things about this woman who raised her. I remember spending less than ten days with my grandma Blanche in total before she died. I remember making two types of cookies, sweet pickles, and a cucumber salad, in her kitchen. I remember being happy, but also strange getting all the attention. I grew up in a home that did not focus on the children. My brother and I learned many survival skills, such as spending a lot of time at friend's houses, playing outside from sunrise to sunset, and finding school a place of comfort. My father's traumatic brain injury rattled our family's stability. My mother was very successful in her career. She took care of us on her own terms and timeline. When I was her focus, she spent that time micromanaging my visual appearance, questioning my choices, and scrutinizing my actions. I felt she preferred me being her work assistant instead of a daughter. As a child, I learned it was best to conform and comply silently, and in that silence, I found the saving grace of meditation.

My biological grandmother, Charlene, and Blanche worked together and had become close. When her friend had not shown up to work, Blanche decided to check on her. The door to the apartment was ajar, so Blanche cautiously called out and got no response. Worried her friend could be hurt, and in need of help, she entered the apartment and found my infant mother, dirty and crying out. Blanche scooped her up and took her home. She and her husband raised my mother until she was kidnapped at age three from the daycare center by Charlene. Charlene did not take back her child to raise her. Instead, she took her across the country to torture her older sister and her family. She devastated Blanche and my grandfather.

My brother and I grew up isolated from our extended family on both sides. When my grandmother Blanche and grandfather had both passed away, my mother finally gave me permission to investigate her adopted side of the family. She said she wanted only her medical background and had no interest in meeting either of her biological parents, but I wanted more family. At that time, my mother had no knowledge or memory of her infanthood, but she did have her birth certificate. She also revealed to me that her adopted parents had not finalized her adoption. I was able to locate her biological aunt and learned her biological mother had passed away less than fifty miles from my parent's house. I learned a lot about my biological grandmother in my investigation, but my mother had no interest in hearing any of it. She was interested in the aunt. My mother recognized her aunt as the neighbor lady she liked so much as a child. I went with my mother to reunite with her biological family, and it was healing until it wasn't. While my mother and I were welcomed unconditionally, my mother's reaction was strained. It was during this visit I recognized a pattern of maternal behavior.

Out of earshot of my mother, our newly found biological family described Charlene as a narcissistic personality. As they filled in the missing parts of my mother's childhood and family history, I learned Charlene was an infant, and her sister was six when their mother died of the Spanish Flu in the 1918 pandemic. Their father remarried, and the decision was made to send off the older sister to work in a series of relatives' homes as a mother's helper. Charlene was raised by her stepmother and father. The family reports of her behavior are not flattering. She was described as selfish, wild, and mean-spirited. A petite and attractive woman, Charlene was married three times. Her second marriage ended the same year she abandoned a child to the state who had Down Syndrome. Two years later, she had my mother out of wedlock in 1945. She lived under variations of her name and set out to destroy her older sister by having a child with her husband. Yes, my mother was created in a scheme to steal a husband; but that did not work. My mother was also used in an attempt to trap a former boyfriend into claiming his parenthood listed erroneously on the birth certificate; that did not work either. So, my biological grandmother once again abandoned her three-year-old child at her sister's doorstep and disappeared for the rest of her life.

When my mother was nearly five, she was returned to her adopted parents in a secret deal. Blanche and my grandfather accepted the biological aunt and her family to be part of my mother's life. They moved into a house on the same street, and their daughter taught my mother to ice skate. My mother did not know that her favorite neighbors were actually her biological aunt, uncle/father, and half-sister. Clearly, my mother had been put through a childhood trauma but was very much loved and wanted by Blanche and her biological aunt. I feel that both these women compromised and sacrificed to be with my mother.

It can be debated how much nature plays in a child's development as compared to nurture. In my maternal biological line, the mothers prioritize themselves over their children. My entire family flows through me; their gifts and their toils line my path on how I approach all aspects of my life. I mimicked them in some respects and spiraled away on my own path too. At that moment in Kazakhstan, I found two distinct pieces of knowledge. First, my brother was the only person I could trust. Second, my life had begun anew in Kazakhstan when I was asked to choose to prioritize myself or my child. It was a flash, an instant in time when I was given the opportunity to heal those maternal patterns. It was my hope that in doing so, my deep love for my adopted child would somehow heal my mother.

Within three months of our return to the United States, Dinara and I sold our house and moved across the country, a block away from my parents. I got a teaching job, and Dinara was watched by my parents before and after school until she was in middle school. Dinara was a magical addition to our family, and she changed the entire culture of our family to include hugs and the words, "I love you." Those actions and words were not part of my world growing up, and when they arrived, it was healing and became an established family norm. My father and mother had a "do-over" with their grandchildren. My brother and I commented about it one night after a few stiff drinks. We agreed that it was easier for us to put our childhoods behind us and just be grateful that they could both be present and loving grandparents. The terminal sentence of one year given to my father stretched on to fifteen years. When he passed, all his grandchildren gathered around his hospice bed. As his daughter, I was relieved his journey was over. As a mother, I felt blessed that he had given his best self to the four teary-eyed young adult grandchildren. Dinara's soul cried with his passing, and my heart soared with gratitude for their strong bond.

It should not have been a surprise that Blanche came to my life as a spirit, but she did. It was my first reading from a medium, and I was skeptical. I felt I was committing an irrational act and expecting something I would somehow accept logically. When I was free from my repressive childhood home, I sought to learn all I could about God, and I studied my way right out of traditional, organized religion. So, as I sat in the chair trying to achieve a meditative state of openness for the medium, I simply stated, "Ask the universe if it has something it needs to share with me."

She gave a long pause, seemingly processing my request, then said, "Your grandmother is here, and she wants to work with you."

I asked, "Which one?" I drew in a half breath, "I have three."

Although she did not open her eyes, the medium gave me a strange look then said, "She says she is the fun one."

I had a follow-up question that I said inside my mind only. *Do you think you are the fun one, or did you have fun with me?*

Still, with her eyes closed, the medium raised her eyebrows and gave me the "what did you just say" face. "She says she wants to work with you using rose quartz."

At this moment, Blanche appeared in my mind, like a daydream. I noticed her hair was light brown and soft around her face. She appeared to me about my age and wore a light blue top and pink lipstick. I felt her cheek on mine. I smelled her familiar Chanel perfume. I held that moment in my mind for as long as possible. Time melted away, and I forgot my surroundings. She was smiling at me. The medium did not need to answer my question; I answered it myself. Whether a person has developed their natural gifts of spiritual communication or done a deep dive into family history on Ancestory.com, all people can receive ancestral guidance.

It is my belief that all people are on a journey for knowledge and spiritual growth. It is also my belief that as humans, we pass along knowledge through our shared DNA and life experiences. I firmly believe that humans have a greater capacity of communication than is utilized.

Intuition, energy flow exchange, the ability to read the room, to read a person, and to go with your gut are all skills that can be honed. Some people develop these skills inside a practice, such as a religion or through a mentor, while others grow it naturally as they grow over a lifetime. All that made up my biological grandmother and my mother is integrated into my cells and weaves in and out of my life experiences with an equally powerful flow of love that nourishes me from my adopted grandmother and daughter. Patterns develop and flow from one generation to the next and enhance or impede a person's journey. Choose a journey of healing and growth.

MY TOOL

Meditation is both spiritual and physical; it removes the stress and negativity of life, opens the mind to the sacred forces of the universe, and strengthens the body. I use positive affirmations in my daily ritual mediations to help me utilize all that God has given me in my mind, body, and spirit. I shared my story to illustrate the power affirmation and mediation have in positively guiding one's path. I believe that infants come into the world with all these gifts, and they are silenced by events, societal norms, and life trauma. I challenge you, the reader, to regain your gifts and promote them in your children.

My spirit grandmother continues to guide me through my life journey. Blanche's life lessons are mine to learn from; she is my affirmation chant. However, it was not easy for me to initially connect with her. I first had to bring a positive light into my life. I achieved this through learning to meditate, then to journey. My communication is held in my thoughts and physically gridded in stone. I maintain rose quartz as a central part of my daily meditation grid. Stones and crystals have long been utilized to enhance meditation and are often carried in pockets or worn as jewelry or amulets. These natural stones and crystals are ascribed meanings used to promote affirmations of good fortune, healing, protection from negativity, and increased energy. As my ability to journey during meditation grew, I utilized my affirmation grid messages to symbolically speak my words very clearly. I also wear my affirmation messages in the form of metaphysical jewelry to openly state the affirmations I am striving to achieve.

Try this tool:

Start with a free affirmation pendant of rose quartz (https://earthaffirmations.com/freebies) and my morning affirmation meditation ritual.

THE MORNING AFFIRMATION MEDITATION RITUAL

Rise with the sun naturally. Free your windows from heavy curtains and blinds and let the natural sunlight move around and cast light into your home. Let your body absorb the energy the light brings each day. Upon wakening, lay in bed with your eyes closed for ten minutes and enjoy the comfort and security. Mentally travel around your house, picturing each room. As you find a person, animal, or treasured item, leave this mental affirmation, *Peace, love, and joy in my house and to all who dwell within it.* Or find one that states what is in your heart and rolls off your tongue easily. Do this every morning of your life. Extend the morning meditation to your loved ones outside your home. Place rose quartz and black tourmaline in the four corners of your home, and mentally draw lines between them while saying the morning affirmation. Repeat daily.

For more affirmation meditations, sign up for Earth Affirmations free seasonal newsletter.

Lisa A. Newton, is a lifelong learner and educator, specializing in the field of special education and English language acquisition. She has gifts in the area of communication, and has published three language arts courses. She is a metaphysical jewelry and amulet designer, and student of reiki and shamanism.

https://www.facebook.com/earthaffirmations/

https://www.etsy.com/shop/EarthAffirmations

https://earthaffirmations.com/

Chapter 7

CUTTING THE CORD
Release Ancestral Karma through Spiritual Hypnosis

ALLISON BROWN, ED.D

MY STORY

Holy shit, this really works!

I sat there, flabbergasted, staring at my husband Will, who was lying in front of me in a deep trance state. To say I was shocked would have been an understatement. But I was also giddy with excitement! As a newly minted practitioner of a spiritual hypnosis modality called Beyond Quantum Healing (BQH), I naturally relied on Will to be my first guinea pig. Although I knew that hypnosis worked, and I trusted my training, I wasn't 100% convinced that I could put him "under." After all, it was ME! We had been married for 30 years. He was used to my voice! What if he just felt...weird?

Almost two hours later, after an incredible, in-depth conversation with his team of guides (who, we now know, call themselves The Collective), I brought Will back to a waking state.

"Do you have any idea how long you were out?" I asked him, still amazed at what had just transpired.

"Oh, I don't know...15 minutes?" Will replied nonchalantly.

You see, Will is a *somnambulist*. That means he is among the 5% of the population who go so deeply into a trance state that they don't recall their hypnosis session when they awaken. Most folks, however, remember everything, which is why they often don't believe that their hypnosis session even worked. They claim they were "awake" the whole time and think they "made it all up!"

Well, I know differently.

***

My journey to that point – that eventful day – might seem rather unremarkable to an outsider, but it was quite extraordinary for me personally. I grew up in a loving family with two parents and a younger brother. Although my parents eventually divorced, I was away at college by then, so the impact wasn't as traumatic as it might have been otherwise. I was raised within a conservative Christian framework; though it served me well for a time, I eventually realized that much of my belief system was grounded in fear: Fear of displeasing God, fear of going to Hell, fear of making the "wrong" choices.

My spiritual awakening was gradual. And by awakening, I mean reconciling with the fact that I was a spiritual being, temporarily housed in a physical body – understanding myself as a piece of the Divine, with gifts and abilities that extend well beyond what can be experienced with the five senses alone. Throughout my awakening process, I was eventually able to let go of the fear, operate from a place of love, and expand the "box" that I had placed around God/Source/Spirit.

It all started with a *knowing*. One day, I simply "knew" that I was supposed to start a hands-on healing team at my church. I now recognize this as an instance of *claircognizance*, knowing something without knowing why. I made an appointment with my pastor, who confirmed that he had gotten the same message; he just didn't know it would be *me* coming to see him. Wait, what?! This was huge! Not only was it the first time God had *spoken* to me, I realized I was being used as a conduit for healing; this was my path of service. Over the next fifteen years, I migrated away from mainstream religion and into the greater spiritual community. Truth be told, it took me quite a while to shed the fear-based constructs I had adopted, but my "box" gradually began to expand in miraculous ways!

My first point of exploration was Reiki, a Japanese technique for stress reduction and relaxation that also promotes healing. Typically administered through the laying on of hands, Reiki naturally piqued my curiosity – I wondered how it would compare to the "Christian" energy healing I had been practicing. I came to understand that no matter what I called it—Reiki or the Holy Spirit—the energy originated from the same Source. It was simply an overwhelming expression of intensely healing Love.

I like to joke that Reiki is a gateway "drug," because it tends to fling open the door to all sorts of metaphysical exploration. And, boy, was I addicted! I began practicing on my most convenient client, Will, of course, and that's when things really started to heat up. The Reiki energy quickly unlocked many of Will's latent gifts and abilities. His intuition heightened, his body vibrated inexplicably, and he began to perceive others' thoughts. It seemed as if something (or someone) was trying to get his attention.

The changes that were happening caused Will to reflect on his own childhood; although he had not been raised in the church, he always had a strange feeling, a distinct *knowing*, that he was not alone. It was a sensation of being guided and protected. Now, as he opened up to his spiritual nature, the Universe put specific people and experiences on his path. One afternoon, as he perused Facebook, he noticed that a freshly trained Quantum Healing Hypnosis Technique® (QHHT®) practitioner was soliciting "practice" clients. QHHT® is a past life regression process founded by the late Dolores Cannon, an extraordinary pioneer in the field of quantum healing. Will had never heard of it, so, naturally, he volunteered. It turns out Will is really good at this guinea pig thing!

During his session, much to the practitioner's surprise, Will dropped into a somnambulistic trance and began to channel his primary guide, Enoch – Noah's great grandfather! (By channeling, I mean that Enoch used Will's voice to communicate.) Enoch was the one Will had sensed around him as a child and who guided him from behind the scenes all of his life. This was particularly noteworthy, as Will had not been raised in the church – he didn't know who Enoch was, nor had he ever read the Bible. After a few more sessions, Will understood that he actually had a small "team" of guides – The Collective – and was able to bring them forth through channeling.

Around the same time, my own guides were leading me towards the BQH course that I spoke about earlier. BQH is, from my perspective, an evolution of QHHT – very similar in process and outcome but a bit less structured, with fewer rules to follow. I assumed that my guides wanted me to learn the process to assist Will with his channeling, but during that very first session, the one I described at the beginning of this chapter, I was told that I would be using this modality to help others on their healing journeys. The Collective assured me that they were there to guide and assist me along this new path.

**

I completed BQH training in July of 2018 and began seeing my own "practice" clients to hone this new skill. As promised, The Collective placed the perfect people on my path; folks who came from all walks of life with a variety of issues, challenges, and goals. Little by little, I increased my comfort level and fine-tuned my ability to stay calm and think on my feet. In a spiritual hypnosis session, you never know what you'll be presented with!

I like to call this modality spiritual hypnosis, in contrast to traditional therapeutic hypnosis. First of all, I am not a certified hypnotherapist, and truthfully, the two roles are quite different. Rather than tackling issues from a purely scientific, clinical perspective, BQH allows me to take a metaphysical approach. In other words, as energetic beings, most of our physical ailments and emotional issues have an underlying energetic origin. And as any gardener knows, unless you kill the root, you'll simply keep treating the weeds that sprout up on the surface. (Please note: it is not my intention to imply that conventional medical intervention isn't necessary. Traditional Western medicine most definitely has its place and is a critical component of a balanced health plan.)

Take, for example, a client who wishes to lose weight. During our BQH session, we would search for the origin of the weight issue. Quite often, the origin pertains to a past life. Perhaps, in this case, the individual had perished from starvation in a previous lifetime. The soul's remembrance of that predicament could unwittingly filter into the client's current life, causing an unconscious compulsion to eat. Once that information is brought forward, and understanding has taken place, the issue can be released. In many cases, it truly is that simple!

What does all of this have to do with ancestors, you ask? Well, when we tap into past lives, we can also explore previous familial relationships with those who are (or were) present in our current life. Through reincarnation, human souls have the opportunity to explore karmic themes and play out various roles from lifetime to lifetime. If your soul wanted to learn about compassion, for example, you could choose to play several roles: once as a disabled child, another as the child's parent, and again as the child's sibling. Within those roles, you'd be able to explore receiving (or not receiving) compassion *and* providing (or not providing) compassion. By incorporating all of those different perspectives, your soul would acquire a more balanced understanding of compassion. And truly, that is what karma is all about – balance. Not payback or revenge. Therefore, when we can peer into past lives, we gain a new perspective, ultimately making forgiveness and reconciliation much easier.

Before incarnating into human form, all souls create a life plan. We design our own "play," if you will. We write the script and make agreements with other actors (souls) to explore a particular theme, undertake certain experiences, or learn specific lessons. Likely, you and your family members incarnated together to "act out" those roles – all at your request. Part of these agreements include your family's genetic make-up and behavioral proclivities. For example, you might have chosen a birth family with a history of alcoholism or drug abuse. Or, perhaps the men in your family all tend to die early from heart disease. In other words, your birth family and ancestors, along with their genes, traits, and behaviors, are working FOR you, not against you, as it sometimes seems. They help create the foundation through which your soul learns and grows. Keeping this in mind can help you find peace in times of turmoil.

Don't misunderstand; this is not an attempt to blame the victim. You should *never* remain in any abusive situation, thinking that you somehow *asked* for it. Always remember that our souls are pure Love. However, when we incarnate into the physical body, a veil is created; we "forget" who we *really* are. What's more, each and every one of us has free will. All too often, we get lost in our roles…we become too immersed in the "play," and we forget that, at our core, we are Love. When we become courageous enough to undertake this type of healing work, we must remember that there is a *huge* difference between attempting to understand (and possibly forgive) an abusive family member and allowing that family member to continue to abuse us.

A spiritual hypnosis session can lead to profound healing in a variety of ways. First of all, you can unravel the mystery behind any genetic or behavioral threads you've inherited as part of your ancestral lineage. In the case of karmic ties, oftentimes, you may not even be aware that there is an ancestral "history." Sometimes, awareness alone is enough to loosen the grip of the past and allow for emotional healing. In other cases, connecting with your ancestors through hypnosis can open the door to a new relationship with them, tapping into *their* assistance from across the veil. Once they lose the physical body, your ancestors in Spirit have a much deeper understanding of the impact their actions had on others.

What's more, souls never stop evolving—so helping *you* heal benefits them, as well. It's a win-win!

THE TOOL

During a spiritual hypnosis session, the practitioner induces the client into a light trance state, similar to what is experienced upon waking. Most folks simply feel extremely relaxed. Being in a light trance is quite common, actually. Have you ever been so engrossed in a book that you didn't hear someone speaking to you? That's what being in "trance" feels like! Relaxing the conscious mind (the left brain) in this way allows for the subconscious mind (the right brain) to take center stage. And *that* is the gateway to the Quantum Field, where *everything* exists.

Some people feel that they are too left-brained, analytical, or skeptical to completely relax; they may also find it difficult to meditate. If this describes you, it can be incredibly helpful to practice inducing yourself, taking the time to walk your body through a progressive relaxation exercise. This is an important first step in being able to access valuable information from the Quantum Field.

What follows is a simple relaxation exercise designed to progressively guide your body – and subsequently, your mind – into a state that imitates the hypnotic trance. Practice this as often as you wish; the more consistent you are, the more successful you'll be. Once relaxation comes easily, head over to my website www.drallisonbrown.com, where you can download a free recording that will guide you into a past life regression. Have a pen and journal handy to record any impressions or insight you receive as you listen to the recording. You will be prompted to remember everything you experience.

How to engage with this exercise: After reading through the exercise below, you may want to record it so you can fully engage without having to glance at or memorize the instructions. Once you've worked your way through this exercise, you will be in a completely relaxed and receptive state. Therefore, it can be helpful to set an intention prior to each session, whether that be to simply relax and let go, gain insight regarding a dilemma, or receive a message from an ancestor. Remember, an intention is not the same thing as an expectation. So, release the need for a specific outcome. Now, let's get started!

RELAXATION EXERCISE

Begin by finding a comfortable, quiet place to sit or lie down. You may choose to play soothing instrumental music if you wish. Turn off your phone. Ensure there will be no distractions for the next 15 minutes.

Focus on your breath. Breathe in and out deeply but comfortably. Do this for a few minutes, allowing your breath to find its own rhythm. Feel your body become heavy, sinking into the floor or chair. Allow any cares of the day to flow out with each exhale.

Now, focus on your heart space. Imagine that your heart itself is doing the breathing…breathing the air in…and out. The air flows in through your heart, circulating it throughout your entire body. Take a moment, while immersed in your heart space, to feel a sense of gratitude – for your body, for this quiet time…for whatever is going *right* in your life.

Now, I want you to imagine a beautiful shower of warm, golden light streaming down onto the top of your head. This crystalline light is magnificent! It heals and relaxes *everything* in its path.

This warm light flows down, now, into your head and face, relaxing the muscles of your forehead, your eyes, your cheeks, and your mouth. Your throat is now bathed in this light.

The light moves down into your neck and shoulders, releasing any tension and relaxing the shoulder muscles.

This golden light travels down your arms, relaxing the muscles of your arms, your forearms...all the way down to the tips of your fingers.

This healing energy flows, now, down your back...releasing and relaxing the big muscles of your back...down, now, into your lower back, allowing any tension to drain down into the floor.

Your torso is now bathed in this warm, glowing light...filling every organ, every system in the body.

This beautiful light flows down, now, across the hips...relaxing the hips...moving down, now, into the legs...this warm energy releasing and relaxing the muscles of the legs, the shins, the calves, and the feet.

This healing light streams out of the feet and down into the floor, carrying away any remaining tension...negativity...anything that doesn't serve you as you lie in this comfortable, warm, relaxed, and peaceful state.

(Remain here for as long as you wish. Take note of any impressions, feelings, or sensations you experience.)

When you are ready, gently return back to your room, becoming aware again of your physical body, aware of this current day and time. You may wiggle your fingers and toes and open your eyes when you are ready.

Dr. Allison Brown is an educator, writer, and seeker. Her search for reconciliation between a newfound spirituality and her traditional Christian upbringing led her on an amazing journey of self-discovery. Her passion is to share those lessons and insights with others.

As a Reiki Master Teacher and a Quantum Healing Practitioner, Allison employs a spiritual hypnosis modality called Beyond Quantum Healing (BQH). Holding a master's degree in counseling psychology and a doctorate in educational leadership, Allison's use of metaphysical practices within a framework of traditional counseling gives her the unique ability to gently uncover and address her clients' underlying issues.

In addition to being a syndicated contributor to the *Good Men Project* online magazine, Allison's work has appeared in numerous publications, including *Focus on Fabulous, Natural Awakenings, and Heart and Humanity*. She has been a twice-featured guest on award-winning author Debra Moffitt's Unity Online radio program, *Divinely Inspired Living*, discussing the inspiration behind her first book, *The Journey Within: A Christian's guide to 14 Non-Traditional Spiritual Practices,* published by Cactus Moon.

Allison and her husband, Will, a psychic medium and trance channel, are partners, working together to help folks heal, discover, and awaken. Using complementary skills, they facilitate communication with their clients' higher selves, spiritual guides, ancestors, and even pets! In 2016 Allison and Will, both veterans, co-founded Reiki For Vets (RFV), a non-profit that works within the Veterans Administration to provide free Reiki clinics to disabled veterans. Connect with Allison directly at drallisonbrown.com or visit palmandlotus.com to find resources that will assist you on your journey!

Chapter 8

UNLOCK YOUR ANCESTRAL STORY
Take Charge of YOUR Life

JACQUELINE KANE, R.T., LMT, EFT, BP

MY STORY

I was at the Old Corner Bar at Thanksgiving 2015 with my husband Don, his parents, brother, and wife, Pam. It was cold outside, but inside the air was noisy with my favorite singer, Mark James, playing Irish tunes. We were trying to cheer Pam up from her father's illness and subsequent recent death. Even though he was 80 years old, it was still tough after her sister's sudden death earlier in the year.

A part of me is always looking to make people feel comfortable. Some people call it the "team player" part of the psyche. I knew my sister-in-law was very close to her family and that the holidays would be tough.

My solution was to plan a family trip for the thirteen of us. Over frosty glasses of Guinness, I said, "Let's go to Ireland for Christmas." The more we talked as the beer slid down our throats, the more excitement bubbled up for some of us.

Since my mother-in-law was born in Ireland, I thought they would enjoy a family trip to her hometown. The grandkids were at a great age to travel. I thought it would be the perfect time to show them where their grandmother grew up and also introduce them to their Irish cousins and family. Some remarked on where to find a house to accommodate 13 of us, with a big kitchen for communal cooking and a table to gather at for card games. We also needed enough personal space to accommodate six teenagers and their hormonal mood swings.

It came as a great surprise when I heard my inlaws say, "We don't want to go back to Ireland, especially at Christmas time. It's too cold to be going there to visit. It'll be too hard to get the family together. And will we all get along?"

I was so disappointed hearing this great idea, and excitement fizzled out. So many times in my life, I had ideas, then experienced rejection, then disappointment. Because I was doing so much personal development work, I recognized the following as a deep-seated belief: *No one ever wants to do what I want to do.*

Wow, really? I thought. So many questions flooded my mind. *Why not?* After some discussion, we dropped the subject and moved on. My husband and I decided that if we really wanted to go, we would take our two teenage sons, and the four of us would take the trip.

Christmas came and went with little discussion about vacationing in Ireland.

In January of 2016, I had the pleasure of going to visit my mentor and friend Alan Davidson in Houston, Texas. He was hosting a three-day retreat, and I was excited to spend the weekend with friends to experience Alan's Mystic Meditation processes.

On the second day of the retreat, he took us through his Ancestral Karma Energy Clearing process. I don't remember feeling or noticing anything during the process. It was immediately afterward when I became aware that something amazing had just happened.

As I was leaving the event hall, my phone started buzzing. My son was texting to say that he found a house to rent in Ireland, perfect for all 13 of us. It had enough bedrooms, bathrooms, and space so we could join for activities, but not so close that we'd want to kill each other.

My first thought was, *that's nice, but we aren't going.* Then, I was shocked to read the next text from my husband saying that the family had reconsidered. Everyone, including my inlaws, agreed to go on vacation together, all thirteen of us!

I shook my head, walked up to Alan, and asked, "Okay, what just happened? What on earth did we just do to create this kind of shift?"

Alan replied, "No mistakes," as he nodded with quiet satisfaction.

I know there are no coincidences in life. Something inside of me said, "Pay attention, Jacque."

From the moment I received the text from my son, everything became easy planning for our upcoming vacation. We found the perfect, large house which had bedrooms to accommodate everyone's needs. It had a huge kitchen where we could cook together, and I envisioned playing card games and drinking wine while socializing with the Irish relatives. And that's how it turned out.

A couple of my special moments were simply being with my sons, my husband, and the extended family. Being able to hang out and spend time together was something I was longing for, and it filled my heart.

The trip included flying to Dublin, where we spent a couple of days. It was a bittersweet time as my husband's uncle was close to passing. This was another sign that our trip was divinely guided, so he could be there to say goodbye. It was a blessing for my mother and father-in-law to spend time with their cousin before he passed.

There was so much to see and so many relatives to meet. It was a joy to meet so many new cousins and their children. I was so impressed as I watched my sons meet strangers and become friends with their new cousins.

We enjoyed a trip to the Guinness factory that had Dublin's most amazing view from their scenic bar. Of course, there were too many pubs to mention, and we enjoyed as many as we could in the two days we were there.

One of my favorite parts of going to pubs in Ireland is the music. Each pub has its own local talent that graced us with perfect pitch singers whose job was to get the audience engaged. That was easy to do when the Guinness was flowing.

The time came to leave Dublin and drive to Killarney to see if the house we rented was real. The family had many skeptical conversations wondering, "Is this house we rented online and paid for even really there?"

We boarded a 20-person rented van with a driver hired to take us across Ireland to Killarney. We were beyond excited to see that the house really did exist. It was beyond our wildest dreams. It even came with a horse called Cora, who visited us daily in the backyard.

The most important question the teenagers asked was, "Does it have WIFI, and is it working?" The days were better for everyone when WIFI cooperated.

It was bitter-sweet to watch our children play in the same area my husband and his siblings used to play when they visited their Nana. Visiting her home brought up so many memories for my sister-in-law and her mom. I loved being able to experience this with them.

This vacation was divinely guided as we met so many old friends and family. We took scenic tours to the Cliffs of Moher, driving through the Burren and sharing pints of Guinness and so much laughter. The trip to Ireland helped Pam so much with her grief and brought us all together.

It is such a blessing to think that it all became real with one ancestral energy clearing. I learned I could turn my pattern of disappointment into excitement to create unlimited possibility. I believe it changed my energy enough so that it helped change my families' minds from a "No" into a "Yes!" And I've had the honor to provide Ancestral Energy Clearings for my clients so that they release limiting patterns to create their unlimited possibilities. I love witnessing the "Yes!" in their lives.

Today I would like to help you clarify what your Ancestral Energy story is, and then let's begin to unlock it.

"What is Ancestral Energy?" I define it as our ancestors' unresolved emotional issues from situations or events that caused hurt, pain, or trauma. These may have included illnesses, accidents, financial troubles, broken relationships, etc. This consists of any "emotional baggage" that was unsettled, pushed aside, or not talked about in their lifetime.

This Ancestral Energy impacts five key areas:

1. Your physical, emotional and mental health.

2. Your ability to create wealth and cash flow.

3. Your ability to have deep connections.

4. Your spiritual connections and ability to have faith no matter what.

5. Your ability to step into your power, own who you are, and communicate your needs.

Standing in your power is being able to succeed in all five of these areas. The cost of not healing ancestral energy is:

• The lack of a strong healthy, vibrant body.

• An abundance in income and wealth building.

• Fulfilling relationships.

• A deep spiritual connection with your soul purpose and trusting your divine guidance.

• Setting healthy boundaries for optimal living.

Indications that there are deficits or impairments are crippling self-doubt, confusion, lack of clarity, and lack of action towards your soul's purpose and your sacred calling.

Let's uncover your ancestral energy story and see how it impacts your physical, emotional, and mental health.

First, know that we are all energetic beings susceptible to the energy of others.

It starts in the womb from conception. As a fetus, we lived in our mother's womb, where we were exposed to her hormones, nutrition, and emotional state. All of her worries, concerns, joys, and excitement surrounded us.

Some mothers enjoyed emotions and thoughts like, "a child is a blessing." They enjoyed good nutrition to nourish the growing infant.

Compare that to the angst of a mother with "too many mouths to feed," struggling to put food on the table or a roof overhead. A lower-income level meant overwhelm, crowded living conditions, noise, and perhaps issues of alcoholism, abuse, or neglect. This contributes to the infant's environment in the womb.

Whichever environment existed for our great grandmother's, grandmother's, or mother's babies, it wasn't a choice. Babies are exposed to what their mothers and fathers are exposed to!

And that's where your ancestral energetic story begins because your mother carried her mother's energy, pain, suffering, beliefs, and programming, as well as her mother's mother and back through time.

There were even ancestral health conditions, pain, and suffering entering into you in the womb. It became your DNA. Your cells were infused with it. Your nervous system and every system in your body were created from that energy. You inherited the DNA of your personal family trauma, which is passed down from generation to generation.

These patterns can inhibit or disrupt your success today. They show up as obstacles, blocking your pathway to joy, abundance, authentic power, and unlimited possibilities.

Scientists are now studying how the grandchildren of the Holocaust are impacted by ancestral energy leading to grief, sadness, or pain. It's been written that they experience guilt around being alive.

This survivor's guilt shows up in every area of their lives. They feel bad about being successful and doing well. They could experience a lot of sadness in their lives and not understand why. They could have trouble taking action because they're confused, doubt themselves, or lack clarity, thus preventing taking action and not feeling empowered to speak up to get their needs met.

I remember growing up with fear and worry. I was always nervous but didn't understand why. This high level of worry and fear caused me to be exhausted and depressed for years.

I suffered from physical pain in my hips and lower back. I went to many doctor's visits without getting much relief. Finally, I was diagnosed with Chronic Fatigue Syndrome.

My Ancestral Energy story includes my grandmother raising her family in Sardinia, Italy, during World War II. My grandfather was a soldier fighting at the front while Nonna was home alone raising three children, including my mother. Nonna lived in fear and worry about her husband, struggling to feed her family. Like other villagers, she lived with the constant threat of the German soldiers who invaded her town and what they could do to her or her loved ones. Fear was the norm for her.

As I was growing up, Nonna never spoke of those days in Italy. I could only imagine her daily level of fear, and I wondered how it impacted her life.

I know that back then, everyone suppressed their emotions. They had to just to survive. Fear became a part of them. It affected their neurons, programming, DNA, hormones, and all systems of their body. When they became pregnant, their babies inherited these states, and so on. All of this becomes so ingrained and programmed into us that we don't even question it.

I witnessed my mother living with worry, fear, and feeling like she was powerless to do anything about healing it. She said things like, "The doctor can't help me to hear better," or "Nothing will help me get rid of the pain in my hips and legs." That is the impact of her mother's experiences.

You may hear people say, "That's just the way it is." Or, "My family has heart problems; that's just how it is for my family." These are statements of ancestral energy stories. And there are ways to transform and clear these. This can help stop the passing of those patterns to the next generation.

Ancestral energy clearing may be the missing link to free you from what you've inherited so that you can begin living your life with ease, flow, and abundance; so that you enjoy personal fulfillment.

THE TOOL

Here is a process you can use to unlock your inherited ancestral energy story, causing physical, emotional, or mental challenges in your life.

Instructions: Set aside some quiet time, grab a pen and your journal or writing device, and ask yourself the following questions. You can also go to my resource page at www.jacquelinemkane.com/resources and listen to a video I recorded for you to take you through this process.

1. Your Physical Health

- How is your physical health?
- Do you experience daily physical pain?
- When you think of this physical pain, how does it make you feel?
- How is your energy level?
- Do family members have similar complaints or conditions, like heart disease, diabetes, headaches, arthritis, or infertility?
- What's the common complaint that you hear in your family? You may hear people say, "Yes, heart conditions run in our families. That's just the way it is."

2. Your Emotional and Mental Health

- How is your emotional health?
- Do you experience confusion, self-doubt, or lack of motivation frequently?
- Do you suffer from emotions of guilt, blame, and shame?
- How is your level of openness or trust towards others? Does this help you build nurturing relationships?
- What is the level of resilience you have to overcome obstacles, learn from mistakes, and move forward?
- Do family members have similar complaints or conditions, like depression, anxiety, overwhelm?
- What is the belief that you created about your life?
- What's the most common emotion you feel?

3. Your Ancestral Energetic Story

- What awareness about your family have you uncovered?
- What's the emotion that keeps coming up for you as you went through this exercise?
- What was the most common emotion that you saw your parents experience?
- What was the energy, belief, and thought felt in everything?

4. Release the Old

- What's the common emotion and energy that has played out in your family?
- Where does this energy sit in your body?
- Is there a color or texture to it?
- Scoop and pull this energy outside of your body into a ball in front of you.
- Ask this ball of energy what it needs from you?
- Who does it belong to?
- Now send it back to that person with love.

5. Embrace the New You

- Decide what new energy you would love to bring into your body. For example: Unconditional love, compassion, excitement. Bring this new energy into your body and allow this new energy to expand into your entire body.
- Take a few deep breaths and breathe in this new energy.
- Visualize your new life as you expand into this new energy. Visualize the new you.
- Take a few minutes to come back to the present moment.
- Journal your new thoughts and ideas.
- Decide today and claim that this is the new you and that you get to have all you desire.

This is a powerful process that can make a huge impact on your health and your life. The more you do it, the more you will trust the process and notice your health and life improve for the better. Basically, all areas of your life will improve.

I would love to know what you noticed during this process. Feel free to send me an email and let me know what you noticed or ask any questions. Email me at jacqueline@jacquelinemkane.com

Jacqueline Kane, Medical Intuitive, Stop The Pain Specialist, wants to know what's going on underneath the surface. After 35 years in health care and 20 years in private practice as a healer, she knows that one of the keys to a full life is to look past the symptoms of a problem to access the cause.

Along her journey as a Bowenwork Therapist, Tapping Into Wealth Expert, Soul Clearings, Massage Therapist, and Emotional Freedom Technique Practitioner, she discovered the crucial hidden links between physical pain, finances, and our ability to live with joy and ease. Her research led her to create unique, results-oriented methods for uncovering these connections. Her programs liberate clients from physical pain and financial struggle, so they create a path to energy, health, ease with money, and personal fulfillment.

Jacqueline works with individuals, groups, and organizations. She is the creator of the Healthy Wealthy Success Blueprint© for creating a joyful, pain-free life full of energy and financial success.

If you're ready to reach your health and wealth goals today visit www.JacquelineMKane.com.

Chapter 9

HEAR THE WHISPERS OF YOUR ANCESTORS

Connect and Embrace the Power of Your Gifts and Talents

DEENA CHESTER, A.S., B.A., M.C.S, C.HT

MY STORY

A little girl, maybe five years old, is sitting alone in a meadow. Her tiny body is almost hidden by the tall grass and flowers. The sun reflects on her dark brown, braided hair. There doesn't seem to be any adults nearby. Who would have left a child alone like that? Is she okay? What is she thinking? Is she scared and afraid?

That little girl is me in a former life and showed up in a past-life regression hypnosis session in my hypnotherapy certification program. I must admit that I was extremely skeptical. I wasn't sure about reincarnation and did not expect to have such a powerful, life-changing experience.

It was explained that even if you don't believe in past lives, the process can tap into your subconscious mind. Your subconscious mind understands stories and metaphors. The hypnotherapist guides the client through the steps to go into deep relaxation. It's there that the client can connect with her subconscious mind where the memories reside.

As I settled into the comfortable chair, I became more relaxed even though I was a little anxious. Athena, the Hypnotherapist, spoke with a calm and soothing voice. She provided an overview of the session and gave me the opportunity to ask questions.

Athena: "Today, we are going to do a past life regression session with the intent that you connect with your ancestors in this lifetime or a past lifetime. Are you ready to begin?"

Me: "Yes"

Athena proceeded to guide me through steps to relax and then lead me on a journey to connect with a past life.

Athena: "Where are you?"

Me: "In the meadow." *I am not sure why she is asking. Can't she see it is a meadow?*

Athena: "Tell me about the meadow."

Me: "I am sitting on soft, green grass. There are yellow and white flowers. Do you hear the birds and the animals?"

Athena: "I did hear a bird. How old are you?"

Me: "I am a little girl."

Athena: "Do you know how many years old you are?

Me: "Little." *Can't she see I am little?*

Athena: "Are you alone?"

Me: *Someone is talking again. I can't hear the birds.*

Athena begins to think that maybe I'm going to a time when I felt alone or abandoned.

Athena: "Can you hear me? Are you alone?"

Me: "I am not alone."

Athena: "Who is with you?

Me: *Sighs.* "My earth family, like butterflies, bees, rabbits, wolves, deer, skunks, dragons, fairies, wind, moon, and sun."

Me: *I don't understand why she can't see them. Maybe she has old eyes.*

Athena: "Where are the adults?"

Me: "I don't know what that is."

Me: *Bunny and skunk are playing a roll and tumble game. I should go play with them. Sometimes skunk gets stinky.*

Athena: "Where is your mother or father?"

Me: "I don't know. Probably over there at the tepees doing what big people do."

The little girl is giggling as she plays and talks with the animals. She thinks it's so sweet when wolf nuzzles her ear. She feels so pretty when butterflies sit on her head.

Athena: "Do they know where you are?"

Me: *I wish she would leave and quit talking to me.*

Me: "Yes. Grandmother will come for me later. She is funny and smart. We play games in the woods. She teaches me to listen to the wind and the animals. She tells me which plants are good for me. She shows me how to make flower necklaces. She tells me I'm a special little girl. She says I'm smart like her. I'm important, and I matter. Someday, I will have wisdom like her. She says I will heal and help others."

Athena: "I see. Are you happy here?"

Me: "Yes. Do you have to keep talking? You are bothering the animals."

The little girl is feeling bothered and annoyed. She just wants to play and be with her friends.

Athena: "Just a few more questions. What makes you happy here?"

Me: "My earth friends love me, and we have fun. We talk, sing, run, jump, play, and see the magic. Sometimes, we are quiet and listen to each other, the wind, the grass, the trees, and the sun. You can leave now."

Athena: "Are you ever afraid?"

Me: "Grandmother says that I'm safe, protected, and loved. I'm a little sunbeam."

Athena: "Very well then, child. Thank you for talking to me."

Me: *Earth friends, it is happy time.*

During the session, I felt frustrated because the woman kept talking and was bothering me. I wanted to be with my earth friends because it made me happy.

Athena seemed concerned that I was alone and maybe abandoned. I couldn't understand why she would think such a thing. I had such a sense of safety and love. Every time I think about the session, I can immediately connect to those feelings.

The session was so powerful as I realized and felt so connected to that time and place. My oneness with nature, the animals, and grandmother brought me so much comfort and peace. It was such a comfort to have my ancestors there, especially my grandmother. Even as that child, I knew she was smart. It made me smile that I mentioned her being funny. Even though her skin was weathered and wrinkled, her smile was precious, and her eyes twinkled.

She is an ancestor who is still in my heart and has traveled many lifetimes with me. It seems like such a simple message to know I'm safe, protected, and loved. Hearing her tell me that I was important and that I matter had huge healing benefits for me.

When I did this session, I was at a very transitional point in my life, and these were feelings I totally lost touch with. I recently divorced after 20 years of marriage and was starting the journey of moving out of traditional healthcare and feeling stuck and frustrated in my job. At that time, I was still confident in my abilities as a systems analyst in healthcare information technology. It was easy to be a manager or consultant, but there was no longer any fulfillment there, and it drained my soul.

I was taking classes in reiki, metaphysical reflexology, shamanism, and other holistic modalities. But I had the false belief that I couldn't leave healthcare and work in the holistic field. Remembering grandmother telling me I would have wisdom like her and help heal others was a life changer for me. Once I quit sobbing and shaking, I knew that I came to this world to be a healer. Part of my purpose in this lifetime is to guide others to remember their unique life purpose and take action to live it. Part of the process is teaching them to accept their power by connecting and embracing their gifts and talents.

As I write this story, I realize grandmother is bringing to my awareness earth connection and magic. It's in nature that I connect, and I haven't been doing that lately. It's there that I will continue to find healing, connection, and magic.

This is just one example of the power of the subconscious mind's ability to connect with ancestors, other lives, and to heal. When a person heals, the ancestors heal, as do future generations.

THE TOOL

This tool can be used to better understand your gifts and talents you may not be aware of or have forgotten. This is a method of tapping into ancient and ancestral wisdom and guidance. It may also be used when struggling with feelings, going through changes, or dealing with a challenge.

A free recording of this exercise is available at www.acceptyourpower.com/ancestorswithin. If you listen to the recording provided in the link, do not listen while driving.

The steps in the exercise are amazingly simple. Read through the steps first. The first few times you do the exercise, you may want to open your eyes and look at the steps.

Steps 1-10 can be used anytime to relax, meditate, or connect with your higher self.

1. Find a quiet location where you will not be disturbed. Sit or lie in a comfortable position.

2. Set your intention for this exercise to connect to your ancestors to explore your gifts and talents.

3. Put your thumb and index finger on your left hand together.

4. Look up and focus on a spot on the ceiling. If you are outside, focus on a spot in the sky. If you are in a dark room, look up.

5. Take a deep breath in and hold it for a moment.

6. Say to yourself, "Relax."

7. Exhale as you close your eyes and relax your hand—tension releases from your body.

8. Take two more deep breaths. Each breath relaxes you more.

9. Imagine or think of a beautiful golden beam of light and relaxation above you. The light softly and slowly descends and moves down to your head and shoulders. As it descends, you feel each part of your body releasing and relaxing. That's right. The light continues to gently flow down your body all the way to your toes.

10. This light will also protect you, and you will only make connections that are for your highest good and benefit.

11. Imagine or think about a long hallway in front of you. The hallway has doors on both sides. Each door is different. Some may seem ancient, and others more modern. Some are made of wood, and some are metal. Some doors are tall and wide, and others are smaller. The doors vary in color. The doorknobs are different on each door. Some are round, some are elongated, and some are larger than others. They may be made of different materials like wood, brass, or crystals.

12. Take your time and notice which door or doors attracts you. At first, there may be more than one. Move toward the door that is attracting you the most.

13. Reach out and touch the doorknob. Easily turn the knob and open the door. You may feel excitement as this journey begins.

14. You are in a safe place. Step inside and observe. Look all around you, including up and down.

15. The place may be familiar or maybe not.

16. Does it seem like a time in the past or the future?

17. Hear what you hear. See what you see. Smell what you smell. Feel what you feel. If there is food or drink, taste what you taste.

18. Notice that there is a group of people nearby. One of the people or beings starts walking toward you. There is a feeling of connection and familiarity. There is a bench on the path between you. The person gestures for you to join them on the bench.

19. Follow your feelings. You may want to hug them, touch their hand, or just sit beside them. Know that this meeting is a connection for your highest good at this time.

20. Listen for a moment. They may share a story or information with you. Even if it seems strange or odd to you, just allow yourself to take it in. They may tell you of a story in their life that resonates with you. They may tell you what gifts and talents they experienced in their lifetime.

21. If they did not already provide information on your gifts and talents, then ask them questions (examples below).

    a. Are there gifts and talents that I am not aware of or have forgotten about?

    b. If you knew me as a child, what did I like to do or play?

    c. Are there gifts or talents that you know you passed on to me?

    d. Did you have challenges in your lifetime with the gifts or talents that we share? If so, how did you handle them?

    e. Do you have suggestions on how I should use my gifts and talents?

    f. Are there any other words of wisdom or guidance you have for me?

    g. Take a few moments and enjoy this interaction.

22. Thank them and make your way back to the door and step back into the hallway.

23. Now become aware of your body. Say to yourself, "One, two, three, awake." When you say, "Awake," you will feel energized, connected, and alert.

After doing this exercise, it is a great time to contemplate your experiences. Writing down your thoughts and feelings will often connect you even deeper to your gifts and talents. Sometimes after this exercise, you may get more information in the coming days or in dreams.

How will you take action to continue to connect and embrace the power of your gifts and talents?

Deena Chester is an expert healer and owner of Accept Your Power. She's a certified hypnotherapist, past life and age regression specialist, certified transformational life coach, Reiki Master, EFT practitioner, providing intuitive, transformational guidance for spiritual connection, past lives, and unique life purpose. Deena's powerful blend of modalities and skills will help you live the life you were born for. She offers individual sessions, workshops, and group sessions online and by phone.

Deena's journey began in the rural mountains of Virginia, where opportunities were limited, especially for females. She never felt like she fit in, nor did she really want to. She felt a longing and calling for a different path. She found the courage, took a chance, and stepped out into the unknown, achieving an associate degree in science, bachelor's degree in medical technology, and master's in computer science.

The structured, analytical, and logical math and science career path served her for many years, but there was always a feeling that there must be something more. And there was! She reached deep within and found the courage that she didn't know existed. As she connected with her soul and higher guidance, she stepped into living her unique life purpose. Deena's heart's desire is to help others find what makes their hearts sing sooner and with fewer side journeys.

Try this FREE quick exercise to discover if you are connected with your Unique Life Purpose and receive a FREE bonus guided imagery download at https://www.acceptyourpower.com. You will also find a full list of Deena's life-changing services.

Chapter 10

RAPTURE JOURNALING

Surviving Your Ancestral Story:
Recognizing the Opportunity for Change

CAROL DUTTON, SUBTLE ENERGY MEDICINE
SPECIALIST, AND REIKI MASTER

MY STORY

Keep thinking positive! We trust this neurologist. She will have a solution.

It's been 16 years since the onset of symptoms, and five years of doctor visits, physical therapy appointments, numerous EMGs, two muscle biopsy surgeries, pulmonary tests, and many MRIs, that have brought us to this point.

His name is called.

He slowly rises from his chair and concentrates on his gait. We follow the nurse through the maze of hallways to the exam and consultation room. After the nurse asked the intake questions and recorded his vital signs, we wait for the doctor.

"Are you ready for this?" I ask. He stoically replies, "It is what it is."

My husband and I are at Mayo Clinic Rochester, Minnesota. After seemingly endless rounds of testing and months of waiting, we will finally have an answer.

This appointment will reveal their findings and course of action.

Don't let my fear show. He needs my support. Stay strong!

The doctor arrives. Going through all the test results with us, she draws pictures and explains. Finally, it is time for the diagnosis.

She compassionately says, "So what we think you have is a form of Mitochondrial Myopathy. But we haven't been able to identify the gene source causing your condition. What we do know is it is located in your nuclei DNA, not the mitochondrial DNA. That means it comes from both of your parents, not just your mother. This makes your case exceptionally rare."

Okay, so what does this really mean?

She completes the diagnosis with, "There is no known treatment, no known cure. Now, do you have any questions?"

What the HELL? How can we absorb what you just said, let alone form any semblance of a question?

Ever practical, he asks, "So what's that mean? Tell me what will happen." She replies, "Your muscles don't rebuild. A muscle tear, no matter how small, will never mend itself. Also, remember that your heart is a muscle. It is important to never allow your heart rate to exceed 100 bpm. Heat makes your muscles work harder trying to cool your body, so avoid getting hot. But don't stop moving, just don't overwork the muscles." She continues with, "We can do more extensive gene testing, but it would be at your expense. Insurance won't cover it because your prognosis won't change regardless of what we find." After discussion, we choose not to proceed with this $15,000 testing.

My heart falls into my stomach. Speechless and devastated, I view our world completely falling apart and realize our future will never be what we planned.

The doctor continues talking. My mind is beyond comprehending everything she's telling us, blurring the rest of the appointment.

I leave with the impression he will end up in a wheelchair within six months, a care facility, and might survive for a year.

Our life is over. My heart is breaking for him. I don't want to see him suffering. I especially don't want to become a widow. Remember, this isn't about you; it is about his needs. Keep quiet. Let him lead the way on how we work through this.

Gripping the steering wheel, I navigate the car out of the parking ramp to begin our four-hour drive home. Feeling the strain, I concentrate on the traffic. Slumped in his seat, defeat written on his face, he is uncharacteristically quiet. We are each absorbed in our private thoughts. Our conversation is sporadic and covering several topics. At times the silence is palpable as we avoid bringing up the ELEPHANT.

"I agree with your doctor when she said it makes no sense that having seven siblings, you are the only one in your family that has inherited this." "Yeah, she was certainly thinking the odds are that with eight of us, it should be showing up in someone else too." "I know you are unique, but you didn't have to go this far to show it. I wonder how you could be so healthy for the first 50 years of your life and then get this." "Yeah, I think the odds have been in my favor. I've lived a very full life except when I was seven years old. I had Rheumatic Fever and spent six months in the hospital. I have been very healthy." My husband and I have exchanged this conversation many times since that initial diagnosis.

Have you ever loved someone so much that their problems become your problems? That you would do anything to fix it?

Since that diagnosis in 2014, I have studied and trained to do everything I can to bring some relief to my husband. I learned about meridians and chakras and studied Reiki. I became a Reiki Master.

Like magic, the clearing of energy flow and chakra balancing provides him with some temporary relief. His body melts into the padded massage table like butter melting into toast fresh from the toaster during some sessions.

Glimmers of hope. Maybe we will be able to arrest these symptoms. But those times are becoming rare.

Being his only advocate, I have an ongoing, never-ending search for ways to help him. I took my first training in Subtle Energy Medicine at a local community college. A whole new world of possibilities for healing is now at my fingertips.

Intrigued by the expansiveness of this training, I continued with an apprenticeship program for the next three years, becoming a Subtle Energy Specialist.

Every new technique is a tool I can use to expand his life. Molecules of JOY, epigenetics, heyoka traits, shamanic techniques, and so much more from that apprenticeship program are now in my healing toolbox. I can offer these techniques to help him deal with the symptoms, especially peripheral neuropathy, which is so bad that even with medication, he can't sleep with anything covering his feet, not even a lightweight sheet.

In 2019, he had a follow-up appointment with the neurologist at Mayo Clinic. She noticed a bit more weakness in his peripheral muscles. His gait is less steady. He now also has fluid retention. Again, she discusses the genetic traits and how they should be showing up somewhere in the family.

There is still nothing they can do for him besides prescribing medication for neuropathy and edema. He is still walking unassisted and living at home. We have purchased a lift chair, so, as he says, "I'm not wasting my little bit of energy struggling to get out of my chair."

Thank you, Universe!

The work I've done for him has helped. He exceeded the lifespan predicted at that appointment several years ago.

But the disease is continuing to take a toll on his body, especially showing in his lack of stamina.

One sleepless night, I sit quietly, thinking about what we might be missing. While drumming my fingers on the arm of my chair, thoughts are swirling in my mind.

There MUST be something MORE I can do for him. Why would a gene be fine for 50 years and then suddenly not work? There must be something that acted as a trigger. Science doesn't seem to have any answers! What can I do? Where can I look? Well, duh, since it is genetic, you need to look more closely at his family. Why didn't I do this sooner?

Finally! Once again, I can focus on doing something. What a sense of relief to have a concrete project. *What is singly his that none of his siblings have?*

Grabbing a pen and paper, I start by writing his name. Pursing my lips and tapping the pen on my cheek, I concentrate on what to write next. And the list describing him begins:

1. Tall and lanky (until he was told not to exercise).
2. Engineering/mechanically minded. He thinks things through and knows how to design, build, and fix nearly everything.
3. Gruff, nearly rude, protective exterior hides a very loyal, kind, and compassionate heart.
4. Hardworking, strong work ethic.
5. Willing to attempt new things.
6. Stubborn and hard-headed.
7. Married three times and has three children.
8. Has a positive attitude.

Picking up a red pen, I cross off the traits that also describe one or more of his siblings. Gone are numbers two, four, five, six, and eight. This doesn't lead me anywhere within his immediate family except that at 6' 6" he is taller than any of his siblings. And he has created a hard exterior that hides his vulnerability of caring too much. He is also the only one of them who divorced.

What does any of this have to do with muscle disease? Nothing I can connect to his condition.

You did all that family genealogy a few years ago. Maybe that is where the answer lies!

We have a history of thirty generations, ten of them are in this country.

But what clues am I looking to find? Muscles are connective tissue, so what are the connections within his family ancestry? Perhaps there is more hiding in the information than just their names.

It is time to boot up the computer and open my genealogy program. *It takes forever to load this program. Be patient. Think positive. It will be worth the wait.*

Looking through the genealogy records, I find patterns emerging from the data.

His paternal grandmother:

➢ was married three times.

➢ raised three children.

➢ died at the age of 51.

His paternal great-grandfather:

➢ was married three times.

➢ raised three children.

➢ died at the age of 51.

I am seeing a pattern that could have passed on to my husband. Only he did not die at the age of 51. Interestingly though, that was when he started showing symptoms of his muscle disease.

I might have found his ancestral energetic connection.

Jumping up from my chair and doing a happy dance into the living room, the words burst from me, "Aha, here it is! I think I've found it! This looks like too much of a coincidence."

Could epigenetics be playing a part in his condition? Could it simply be the energetic connection between these two ancestors and my husband? They must have shared similar life events that they wanted to connect to him as a way of protection!

If this is an ancestral story he is fighting and surviving, what is our next course of action? Acknowledging and honoring their experiences in a journaling exercise seems the best way to move forward. Creating the exercise was easy; implementing it was more difficult as writing is laborious for him.

Wow! This has helped. He has changed. Even though his muscles are still weak, his attitude is more positive.

Over time, we have repeated some of the steps in the journaling exercise. It helps to solidify the change, and it never hurts to say thank you to your ancestors.

I hope this tool can be useful to others. You can get a free PDF download of my RAPTURE Journaling Exercise under the resource tab at https://beingyouenergetically.com/resources/

THE TOOL

Journaling is a focused way to capture your thoughts and feelings. It can be done with paper/pen, a word processing program, or dictation. The important thing is to get it where if you choose, you can refer back to it.

Your ancestral experience does not need to be verified with any genealogy information. The ancestral link you have may be as simple as a repeating occurrence, such as if one of your ancestors was trapped in a cellar, you accidentally get locked in a closet.

To give thanks to the ancestors and their influences, I created a very specific journaling exercise called RAPTURE.

RAPTURE Journaling Healing Tool

R: Recognize the repeating pattern happening in your life. Some examples may be: Do you constantly lose things (keys, pens, notes, etc.)? Are you always early or always late? Do you often find yourself drawn to a life of a different time/era?

A: Acknowledge how the pattern may have developed for your ancestor(s). Did they emigrate to a new country? Did they leave behind their family and all their community connections? Consider what the impact was for them to survive because of the pattern. How does the pattern serve you? Is it a hindrance, or is it helpful?

P: Praise your ancestors for the struggles they endured that led to the creation of the pattern. This can be said in a few words, short and sweet, or a lengthy and honoring paragraph. Whichever you choose, it should be done with loving words.

T: Thank your ancestors for their caring. They passed on this pattern because they thought it would help you. Again, no matter what words you use to express your thanks, lovingly offer them.

U: Understand how the repeating pattern is and is not serving you to live YOUR best life. Write how you feel when experiencing the pattern. Are you frustrated? Grateful? Annoyed? Unaffected? Be honest about your feelings.

R: Release the pattern for your ancestors and yourself. An affirmation that I have found helpful is, "I release (state the pattern) from my life, from the lives of my ancestors, and the lives of all others affected by it." It may be deeply embedded. If this is the case, repeat this exercise until you feel you can move on to the next step. Journal when you do this exercise and how you feel afterward.

E: Expressing and Envisioning. Express your love to your ancestors for their impact on their world, descendants, the universe. But especially for their impact on YOU. Envision your new life with patterns that only enhance you to live YOUR BEST LIFE. Journal how you expressed your love and the vision of your new life.

As I sit here, writing my story (his story, really) and providing this tool, gratitude fills my heart. I feel gratitude for the fact that my husband has survived his ancestral story, for the emotional purging I got from reliving this experience, and for the opportunity to share this with you.

Carol Dutton is the owner of Being You Energetically, LLC and an expert Subtle Energy Practitioner, Reiki Master, Crystal Grid Healer, and a trained Irigenics™ Ancestral Eye Reader. As a non-denominational ordained minister, she also performs spiritual oil anointing.

Whichever modality you choose, her powerful sessions will immediately give you the unique and specific missing links to clearing the traumatic and ancestral patterns keeping you from living an extraordinary life.

While spending her working career in the corporate world, she started her journey into the holistic healing world to bring comfort to her husband, who struggles with a rare muscle disease. Seeing the relief he felt after a session, Carol decided to offer the sessions to friends and family members. With their encouragement, she started offering sessions to others.

In January 2020, her corporate job was eliminated. This was the impetus for her to seriously consider opening her own business doing the work she loves. After educating herself on being a business owner, she founded Being You Energetically, LLC in January 2021.

She lives in rural Minnesota with her husband. Her hobbies include gardening, preserving food from her garden and farmers market, reading, fishing.

She is a storyteller and recently rediscovered her love of writing. Spending time in nature is her way to refuel and feel energized.

You can find her at:

www.beingyouenergetically.com

www.carolduttonusa.com

www.facebook.com/BeingYouEnergetically

Chapter 11

SHAMANIC JOURNEYING
Breaking Limiting Patterns
by Connecting With Our Ancestral Guides

TANYA L. COLUCCI, M.S., LMT

MY STORY

I am sitting in a circle on the floor at a shamanic workshop. We're learning how to use shamanic journeying to assist souls after they transition to the upper planes. The instructor is sitting calmly, firmly holding space. She cradles her deerskin drum and guides us to go deeply into the journey with the intention to connect with a deceased loved one to check on them.

Up until this point, we have each made several journeys, our guides showing us the various levels and layers to the souls' ascension process after death. I slide my blindfold over my eyes, blocking out any hints of light, falling into complete darkness as I lay back on my soft mat on the floor. The drumming sends me into a now-familiar trance state. Slowly I begin to travel to my guides so they may lead me to the upper worlds.

I fly up layer by layer and land in a castle made of clear crystals. This place is familiar. I've been here many times before. I go here as a shaman to power up and bring energy back into a client.

In front of me, there is a staircase, and I sit down. A tall man dressed in brown Franciscan order robes is walking down the stairs towards me. At first glance, I thought, *Saint Francis of Assisi?* But, as the brawny man got closer, I realized it was my deceased father. I thought, *well, isn't this going to be interesting,* in a half-cynical way.

My father passed away when I was 16, and I was daddy's little girl. He was a firefighter, golden-glove boxer, and an athletic man with a strong, disciplined temper. Yet he was a protector with softness inside and was quite the charmer, befriending everyone he met.

Being raised Roman Catholic, he was a devout Catholic. Towards the end of this life (after his cancer diagnosis), he started praying, attending prayer groups and went deeper into theology study than I remembered previously. He kept it very private.

Our eyes were locked as my father walked over to me and took my right hand in his, placing his left hand on top of mine, cradling it in his. Immediately we went into a telepathic conversation covering about 26+ years of my life at a rapid-fire pace, playing "catch up." He confirmed, "When you see me out of the corner of your eye riding in the back of your Jeep, that is me."

Most significantly, he wanted to address my ongoing beliefs around money and subconscious beliefs about not having enough. He said, "You are always worrying about money. You have nothing to worry about, Tanya. Spend your time and energy with your son. Rest, relax, and have no regrets about how you spend it or your time. Matteo makes me laugh; he is so good with women, he is sweet, and he loves so much from his heart. With the healing work that you do, it is such important service work to humanity helping others heal from your heart."

He reached up and placed his right hand on my cheek. The same place where he had once struck me. My stubborn and strong nature had pushed him to the edge, and his temper got the best of him. It was the first, last, and only time he hit me like that. At that moment, he said, "Please forgive me. Use love and forgiveness always, and don't hold onto things. Thank you for working so hard to break this cycle of anger."

Tears streamed like a waterfall down my face, and the blindfold that covered my eyes was dripping in my tears. I could feel this pure, divine,

Christ-like energy streaming through his hand into my body, clearing my entire being, including my heart. At that moment, I could feel and sense the energy clearing his life, my life, my son's life, and our ancestors' lives.

"What are you doing in that brown Franciscan robe?" I asked. He said, "I spend all my time chanting, praying, clearing energy, and working on your behalf, clearing the path for you. If you need anything, all you need to do is just ask for it, and I will work on your behalf for you. Don't worry about Matteo; he will be okay no matter what; he has an old soul and is strong and happy."

Rapid-fire communication is happening on multiple levels simultaneously as I feel this immense weight lift off my energy field with the supportive nature of him. I think, *wow, it's our ancestor's responsibility and duty to help assist us from the spirit realm in clearing our path.* My attention is grabbed by the sudden change in the drumbeat, which is our alert and call back to transition our energy back into the physical body to come out of the journey. I say goodbye, for now, coming back with a sweetness filled with support and love.

During that journey, it was made apparent that I needed to heal the pattern of financial lack around abundance and anger. Throughout my life, money has always been a huge stressor, distracting me so much from experiencing life. In reality, I haven't ever truly experienced a lack, and during times of challenge, things have always seemed to work out. Often I was unaware of the limiting subconscious beliefs holding me back from taking chances.

Patterns are funny things. They keep us bound and wrapped so tightly we can't breathe, move, or feel as deeply as we would truly desire. Do you know that feeling of desire to deeply connect inside, know yourself, heal yourself, serve others, have a deep connection with God/Source, and enjoy life to its fullest with deliciousness? You want it but don't know how to access it. These limiting patterns are the very threads preventing us from experiencing those depths. Through the art of learning how to do shamanic journeying, you can develop these connections with your ancestors as I did.

Perhaps one step we can take is to unravel those tightly-wound patterns keeping us from experiencing all the multidimensional aspects of ourselves emotionally, physically, energetically, and spiritually. This burning desire to experience more is calling us inwards to connect with the ancestors to heal generational wounds so you, right here and now, can break the inherited patterns. Spirit is always calling us, whispering to us softly and sometimes loudly.

Some examples of intergenerational pain and trauma that can stay alive for generations are health issues that won't go away, unexplained sadness, fear, grief, unsuccessful careers, failed relationships, addictions, anger issues, and various unconscious belief patterns that aren't in alignment with our true beliefs. These traumas can all disrupt our lives. Our ancestors want to assist us in healing generational beliefs. We can call on them from our heart and travel to meet with them with the powerful tool of shamanic journeying.

In indigenous cultures, it's believed that we are all shamans and should use the tool of journeying to travel to non-ordinary reality to seek guidance and healing. Shamans regularly use journeying to gain insight, spiritual knowledge, receive and perform healings, and contact the spiritual realm itself to receive healing from the spirits. Shamans use the repeated drumbeat of three to four beats per second which is played to get us into an ecstatic trance state as to allow us to connect easily with another dimensional reality (non-ordinary reality).

Once you learn the skill of journeying, it becomes a skill that never leaves you; there at any time for you to access non-ordinary reality to help guide you and heal. It's through the seeing of life through our heart lens that we can begin to shift generational patterns of resistance that manifest daily in our life.

THE TOOL: SHAMANIC JOURNEYING

HOW TO DO A SHAMANIC JOURNEY TO THE LOWER WORLD

To make shamanic journeying easier to enter into non-ordinary reality, we use drumming and rattling to bring the brainwaves into a delta trance state, an altered state of consciousness. The drum is played at a rapid drumbeat of three to four beats per second.

In shamanic journeying, there is the lower-world, the middle-world, and the upper world. Beginners learn how to journey to the lower world. Prior to starting a journey, it's important to pick how you will enter into the lower world. Examples include a hole in the earth, tree stump, cave, waterfall, rabbit hole, and any other opening that resonates with you. Once you have this in your mind, you want to visualize and have the sensation that you are going DOWN. The most important feeling is having the sensation that you are traveling DOWN into the earth. Once you travel down, you will land in a "landing spot," which will be the same for every journey to the lower world. Once you are there, you will ask for an ancestor, power animal, or guide to show up and lead you to an ancestor cave. Once you arrive, you will state your intention to your guide or ancestor and request healing or insight on how to heal this pattern. You will spend some time receiving the insights you are meant to receive. Once this is complete, you will head back to the landing spot and make your way back up the way you went down (hole, crack, tree stump cave, etc).

STEP 1: CREATE A SACRED SPACE:

Before beginning any ceremony, I recommend creating a sacred altar and specifically one that includes your ancestors. Find a place in your room, on a dresser, shelf, or any area in your home where you will be present to make your shamanic healing journey. Important items to have on an altar:

- Candles (light the candle on the altar)
- Incense/sage/palo santo to burn to clear your energy field before a journey
- Crystals, statues, or any items that have significant meaning or powerful energy
- Pictures of your ancestors, family tokens, heirlooms, religious tokens
- Feathers
- Sacred cloth, shawl, or any other high vibrational items
- Small cup or ceramic bowl to put water in

- Items from nature: special rocks, sticks, leaves, or fresh flowers

STEP 2: GATHER ALL ITEMS NEEDED FOR THE SHAMANIC JOURNEY:

- A comfortable place to lay down (floor, bed, massage table)
- A bandana or eye cover to block out all light
- Wear comfortable, loose-fitting clothes
- Speaker/phone or device to stream drumming sounds or play the guided video on my website leading you through a shamanic journey
- Journal and pen to write down your experience before and after the journey

STEP 3: SET YOUR INTENTION:

It is with our intent and the desire that allows us to connect with our ancestors and ourselves at a deeper level to have inner experiences. I have found that the more open we are to connect from our heart without expectations, miraculous experiences and interactions happen.

Take a moment to light the candle on your altar, breathe into your heart space and ask what is it that you would like to clear and heal generationally that has prevented you from living more freely from your heart without limitations. What blockages have held you back in life? Be as specific as you can with your limiting belief as you can and take a moment to write it down in your journal. Begin to ask for your ancestors to come to you during your Shamanic Journey to lead you to a healing fire ceremony or life cave to reveal which pattern is needed for you to shift and heal at this moment to clear. The more specific you can be with your request, the better. Write these ancestors' names down along with your limiting belief or pattern you're struggling with during this time.

Examples of this might be:

- What ancestor experienced a trauma, hard life, or emotional strife that I want to connect to?
- Write the intention down with the intent to uncover family secrets, events, and timelines.

- Ask the ancestor what legacy or healing they want to receive around this issue.

- Releasing the belief that "I am not worthy to fully receive love."

- Releasing the lack mentality, never having enough, never being enough, never being able to have abundance in all forms (financially, love, joy, etc.).

- "I want to release the trauma of sexual abuse carried on through the female lineage."

- Healing chronic back pain which is connected to a belief that I cannot support myself financially and releasing the fear of failure and not being safe.

STEP 4: CALL IN THE FOUR DIRECTIONS:

Creating a protective space is important when doing any ceremony, and for this particular type of journey, I recommend calling in the four directions of the South, West, North, and East. Connecting and calling in all the helping spirits and protectors of the medicine space before beginning our journey together (see the prayer below).

Take a few moments to center yourself by closing your eyes, bringing your hands to rest on your heart space, connecting down into Mother Earth through your feet, energetically visualizing roots growing down and anchoring into Mother Earths' heart core. Take a moment to light sage or palo santo to burn, and use your hand or a feather to clear the space around your body, circling counterclockwise around your head, down the center of your torso, legs, and feet. While the smoke moves around you, visualize it clearing any energy that is not of the highest good from your energy field, allowing it to clear away. Stand from your heart space while intently calling in all the directions (you may drum or rattle if you have one).

STEP 5: GO INTO A SHAMANIC JOURNEY:

You can listen to prerecorded shamanic drumming or go to my video to have an experience. Typically most shamanic journeys are made in 15 to 30 minutes.

> Access the video recording to have a live experience here:
> https://www.sacredsoulguidance.com/resources

STEP 6: INTEGRATION:

Over the course of the days and weeks after your shamanic journey healing, it's important to tune in. I would suggest:

- Journaling your experiences and how things are shifting in your life.
- Connect with nature as much as possible while integrating.
- Develop a practice of making a journey weekly.

OPEN THE PROTECTIVE FOUR DIRECTIONS:

INVOCATION

To the winds of the South

Great Serpent (physical)

Wrap your coils of light around us

Teach us to shed the past the way you shed your skin

To walk softly on the Earth

Teach us the Beauty Way

To the winds of the West

Mother Jaguar (emotional)

Bring with us love and curiosity

Protect our medicine space

Teach us the way of peace, to live impeccably

Show us the way beyond death

To the winds of the North

Hummingbird (Mythical level offering your contribution without comprehending how it fits into the collective dream), Grandmothers and Grandfathers

Ancient Ones

Come and warm your hands by our fires

Whisper to us in the wind

We honor you who have come before us

And you who will come after us, our children's children

To the winds of the East

Great Eagle, Condor (Spirit level. They see the larger picture before them and understand the totality of the dream without being able to express it or define it. They feel immersed in love, connected to all. No longer experiencing "I," but the power and wonder of Spirit. They become the moon and the stars, fire, smoke, each other and themselves, no one, and everyone).

Come to us from the place of the rising sun

Keep us under your wing

Show us the mountains we only dare to dream of

Teach us to fly wing to wing with the Great Spirit

Mother Earth

We've gathered for the honoring of all of your children

The Stone People, the Plant People

The four-legged, the two-legged, the creepy crawlers

The finned, the furred, and the winged ones

All our relations

Father Sun

Father Sun, Grandmother Moon, to the Star Nations

Great Spirit, you who are known by a thousand names

And you who are the unnamable One

Thank you for bringing us together

And allowing us to sing the Song of Life

Tanya Colucci, MS, LMT is an Expert Shaman, Ordained Minister, Author, and Speaker, and owner of Sacred Soul Guidance and Tanya Colucci Myofascial Release Therapy. Her powerful Sacred Soul Coaching and Healing methods use an extraordinary combination of shamanic, bodywork, vibrational sound, and ceremonial healing modalities to be your solution for living with joy, purpose, and passion. Tanya is most passionate about individuals tapping into their inner wisdom and power to heal past trauma to heal pain and start living a joy-centered life.

Tanya has been in the fitness and wellness industry for over 22 years as an international conference speaker, trainer, healer, adjunct professor, and retreat leader. Tanya holds a Master in Health Promotion Management from American University. She hosts powerful online & in-person groups and private 1-1 healings, workshops, and retreats. Find out more here: www.sacredsoulguidance.com

To access Shamanic Journeying Tools and Additional Resources: https://www.sacredsoulguidance.com/resources

Chapter 12

THE WOVEN WEB

Discovering and Removing Energy Strings

MARCIA COLVER REICHERT, CHT, LMT, NMT, SHAMAN

MY STORY

My life has always been filled with fascinating, vivid imagery. I believed a lot of it was real, although I was often informed that it was simply in my imagination. The imagery I see in my mind's eye is absolutely stunning, and it's a great place to live. This imagery enhanced the healing abilities I have, and as a child, I helped animals heal by keeping them calm and visualizing the healing happen.

When I was a child, my parents—my dad especially—attempted to convince me my dreams were not real, at times spanking me. "You need to live in the real world and get out of your head!" my dad would yell. At that time, I didn't understand that my grandmother was institutionalized for what they perceived as mental illness, and my parents feared I was behaving like her.

Healing is a constant calling in my life. My earliest memories include regularly laying my hands on others to offer comfort or relief in the form of massage. Interestingly, my favorite jobs were bartending and working as a laborer in one of the several refineries in my town. Upon reflection, I realize I liked those jobs because I could be combative without fear of getting in trouble for it. In retrospect, I can see I had a truckload of unresolved anger issues, but I was a "biker bitch" so it was not really a problem. Several people thought I was a hero for being a 5'4" woman with no qualms about bodily removing a six-foot-plus-tall adult man from the premises. Eventually, however, I did some soul searching and realized I needed to focus on the healing work that came so naturally to me as a child. I made the huge (for me) leap to enrolling in massage school.

Massage school changed my life, and it was terrifying. I was supposed to get naked under the linens around strangers, and suddenly I could prove once again that I was smart. One fellow student told me, "Marcia, you're so pretty," nearly every day, and another told me that I had psychic abilities, which at the time I did not believe in the slightest. I graduated at the top of my class and then received a few more certifications within a few months after graduating. My client base began expanding, and my skills also expanded. My intuition opened up, and I became a psychic channel without actually understanding what was going on. My life was shifting dramatically as I gained more and more awareness of the magical world I had shoved away from myself for so long. I no longer felt I lived solely in the "muggle" world, to borrow a term from Harry Potter.

One day I was doing a massage and my daughter, who was only about six years old, was in the room. My client, Mary, just had a total knee replacement, and when I finished with the massage, Mary said, "I still have pain in my knee." I enlisted the help of my daughter, Sakara, who came up to Mary, hovered her hands over her knee about two inches away, and moved her little hands around a bit, waving them over Mary's knee for three to four seconds and then said, "Okay," and walked away. Mary looked at me stunned and said, "The pain is gone." I asked Sakara if she would explain what she did, and she impatiently said, "Gaw! Mom, you can see that the colors weren't there; I just moved all the colors in." I could not see what she was talking about but felt compelled to allow Spirit to move my hands to complete the healing necessary and bring all the colors into balance.

Sakara's father and I divorced during this period of discovery and growth, and I felt freer to delve into what was happening to, around, and through me. I experienced more color and more magic. Awareness came. I had been ignoring my gifts and talents, like singing and dancing. Though I was dedicated to helping others heal, new magic was opening up to me.

I began exploring singing and vocal tones. I sang one note at a time, and it was effective, but somehow I knew it was only scratching the surface. Then I had a breakthrough. I was working on a friend who was tutoring me in Gaelic, and it dawned on me that his tight, strong muscles easily melted under my hands when I began singing. Massages became dramatically more effective when I sang or whatever song rose in my mind as I was working. This began the vibrational medicine portion of my healing career. Singing my clients into sacred space and "snake charming" their energy to help relieve trauma and unlock muscle memory is remarkably effective. Together with my client, we navigate hidden magical gifts that collaborate and blossom into their full potential.

I don't remember whether generational healing or alternate lives (I label them alternate because they could be past, future, or even parallel lives) came into my consciousness first. Early in my career, I began to notice patterns of belief systems, choices, and trauma running through generations and alternate lives, which affected the client's current life. I began seeing things in my imagination on the client that I couldn't explain, such as a gaping wound or a knife sticking out of their back. When I informed the client of my experience and performed the work needed to heal the wounds, we could make huge progress in overall healing, and the healing was permanent. Muscle tightness or knots that bothered them ever since they could remember were gone in just a few moments without strenuous work from me. The generational piece of the trauma usually came as a knowing. I always knew there was a connection between trauma passed down from generations and the trauma they continued to experience.

Now that I have been embracing and using my psychic gifts rather than chalking them up to my imagination, I liken what I see when I touch someone to an old-time reel-to-reel movie slowed down so you can see each clip for a split second. I catch glimpses of other lives, generations, and incidents in the current life that show me where and how everything connects. I then verify with the client as much as possible by asking questions. I may tell them the story of what I saw in the vision and ask them if it resonates with them. Usually, that has to do with an alternate life. I then verify what has happened in generations or how that connects with the current life.

When all of it comes together, I ask them if they can see the pattern of trauma and if they would like to remove it. I rarely have anyone say no, but it has happened. The trauma is like the filaments that make up a web, weaving throughout multiple lifetimes or generations. When I have their permission to remove the energy strings from the web between generations, alternate lives, and the current life, I begin to sing and lightly drag my fingertips over their bodies. I begin at the ends of the fingers and toes and top of the head and "gather" the energy in the stomach by continuously moving my hand in a clockwise circle over their stomach, lightly touching so they can feel me "reeling" the energy in. When I finish moving my hands across all the appendages, I scoop my hands into their stomach like I'm scooping water up from their middle and lift the energy out. I envision this as looking like stringy tar. I then release it into the air, knowing the Universe is clearing it before it recycles back into the client, and continue to pull the strings through until I see clean, clear energy coming out. To me, this energy looks like liquid opal. It has all the colors of the rainbow in it and is a shimmering, iridescent, silvery string. The client's own energy is circulating through them, and it really has nothing to do with me. The client feels relief on an entirely different level than regular trauma healing or your basic massage.

THE TOOL

Many cultures believe everything is connected, and we have connections between past, present, and future. We know we're all connected generationally and that even if we didn't grow up with our birth parents, we're influenced by their belief systems and the beliefs of the people who did raise us. The Norse call this the Web of Wyrd. Symbolically it's the interconnectedness of absolutely everything in the universe. Picture it as a huge spider web where everything is actually a piece of a larger thing. We as humans are only cells of a greater being, for instance. If you can imagine that all of those strings that connect us have power as energy, perhaps you can imagine that we could clear those energy strings so that hate and resentment were cleared and love and appreciation remained. Remember that the judgment between good and bad is a human thing and has to do with emotion rather than the circle of life. Energy is just energy, but for our human belief that it can be good or bad, light or dark.

Suppose we have an energy string of abuse that comes in the form of narcissistic behavior on one person's side of the partnership and likely empathy and subservient behavior on the other. In that case, the chaos tends to escalate, and mental, emotional, physical, and even sexual abuse can be prevalent. We tend to learn how to behave from our parents even if this isn't inherited genetically, so these patterns continue through generations. Most people aren't aware that these energies are passed down with the soul as well. Narcissists may continue to be narcissistic, and the subservient soul may continue in that direction. It also may be just the opposite, depending on the purpose of our incarnation. We incarnate in part to clear these energies, which is what karma is all about. Karma is not a punishment but energy that has continued.

Here is an example.

Marie was born to parents of a narcissist and an empath. Both parents are addicts because they have not learned to live with the feelings they experience. Marie is an empath and therefore needs the narcissist in her life to learn the lessons she has incarnated to learn, at least at the beginning. She immediately learns to obey both parents, reinforcing the born-in tendency to be subservient. Her aura glows pink and green, giving the energy of love, but it is slightly dingy, which calls in more narcissists like a lighthouse beacon. She attracts more and more abusive people into her life, and her aura gets more and more polluted with depression, guilt, and shame. She is caught in a vicious circle of abuse and turmoil.

Marie visits her grandmother, hoping she has some insight on why she's continually attracting abuse into her life. Her grandmother tells her stories of the life she lived, and Marie sees the currents of abuse like raging rivers in her mind. She realizes this has been passed down to her and knows her mother went through the same thing as well. She leaves the house, allowing her grandfather, who has always given her the creeps, to kiss her on the mouth and pull her into him tightly for a hug. She doesn't like it, but she is a good little Christian girl, and the Bible says, "Honor thy father and mother," which includes grandparents, right?

Marie knows she needs some help because she has read the psychology books, even has her degree in social work, in an unconscious attempt to try to improve her life. Notice she has chosen a career that takes her further into the abuse she longs to escape in the form of patients who are abusive to their partners. She cannot seem to escape the abuse and chaos. At her wit's end, she makes an appointment with a hypnotherapist who works with past lives. Perhaps there is an answer in the alternate lives she has lived.

During the session, she learns that she has several past lives where she has been raped, enslaved, falsely accused, even murdered. *Can you see how this is creating a pattern of a certain energy?* During each life they go through, the practitioner can clear the energy from that particular life and bring Marie into a state of peace, but only for the life they are working on. Each life has a separate cause for the state of chaos, but does it? Looking from this vantage point, it's possible to see that Marie and her soul have created a web (or perhaps God has created the web) for her to unravel. If Marie can ferret out the hub where all these energy strings of these lives and generations come together, she can begin to unravel the web and release the trauma and the need for abuse in the life she is living currently.

Imagine how much you could improve your life by using this technique. Allow yourself to delve into your past, your generations, and also perhaps alternate lives and envision these energy strings. This technique does not require you to sing, but I highly encourage it no matter what you sound like because the tones of your voice will help you release the energy strings. When you find the hub in the web, you have woven and begin to reel those nasty, tarry energy strings and pull them out to release them to God or the Universe, envision what your life will be like with all that new, beautiful, liquid opal (all the colors of the rainbow in a brilliant iridescent sheen) energy running through you bringing out your own brand of magic, helping you stand completely in your power. For a free guided meditation to help you experience this tool simply click on The Woven Web link at https://marciacolver.com/ancestors-within-book/

Just a note: You do not have to believe in alternate lives for this technique to be completely effective. Even if you don't believe in them, we've all been taught history, and since we're created from the same Earth (we are carbon-based lifeforms), then we're going to resonate with certain things we've learned. When we hear about trauma, parts of our bodies will resonate with that trauma, like the strings on a piano ringing when a person sings in the exact same tone to which the string is tuned. Our bodies are just like that string, and for whatever reason, we latch onto that memory like it is our own. This is why people who don't believe in past lives still believe they were part of, or feel the feelings of, the Jews in WWII; the fear of being captured, the fear of being sent to the gas chambers, or even the feeling of complete defeat.

This piano string analogy explains why vibrational medicine in the form of the human voice is so effective. A voice can resonate precisely with the cells in your body, help them open and release the toxins they carry, thereby releasing the muscle memory and the trauma. Man-made instruments are great, but the voice can go anywhere, and you don't need to buy anything or haul anything around with you. The singing I perform when I'm working with someone to release trauma is just like you can do; I just have a lot of intention behind it. I can see your energy inside of you running like rivers, and when something is blocking it from running smoothly, I help it through by holding a note or moving my fingers until I see that blockage clear. You can use that imagery just as easily; just imagine those strings leaving your body, shifting from dark and tarry to brilliant opalescent, and sing to help them move along. You can even see the energy moving like a snake being charmed if that helps you.

Sing! It's like medicine for the soul!

Marcia Colver Reichert lives in Bridger, Montana, with her wonderfully supportive sister, Donna. When she is not hanging out in the mountains of Montana fishing or helping with the animals, you can find her bouncing all over the country, empowering people, and spreading joy and love through the sharing of her magical voice. Marcia believes every person on the planet was born with their own magical gifts, and she thrives on helping each client discover and move into using those gifts. "Magic is everywhere; we just have to slow down and notice it is happening. I want to help the world notice." For more about Marcia, visit her website at https://marciacolver.com/

Marcia is certified as a Reiki Master, massage therapist educated in eastern and western medicine, reflexologist, NeuroMuscular Therapist, and hypnotist. She is further trained as an astrologer, a vibrational medicine practitioner, and a shaman. She combines all of this training with her psychic abilities to give her clients the most valuable experience possible. Her purpose is to bring to humanity the true power and grace of the Sacred Feminine through healing with love as a High Priestess dedicated to all feminine energies. Among the many ways of forging a path to healing are understanding and clearing alternate soul lives, generational trauma, and limiting beliefs. She assists the client in helping find these traumas or limitations and transmute the energy around and through them to help them step into their own personal power.

Chapter 13

THE HEART SPACE

The Portal to Ancestral Healing

MICHELLE TROUPE

MY STORY

Growing up, I would hear from my parents, "You are just like your father."
"You get that from your father." "You remind me of your mother," and so
on. Sometimes I would hear the same references made about my sisters.
Our parents loved saying, "Wait until you have kids someday," "I hope
they are just like you." My parents were right about that one. Each of my
sisters has three children mirroring aspects of them.

Through my adult years, I could see aspects of my father, mother, and
sisters within my words and actions. It doesn't stop there. Even though I
don't have biological children of my own, I can see aspects of my traits,
behaviors, personality, and actions within my nieces and nephews. As the
saying goes, "The buck stops here." What about my grandparents and
those before them? These memories and questions have been part of my
spiritual journey since 2012.

I wanted to understand where my spiritual gifts of knowing,
heightened intuition, and feeling spirits came from. I also had the ability

to know people's thoughts and feelings. I began asking my parents questions about my ancestors, starting with my grandparents. My parents didn't have much information to offer other than their heritage. I am Italian, German, Irish, Dutch, and Cherokee Indian, to name a few. The Cherokee Indian was the most interesting to me. My mom's grandfather was half Cherokee.

I always felt the presence of native Indians in most of the places I lived and traveled. By traveling I mean, places I have walked and visited almost every day of my life upon the Earth. I also realized that as a child, I could sense, feel, and know the history of the land. I recall a childhood memory of living in Northeast Philadelphia in a townhouse surrounded by cornfields. I did not like those cornfields. I always felt and knew something creepy happened in those fields. I was afraid of them. I loved playing in the cornfields when we moved to New Jersey a few years later. It was the land itself in Philadelphia, not the actual cornfields.

The home I lived in most of my adult life from 1998 to 2019 was built on a dirt-filled swamp. I began feeling the presence of a native Indian family that died on the land. I felt very connected to one of the children. At different times, a few gifted energy workers came to my house for a visit. Before I could say anything, each person felt the presence of the native family in our basement. They also confirmed the land was sacred, and I was there to heal and protect it. I was connecting and healing with ancestors.

A few years later, I began attending full moon drumming ceremonies at my friend's farm. I didn't own a drum, rattle, rain stick, or flute. This was all new to me. I could dance but had no instrument talent at all. Ten minutes into the ceremony, I was dancing, drumming, and shaking the rattle. It felt so natural to me. I could feel native Indians of all kinds dancing with me. It was very freeing and healing. My Shaman friend asked if I wanted to learn shamanism. I graciously declined, knowing I was already connected to the shaman within me.

My spiritual growth took a huge leap in 2018. I traveled to Tucson, Arizona with my friend for a Weekend Energy Intensive. We stayed at my cousin's house in Tucson. We stayed in the spare bedroom, surrounded by pictures of relatives from my mom's side of the family. My cousin showed me old pictures of my great grandparents, grandparents, aunts, uncles, and cousins. It was great to see them all, especially some black and white photos.

The next two days we spent in Sedona with my cousin and her husband. We visited the vortexes of Bell Rock and Cathedral Rock. As we walked through Bell Rock, I stood on an area where the vortex was intense, and everything was moving. It was so multidimensional. I had a blast watching my cousin experience these energies for the first time. She was so fascinated. We continued walking through different sections of Bell Rock.

Just as we were wrapping up the visit, I was guided to go to a nook, a small enclosure within the rocks. As I was standing there, I felt a native Indian presence. It felt strong and protective. I asked to know, hear, see and feel who was with me. I began to get teary-eyed and knew it was my Grandfather Reed (mother's father) with his ancestors. For the first time, I felt the presence of an ancestor I was familiar with. I was so grateful for the connection. Love and peace ran through my whole body. *Feeling is Healing!*

A few months later, I got out of the shower after doing lots of energy work, stood in front of the mirror, and saw my grandfather's face replace the image of mine. It remained there for about ten seconds. *OMG! What just happened?* That was the beginning of seeing various ancestors within me. I also felt I was his connection to my mother, so I told her about the experience. She didn't say much about him, other than he wasn't home much and my grandmother worked full-time. Even though she did not understand the experience I had, I knew it gave her some peace and joy. I felt closer to my mother as well.

In 2019, I met Amy Gillespie at a holistic event in Collingswood, New Jersey. This was a month after Eric and I sold our house. It was the perfect time to get my eye reading. Amy gave me a summary after the photographs. A few weeks later, I received a recording of my reading. *Amazing!* The synchronicities were off the charts; so many things resonated with events of my life, my spiritual gifts, and this very moment.

To summarize, some of my ancestors were gifted writers, and many were from colonial times. Amy also indicated I have a tribal eye. This was very common in native American kids, along with the gift of telepathy. I, too, am blessed with this gift. I know and feel the thoughts and feelings of the connections I make with others and the earth itself. It all makes sense to me now. I am grateful to be connected to Mother Earth in this way. As you can see, many of my gifts are tied to my grandfather and his ancestors.

Also, Eric and I currently live in a home located just outside of Lewes, Delaware. The house was built on swampy land with a lake in the backyard. This land is also sacred and located within a mile of the Nanticoke Indian Museum. The main road close to our home intersects with Indian Mission Road. At night I can feel the native Indians by our sliding glass door. My favorite beach area here is Cape Henlopen State Park. I was drawn to this area by Spirit. I am with my ancestors.

What a ride it has been on my spiritual journey. Looking back on all the tools I have used through the years. Each one led me closer and closer to connecting with my ancestors, known and unknown. For me, the unknown became more about trusting and enjoying the journey. It allowed me to dig deeper without fear and get closer to knowing who I am. I remember that we are all one. We are all connected. These are the same tools I use with my clients, mostly in my multidimensional healing sessions.

THE TOOL

You can download a recording of this tool from my website www.earthangelhealingllc.com/resources.

As you use this tool, you will connect with your ability to heal yourself and your ancestors from within. All healing comes from within. Your external world is always a reflection of your internal one. We're creators of our own reality, choosing the vibration and frequency to live in. Choosing from the heart space is key.

The heart is the seed of your soul. It's your connection to all spaces, places, lifetimes, and dimensions. It is all aspects of you. This is your connection to your ancestors. How do you want to connect to your ancestors to heal? What is it you wish to heal?

STEP 1

Locate and create a sacred space that is relaxing, free of noise and interruptions. You can light a candle and place relaxing crystals for both grounding and connecting. I recommend your favorite red, brown, or black crystal for grounding. For connecting to Source and your higher self, you can use amethyst, clear quartz, or selenite. Everyone resonates with a different crystal. We all have our own unique frequency. You can wear the crystals, hold them, or place them in front of you.

STEP 2

Place your hands in the center of your chest over your heart chakra (heart space). Begin breathing in through your nose and out through your mouth. As you are breathing, direct all parts of you to move into your heart space. You can do so by stating in your head; *I direct all parts of me to move into my heart space, my I am presence, higher self, and all aspects of me. I am here now. I am here now. I am whole.* This grounds you into your body. Keep breathing, so you become more connected to all that is you.

STEP 3

Visualize/sense/feel white light moving from your heart space, creating a sphere of light (your matrix of light) around you. Your matrix of light contains all aspects of you from all lifetimes, spaces, places, and dimensions. Know that these lifetimes include your family and all ancestors before you. You are free and safe in this sphere. This is your Divine Essence vibrating and emanating from your heart. Feel into this energy while it builds within you, increasing the flow of light radiating from your heart.

STEP 4

Send your energy from your root chakra (base of your spine) down into the center of the earth. Know your ancestors have walked this earth since her birth. Feel the connections being made from your heart down into the earth. These connections are filled with pure love and Source energy radiating down to the heart of the earth.

Send your energy up out from your crown (top of your head) to Creator/Source/God whichever you resonate with. Feel the connection to Creator/Source/God increasing with the radiation of light flowing from your heart. At this point, you are in a space of pure Divine connection to all parts of you connecting with your ancestors.

STEP 5

Move into your heart and ask all of your ancestors to create a circle around you. Direct the light from your heart to connect with the hearts of all your ancestors. Create an energetic field of unconditional love and support between you and your ancestors. Sit with the flow of light and unconditional love exchange. In this moment, you have set the intention for healing. Trust in the process and allow all parts of you to embrace the healing through your senses (knowing, seeing, feeling, hearing, and smelling).

Note: Just know all ancestors ready to receive healing with you will be in the circle. In each moment, we heal what we are ready to heal.

We all receive our healings at different levels of intensity. At this point, you may be feeling sensations in your heart or other areas of your body, or you may not be feeling anything at all. You may be crying, laughing, or just knowing it is taking place. Allow it all to move through you with trust, ease, grace, and gratitude without judgment.

STEP 6

Begin sending waves of unconditional love, forgiveness, compassion, and gratitude to yourself. Feel those waves circling in your heart center. Set your intention that it is moving through the cycles of lifetimes with the ancestors in your circle. Visualize the words unconditional love, forgiveness, and gratitude appearing within your heart. If you so desire, say these words in your head or out loud, "I forgive myself unconditionally, I love myself unconditionally, I am compassion, and I am grateful for all parts of me."

Now, send these waves of unconditional love, forgiveness, compassion, and gratitude from your heart to the hearts of your ancestors. Visualize the words shifting to, "I forgive you unconditionally, I love you unconditionally, and I am grateful for you." Know there is understanding with unconditional love, forgiveness, and gratitude. With understanding, there is no judgment of self or others. You are Divine Love.

Take a few minutes to sit in this healing space with your ancestors. Let all hurts, wounds, and trauma be released and transmuted to pure Divine Love. Send gratitude to all parts of you. Feel the forgiveness, compassion, joy, peace, and gratitude.

STEP 7

When you are ready, direct all of the energy flowing from your heart to come back to you. Express gratitude to your ancestors for the beautiful gift of healing. Silently or out loud, state, "I am grateful for our time together in this healing circle. I now disconnect my energy from you. We are free sovereign beings of Light." Slowly open your eyes and move your body. Trust in the knowing that the healing has taken place.

Michelle Troupe spent most of her life dealing with physical pain, illnesses, and feeling lost. After several doctors, medications, and procedures, she began exploring alternative ways to heal. Michelle began her own awakening in 2012 and founded Earth Angel Healing in 2013.

Michelle is a Multidimensional Lightworker, Integrated Energy Therapy Master Teacher®, Certified Sound Healer, and Reiki Master Teacher. Michelle has a unique ability to awaken you to the light within and opening your heart to the truth of who you are. Her work is a catalyst to shifting into higher levels of consciousness. Michelle also teaches you how to live from your heart space.

Michelle lives in Southern Delaware with her longtime boyfriend. She enjoys walks on the beach, fishing, traveling, and creating jewelry. She enjoys spending time with family.

You can go to Michelle's website for additional information on her services, classes, workshops, and resources. You can also join her newsletter and download a recording of the tool from her website. www.earthangelhealingllc.com

Chapter 14

RECONNECTING THE BROKEN BONDS AND HONORING OUR ANCESTORS

Life-Changing Healing Practices

PHOENIX TRUEBLOOD, SHAMANIC PRACTITIONER,
GRANDDAUGHTER OF NATIVE ELDER

MY STORY

HOW I CAME TO UNDERSTAND THE IMPACTS OF MY ANCESTRAL JOURNEY

From birth, we are given an amazing gift. I call it 'The gift of life.' That may seem obvious, but it goes much deeper. The gift comes from our ancestors and is a connection to our soul. We are its caretakers, and then it becomes our gift to future generations. We are immortal spiritual beings only living a temporary human experience. Some of us chose to become healers, teachers, shamans, educators, or even writers to share these gifts.

My personal ancestry is diverse. My father was Native American, and my mother European. I am deeply connected with my Native American heritage, having spent much of my youth in the presence of my grandmother (meoni), who exposed me to the traditions and wisdom of my ancestors, which I hope to pass on to future generations. The ceremonies, rituals, and healing practices of my ancestors are nearly forgotten, which is why this book is so important to me.

My meoni was an elder member of the Apache tribe and had an almost innate knowledge of how to employ sacred herbs. The tribal people believe that all things sacred are animate. Sacred plants, properly grown and harvested with respect to how they will be used, continue to live in the eyes of the indigenous tribal people. My Meoni would never pull the plants from the roots because the roots are tied to the ancestors, and the plants must be allowed to continue to grow for future harvests. My meoni understood the importance of ritual in the preparation of the sacred materials prior to their use. Just as she knew which berries had healing properties and which were poisonous, how to create medicinal teas out of natural elements using things like mesquite and prickly pear cactus, she understood the rituals of the sacred items and passed this knowledge down to me. I regularly use her teachings in my daily life; it allows me to maintain a connection with her which I treasure.

Knowledge of your own bloodline is important when performing healing ceremonies. The best approach is to work directly with those connected to your own ancestral roots. If you are not gifted or a true shamanic healer, you can seek the assistance of one. You can also seek out an indigenous tribal elder to guide you on your journey. An acknowledgment that the use of herbs like white sage and ceremonial tobacco are considered sacred by indigenous people is crucial. Ideally, the use of these sacred herbs should only be done by indigenous people who have used them in ceremonies for thousands of years. If you choose to use them anyhow, grow them yourself to make sure they have been sustainably sourced. If growing your own is not possible, the best option is to purchase them from Native-owned shops to help support their communities and by attending a traditional Native American Pow Wow to see for yourself how some of these traditions and healing ceremonies are performed.

The most memorable pow wow I ever experienced was when I was young and attended the "Gathering of the Nations." It's the world's largest pow wow that originated in 1983. It takes place in Albuquerque, New Mexico, and includes more than 565 tribes from around the United States and another 220 from Canada. To see the multiple generations of ancestral knowledge and wisdom at this event is moving. The ceremony involves singing, chanting, meditation, and dances which represent the sacred expression of one's manifestation into their heritage. Pow Wows like these provide an opportunity for insight, self-reflection, and the absorption of knowledge and wisdom. One night that stands out the most to me was when I spoke with an elder by the fire, and he asked me about my name Phoenix and did a reading and then stated, "Out of death and you will be reborn again and will rise to do great things." Years later, his revelation became a reality.

In 1990 I was brutally attacked and indeed had a near-death experience where I crossed over to the afterlife for a brief time. That experience helped me understand what that 'gift of life' really meant that death is not the end. I knew I needed to share what I learned with others. That moment on the other side forever changed me. In the afterlife, I do not remember my beaten body that died, but instead a place of peace and overwhelming comfort. I believe our bodies are vessels connected to all creations, past, present, and future. When we die, we're transformed into a source of pure light. The actions we took during life will affect our ancestral bonds. I understood we're put here on this earth to make a difference. I refuse to let the traumatic event causing my death become a burden on those in my past, present, or future. I choose to heal all the broken bonds with the gift of love and ceremony. I share my story with you and invite you to accept the gift of life and make a difference in others' lives.

I had my own experience with the powers of ceremonial healing when I was young. My mother was a very prim and proper English socialite. She eventually moved to the states, where she met my biological father, after which I was conceived. I have only a faint memory of my father. I know he dealt with his own ancestral trauma and died before I got to know him. Prior to his death, I was living on the reservation. I developed an appreciation for that way of life and formed a bond with my meoni. I was already as stubborn and wild as a mustang at the time I left the reservation and only got worse after. Being pulled away from the only life I knew caused a wall to form between my mother and me. At the same time, I had horrible nightmares of things that happened in the past that were not my own. When I would visit my meoni, I would share these dreams, and she could feel the pain I was going through. I remember the night she sat me at the fire and guided me through my first healing ceremony. I remember the smell of sage and the braided sweetgrass and can still feel its combined power as it washed over me. Together with the fire, it felt a part of me. I emerged from the ceremony with a newfound respect for my mother. Our relationship improved substantially as my own ancestral trauma began to heal.

Later in life, as a healer myself, I worked with a young woman who was sick for a while and could not figure out why. While doing a reading with her, I felt that her illness was connected to her parents. She was adamant; her parents were very healthy and active. I suggested she get a DNA test to see if there was anything in her lineage or family history that could help her understand what was going on.

Several weeks later, I received a hysterical call from her, saying she figured out the problem. She had thalassemia disorder which is something you can only inherit from both parents. She also discovered that her natural parents had been of Southeast Asian descent, but the parents she had known all her life were not Asian. When she talked to them about the results, her parents admitted they adopted her as an infant. They didn't want to tell her that her birth parents were killed tragically.

With this newly revealed ancestral knowledge, I created a healing ceremony that honored and allowed her to connect to her parents she never knew while giving her peace of mind. The end of her ceremony involves dissolving paper containing a poem to her parents in essential healing oils and purified warm water with rose petals over several days. Its lingering scent reminds her of her parents during the week. She repeats this ceremony every year on her birthday.

THE HEALING POWER OF CEREMONY

Ceremonies have been practiced for tens of thousands of years and are still practiced today in many different forms. Ceremonies are also a healthy, holistic way to heal, whether it allows a grieving family to celebrate or mourn a loved one who has moved on to the next phase in their journey, or is held in connection to the unity of two people in love, such as a marriage. Some ceremonies can be physical and mark a rite of passage.

In traditional Native American ceremonies, we have a deep connection to the Creator and the earth, and all living things. We connect to the universe and journey beyond the ordinary everyday reality. We may enter a state of deep trance where we can experience feelings and perhaps the awareness that our thoughts and intentions are connected to the power of the universe and the Creator.

Ceremonies are truly a powerful thing and are sacred. They should be treated with the highest respect. Once you have attended a true Native American ceremony, I promise you will be moved. Imagine an open field on land that is sacred. You feel the power around you as you gather in a circle around a fire that's six feet tall with beautiful yellow and blue flames. Those vibrant colors are created from the herbs placed in the fire before you begin. You smell sweet grass and sage in the air as the beating of drums, prayers, and chants begin. Your feet begin to move, and you will begin dancing with the earth. The drums' beating has you stepping in a rhythm. You feel alive as the chanting gets louder and the drum's beat gets faster; you're one with the earth. This is ceremony.

THE TOOL

REWRITING YOUR ANCESTRAL SPIRITUAL DECREE. HEALING YOUR LIFE FOR EMPOWERMENT AND FULFILLMENT.

This is a ceremony anyone can do, whether or not you have intimate knowledge of your ancestral lineage. It can be a powerful tool if you are adopted and want to heal any trauma from that discovery. Anyone can still connect with their ancestors with this ceremony.

You may not realize you have a non-physical agreement with your ancestors through your consciousness called a Spiritual Decree.

If you find yourself failing and just not getting what you want out of your life, career, relationship, and finances, there could be some ancestral trauma in your past, blocking your way to success.

Are you ready to release yourself and your future generations from the past ancestral trauma that has you asking yourself, *why is this happening to Me? Why is my life so messed up? Why can't I have the life I want?*

It's this exact moment when you're reading this book and the exact moment in time you're learning this ceremonial practice that will change your life forever.

Whenever I have someone do this particular ceremony for ancestral healing, they immediately feel something is happening as if there's a cosmic shift in energies. Within days, their lives find a new healthier rhythm. They discover what's been holding them back. Maybe it's the realization they're in a dead-end job or a toxic relationship or discover a hidden health problem. It might not even be that obvious, but the change in energy is real.

I love when someone writes to me and says what an amazing difference the ceremony has in their lives. I've heard things like, "I got my dream job," or "I've found the love of my life." People tell me that it not only helped them but their entire family. Whether it's the change in behavior of a troubled child or a spouse finding more energy to get out do things, the change is real and measurable.

RULES THAT MUST BE FOLLOWED WHEN DOING CEREMONIES.

- Do not perform under the influence of any alcohol or drugs.
- Remove electronic devices in the ceremonial area, i.e., phones, cameras, or recording devices.
- Cleanse the land or area where you're doing the ceremony to rid it of any previous energy.

STEPS TO REWRITE YOUR ANCESTRAL SPIRITUAL DECREE

This healing ceremony takes about an hour and involves writing your intentions on paper and releasing all past ancestral trauma while purifying the mind-body-spirit.

List of items you will need:

- A sheet of paper and a lead pencil
- Salt (the more pure the form, the better)

- Abalone shell
- Ceremonial cedar
- Purified water

Step One: PLANNING YOUR CEREMONY

Make sure to find a safe location, one that is private and where you won't be interrupted while performing your ceremony. This could be on your own ancestral land or a place where you feel grounded and connected to the earth. You'll be dealing with an open flame and need to make sure to choose a place that is not in a high fire danger area.

Step Two: PREPARING FOR YOUR CEREMONY

Start this ceremony of purification by sprinkling salt on the ground around you. Himalayan pink salt is known to have deep connections to universal energies. Next, set your intentions. I often say a prayer to the Creator.

Example:

"I choose to step out of this world into which I am bound by my physical form; I have prepared my body and my mind to step into my heart space. I no longer feel bound to the body in which I was held. I seek only good intentions and healing while in this sacred place of light and wisdom from the Creator and the universe as I set my intentions."

Step Three: PERFORMING THE CEREMONY

Take your sheet of paper, and with a pencil, write any negative thoughts, concerns, or known personal or ancestral traumas that you wish to be free of.

Example:

"I, Phoenix Trueblood, grandchild of the Trueblood lineage herby, release my ancestors' trauma and pain. I no longer allow this trauma to continue in this reality. From this day forward and for all future generations, I release the bonds that hold any negative energies. I will only receive positive energy from my ancestors, who bless me with such. I welcome a new positive beginning that awaits me in this lifetime."

Final Step: COMPLETING THE CEREMONY

After writing your intention(s) on the paper, take 15 minutes to meditate and visualize your ancestors being free and at peace. I want you to envision them feeling empowered.

Take your paper with written intention(s) and place it in the shell, fold it if you need to and set it on fire and speak the following.

"May this ceremony release myself, my ancestors, and future generations from the negative energies and traumas of the past. With an open heart and loving intentions, I am rewriting my Ancestral Spiritual Decree so that I might move forward in a more meaningful and fulfilling way."

As the flame consumes the paper and it turns into ashes, you may feel a change in energy, a shift in the universe, a sense of overwhelming joy and gratitude. You may cry and shed tears for all the generations that have suffered. One thing is for certain, through this ceremony, you have just made a clear intention to the universe that you have released the wounds of the past.

Congratulations, you've done it! You have rewritten a more positive decree and released the traumas and pains of the past. Now be ready for amazing things to happen with new positive experiences.

After burning the paper, you can take the ashes and mix them with the soil for a new plant. This will allow a fresh, clean, good energy to grow from the ashes. You may also choose to scatter them in the four winds. Some people have told me they set the ashes free in the ocean to honor their Viking heritage. If you wish to share your way of releasing the ashes, I would love to hear it.

This ceremony is meant to supplement, not replace, whatever other treatments someone may be undertaking, whether medical, psychological, or spiritual.

Phoenix Trueblood is a Gifted Shamanic Practitioner. Working with earth elements and energies since she was a child, she is the granddaughter of a respected elder and medicine woman who lived until the age of 103.

Phoenix has always been truly gifted. Her gifts were recognized by others early in life. In her early 20's she had a near-death experience and believes she was touched by an energy force that's purpose was to make sure her gifts were used. Upon returning from the afterlife, she had a better understanding of her gifts, who she was, and that helping others was at the core of her existence. She believes she must never let the chain of kindness go unbroken and that the links of love, compassion, and kind acts will eventually encircle the world.

Phoenix uses her gifts to help individuals, couples, groups, and even animals with this newfound understanding.

Until this book, her gifts have not been widely known. Over the years, people have been referred to her, either by close friends of Phoenix's or friends of those she's helped. Phoenix helped a disfigured special forces soldier who lost his identity and self-worth on the battlefield and is now remarried with a new lease on life. She assisted a couple with their dream of conceiving a child by performing a powerful ceremony for them. And she helped a woman who had gifts but whose path was blocked. Through readings and an infusion of energy from Phoenix, she broke through and found success. Phoenix is committed to helping people awaken their own gifts with her touch of enlightenment.

For a consultation or personalized ceremony, feel free to contact her.

https://www.phoenixtrueblood.net

Email: energyworker4u@gmail.com

Chapter 15

BECOMING A TRANSITIONAL CHARACTER

Leverage Your Ancestral Gifts to Heal Transgenerational Trauma

ELIZABETH R KIPP, ANCESTRAL CLEARING® PRACTITIONER

A transitional character, a term coined by the late Carlfred Broderick, is one who, in a single generation, changes the entire course of a lineage. Their contribution to humanity is to filter the destructiveness out of their heritage so that descendant generations will have a supportive foundation for building optimal and thriving lives.

MY STORY

I was born with my ancestors' imprints, including a loving heart, resilience, and hardiness. I have a pattern of outrage around injustice, especially social injustice. My grandmother and great-grandmother were suffragettes, so my feelings around inequity and suppression made sense to me when I learned about their history. Religious persecution has also been a challenging area for me. I understood the root of this when I

-discovered French Protestant family members who fled Europe, having been persecuted by a violent Catholic government in the 19th century. Powerful events in our history leave an imprint, a karmic residue that becomes available for the next generation to heal.

My ancestors also imbued me with a profound strength level that could only have come through living and surviving hard times. I had the athletic skills of my parents and grandparents. I was born with a sense of gratitude, which served as a guiding rudder throughout my tumultuous life.

Have you ever learned something about your family's history that you somehow knew in your bones long before you learned the historical facts? By the time I was four years old, I had sensed something was awry in my family. Rather than being based on stories relayed to me about the family, my perception of things gone wrong was more intuitive knowing and a felt experience.

My parents fought with each other. And as children mimic their parents, my brother and I fought reflexively with one another. My grandfathers were stern and stiff, and one of them was perpetually angry. By the time I was five years old, I had discovered that the family was in the munitions business on my maternal side going back to the early 1800s. My mother suffered from chronic pain, bipolar disorder, and alcoholism. So, there was a lot of violence layered into the family dynamics on multiple levels.

I perceived quite early on that my family members had disconnected from their hearts, although I did not have the language for this at such a tender age. I felt it in my heart, and I wondered why and what had happened. But in a household where children were to be seen and not heard, my questions about the depressive environment we lived in were not welcome.

As I experienced more of the family's violence, not knowing how to process any of it, I learned to shut down and hold all the projected fear inside me. Unintentionally, I turned the abuse I experienced from the family into myself. As the years progressed, I developed a fierce and unrelenting inner critic.

My sense of the connection to my heart and the divinity that lived inside faded to a mere flicker. Fortunately, I never lost my awareness of it completely. And so, my heart became a beacon of light in my life. It was not until many years later that I understood that my ancestors were guiding me through this heart space.

Life went on, and the violence continued. My reaction was to harden my heart, armoring it the best I could, and dive into my schoolwork and time in nature. I experienced the world's hardness through my family and friends, friends and teachers at school, and through a world gone mad with the nuclear arms race. Violence seemed to be everywhere I looked. All I ever wanted was peace in both the external and internal worlds.

I kept asking myself, *why is everyone so angry? Why can't we all get along? Why is this so hard? Will I ever find a way to live a life of peace and purpose beyond continuing this cycle of violence?"*

No one wanted to hear my questions. As time passed, like my mother, I suffered from the chronic pain of unprocessed Complex Post Traumatic Stress (CPTSD), although it was not diagnosed for many years. It was not until decades later that I understood that the abuse I experienced in my childhood and my inability to process it healthily had negatively affected my health.

I married and gave birth to a son. I vowed that one way or another, I would do whatever I could not to pass the violence and abuse I experienced to my son. I did everything I could to keep him safe as a child and hold a loving, nurturing space for him. I knew the world would visit its harshness on him, yet I also knew I had agency in how I treated him. I still had self-sabotaging thoughts in my mind, and I did my best not to project these towards my son. I became a transitional character, shifting the violence in the lineage through the power of love.

I was in a pain management program when I first experienced Ancestral Clearing®'s power. Waiting to enter the program, I laid in a hospital bed, feeling old and worn down from years of chronic pain. Yet all the while, I felt held mysteriously and perpetually by grace. I did not know where my life was going, yet I felt inexorably held. My ancestors were here, keeping me on course for the mission I came here to complete.

I went through the Ancestral Clearing® process and immediately felt my pain lessen. I felt lighter in my body. I felt my heart space lighten and expand. Eventually, the chronic pain lifted, my heart grew once again, and I felt its armor fall away. I continued working in this modality. I brought the warring parts of myself to the peace table within me. I turned into a less pronounced version of Benjamin Button since then, thanks to this work in no small part.

As a result of my profound experience, I became an Ancestral Clearing® Practitioner. Through this practice, I learned how to help my ancestors release the burden of violence they carried and all the fallout the lineage experienced as a result of it. I deepened my role as a transitional character. Sitting in silent meditation one day, I heard them softly yet urgently whisper to me:

"We are here with you. We will support you through this healing work. Thank you for helping us."

I realized that all I experienced throughout my life prepared me to serve as an Ancestral Clearing® Practitioner, helping to clear my lineage and help others with theirs.

THE TOOL

We are bound in unknown ways that can hold us hostage unconsciously. All these ways have sources in the past. Let us get some perspective on how deeply our roots genuinely reach.

We each came from the womb of our mother. We arose from the very clay of Mother Earth. If we were just here to examine our ancestry here on Earth, consider this. An ever-so-long and continuous filament reaches from us here today clear back more than three billion years to when the first spark of life arose on Earth. Our heartbeat alone can be traced back to the time of our ancestor's ancestors—about one billion years ago—to the shared genetic information we humans share with the sea anemone.

No matter where we're from or who our parents were, we're descended from survivors, those who made it one way or another, to pass the message of life down through the generations. Each of us is the result of so much, and from so many, it's hard to fathom. Our ancestors live with us. They live in our heartbeat, in the very marrow of our bones, and every cell in the body. They mold us to a great extent into who we are as humans.

Look at all that had to happen for you, even to be here as you are in this moment. You, we, all of us, are living deeply in the wonder of creation. The heart understands this dance of energy. It lives eternally aware of its true identity, vibrating the cosmos with every beat. The soul knows all about this ancient dance, has always known it, and will forever know it. The wonder of creation expressed through the human heart is the eternal dance of love. It pulsed in all your ancestors, and they passed it on to you.

ANCESTRAL CLEARING®

We come into this life with our ancestors' outright markings: eye color, skin color, hair color, and more. We carry other ancestral markings, subtler but as profound. These imprints include unresolved issues from the past, like traumas from emotional heartache, abandonment, and tragedies experienced through war and famine.

Ancestral Clearing®, a process developed by John Newton of Health Beyond Belief, helps us clear these burdens from our ancestors and us. This modality helps free you from your past in this lifetime and from your lineage. Ancestral Clearing® allows you to live up to your true potential in this lifetime rather than reliving your family's old unhealthy patterns. It enables you to live your ideas, your dreams, and your own heart. It allows you to differentiate your inner voice from the many voices around you so you can experience the essence of who you are. Tens of thousands of people worldwide have experienced profound benefits from this powerful modality.

Ancestral Clearing® accesses the field of consciousness in the present moment and, with the understanding that we are all connected, helps us shift old unhealthy patterns and habits. Such shifts are possible because of the truth that we are all connected as one in consciousness. What we do to one, we do to all.

Your ancestors never left. We cannot see them in this three-dimensional reality. Our five-sensory system cannot locate them. The human adventure is one of the Infinite playing finite through consciousness. An effect of that creates a veil of illusion that we are separate. We are multi-dimensional beings receiving and transmitting information in multi-dimensional ways. The mind can only track some of this. In silence and presence in consciousness, a mind-body-spirit understanding and intuitive knowing emerge. The ancestors may have left their karmic residue for us to clean up, but their infinite nature endures beyond the bounds of time.

It is not easy to describe the Ancestral Clearing® process in words because it is experiential by its nature. It's like explaining to someone what it's like to eat chocolate. We can use words, but only in the act of eating chocolate does one fully appreciate the experience of eating chocolate. The process involves asking for help in releasing unhealthy ancestral imprints, being in the present moment, and allowing oneself to experience the sensations arising in the body during the process.

We forego or offer up to a power greater than ourselves. By asking for this help from a Higher Power, we receive it, and then the blocks we carry lift and release. For instance, since unhealed traumas from wars in our lineage have left DNA imprints, they are stored there as an unresolved burden. That imprint is showing up as a limitation in our life. We ask for help from the Higher Power to help us resolve this using prayer and the power of forgiveness. As we connect to our Higher Power, the impulses from these imprints come from within the body as sensations and bubble up to clear, resolving themselves just by asking for help, peacemaking, and forgiveness (offering up), humility, and gratitude. It's both simple and profound. I have used words here to describe what essentially is a direct experience.

Here is an example of an Ancestral Clearing® prayer. When you read this and bring yourself present to it, you will access consciousness itself and the Creator's healing intelligence within it. You can read it aloud or silently to yourself.

Oh, Divine Spirit, Creator of All That Is, we thank You for the countless blessings You have bestowed upon us and our lineages. We come to You, knowing You are always here with us in all Your great and vast nature.

For all of us and all our ancestors and all their relations throughout time, space, dimension, and all realms:

For any time we turned away from another, especially when in need, or times others turned us away, especially when we were in need, and for whenever we felt we did not fit in, when others threatened us, or any time we threatened others, please help us to all forgive each other and allow us to all forgive ourselves. Please and thank You.

For acts of greed, selfishness, superiority, and entitlement, acts of domination, mistreatment, and disrespect of one to another or another to us; for the times others saw us as undeserving of their love, attention, compassion, and respect, and any time we saw another like this, please help us all to forgive each other and help us all to forgive ourselves. Please and thank You.

For the times others took from us without asking permission, and for the times we did this to others, any time we were heavy-handed with others, and for the times others did this to us, please help us all to forgive each other and to forgive ourselves. Please and thank You.

For all the times we felt misunderstood, unseen, or unheard, and for the times we did this to others, knowingly or unknowingly, please help us all to forgive and release each other, and forgive and release ourselves for all of it, fully and completely. Please and thank You.

For all the times we were swept up in and overwhelmed by events beyond our control, and we felt unable or unwilling to do anything about it, and when we felt the weight of such events burden our hearts to the breaking point, please help us all to forgive each other and help us to forgive ourselves, no matter what, now and forever. Please and thank You.

For any time we witnessed violence, had violence brought down upon us, or any time we projected violence of any kind onto another, please help us all to forgive each other and to forgive ourselves completely. Please help us to keep our hearts open and filled with compassion for all beings, including compassion for ourselves. Help us see that 'the other is you' in each other and find enlightenment and illumination. Please and thank You.

For all the times we despaired about not being able to live in peace and prosperity together in the world, as one unified people, and for all that we made it mean about ourselves, each other, society, life in general, even and especially what we made it mean about You, Creator – please help us to all forgive each other, no matter what, for all that happened, help us to forgive ourselves. Help us forgive You, Creator, for the part we felt You played in any of it, now and forever. Please and thank You.

Help us to grow beyond fear and hatred, separation and estrangement into love, unity, and compassion for one another and ourselves, fully realizing that we are all connected to You and each other and are never, ever alone. Please help us to see this in our lives fully. Please help us find resolution in all our conflicts within ourselves and with others and embrace humanitarianism and philanthropy. Please and thank You.

Please help us awaken to and experience our true nature and expand our consciousness. May we live in love, peace, and unity for us all, forever and ever.

Please and thank You.

Please and thank You.

Please and thank You.

Amen.

Notice how you feel now that you have read those words. Do you notice any shift in your energy?

Ancestral Clearing® helps us release our stuck energy to no longer regret the past nor banish it. We recognize the past as part of our history yet do not feel the burden of its weight.

One cannot solve a problem at the same level as created. If we are to find a way to peace, it will be by developing new models and systems. The only way we will see these solutions is first to resolve and release our ancestral burdens and raise our level of consciousness.

Listen to the whispers of the mothers and fathers that came before us. They beckon us and invite us to heal what they could not. We are born with our ancestors' gifts and limitations. It is up to each of us to leverage our strengths, given to us by them, to release our common burdens. They gesture us in so many ways to remember our place under the stars and become transitional characters. When we heal ourselves, we heal our lineage and heal the world.

What are the generational patterns that can change with you? I encourage you to actualize your birthright, all the gifts your ancestors brought you through all their trials and tribulations. They have been waiting for you. It is in your hands. It is already here, waiting for you to claim it.

Here's the link for more information on Ancestral Clearing® and your personal AC® session: https://elizabeth-kipp.com/resources/

Elizabeth R Kipp is an Ancestral Clearing® Practitioner, Addiction Recovery Coach (Recovery 2.0), Stress Management and Chronic Pain Specialist, Bilateral EFT/Tapping Practitioner, Yoga Teacher (RYT/ IKYTA), and author of *The Way Through Chronic Pain: Tools to Reclaim Your Healing Power*. She holds a B.S from the Univ. of Delaware. She pursued an M.S. in Environmental Studies at the University of Kansas, emphasizing remote sensing, ecology, and environmental resource analysis.

Elizabeth R. Kipp is a long-time seeker of truths with a foot in both the spiritual and scientific worlds. Her life experiences and training enable her to bridge the gap between these two worlds.

In the months following her son's birth in 1982, Elizabeth's burgeoning professional career was cut short by the emergence of a structural weakness in her low spine. She spent over 31 years in and out of hospitals pursuing a way to stabilize her spine and find freedom from persistent pain resulting from old injuries.

Her deep connection to the spiritual world, including her ancestors' spirits, supported her through multiple surgeries, decades of prescribed medications, and a long persistent search for modalities that would help her heal. In 2013 Elizabeth entered a pain management program where she was able to free herself of the chronic pain cycle and find a way to live a life free from suffering. The Ancestral Clearing® process was a significant piece of Elizabeth's healing journey.

Now in recovery, Elizabeth helps people step into the power of their healing. She has turned her attention to the alarmingly high population of people who suffer from or are recovering from chronic pain. She uses Ancestral Clearing® as a primary tool in helping people release their past burdens, chronic pain and unleash their healing power.

You can find out more about Elizabeth here https://elizabeth-kipp.com/resources/

Chapter 16

WHEN THE HOMELAND CALLS

Traveling to Your Ancestral Roots

DR. AHRIANA PLATTEN, PH.D.

When I learned the title of this book would be *Ancestors Within*, I thought, *of course – that's the first place to look for them!* I've been teaching people to honor their ancestors for more than 25 years. Their blood runs in our veins. Our bones and skin are formed in their fashion, and we carry both their wisdom and phobias as epigenetic signatures. Cutting-edge science suggests we are influenced by up to eleven ancestral generations and carry within us more than two-hundred years of the experiences had by those upon whose shoulders we stand.

MY STORY

My mother's family immigrated to the US from Italy in the late 1800s. There is so much information about me hidden in that one sentence. Immigrants. My great-grandparents were Italian immigrants. Many of us are the great-grandchildren and great-great-grandchildren of immigrants who left behind their names because they were too hard to pronounce in

English. They left behind traditions and memories to blend into a new culture more easily, and they adopted American ways of living. They left behind people and places they loved and carried forward the wounds of lost identity and familial separation. We carry their losses in our bodies, hearts, and minds.

For most of my life, I had nothing but a few surnames to remind me of my Italian heritage. I knew I was "part Italian," but it meant nothing in my day-to-day life.

Well, almost nothing.

I was born in January of 1961, and mere weeks after my birth, my mom took a train from Montana to Minnesota, where I met my great-grandmother, Cristina, who was very ill. I'm told she held me, but, of course, I can't remember our interaction. I was less than six weeks old when she passed away, soon after our visit.

In reality, I should have no real connection to her, yet as a young child, I can remember looking at her face in black and white photos and thinking, *her hair is wavy like mine.* I wondered if it was the same mousy-brown color and why her eyes held such sadness. I knew her somehow and could feel her watching over me, but why would someone who had only met me as an infant have any interest in following my life from the afterworld? It was a strange connection.

As a Ceremonialist and Spiritual Educator, I've been blessed to experience a wide variety of rites and rituals over the years. One of the most profound is a ritual in which an ancestor is invited to flow into a person's consciousness and use their body to enjoy the sensations of the physical world. The first time I engaged in this sacred ceremony, I knew exactly who I wanted to call in. Speaking her name into a circle of about 150 others, I invited "Maria Christina Stephania Pistilli Fatticci," my great-grandmother. It's wise to be very specific when inviting an ancient one to come forward from beyond the veils.

Almost instantly, I felt a wave of energy pass into my body, so strong I was dizzy and a bit queasy. My eyes filled with tears and, for a moment, I thought I might fall. Instead, I quickly took a new posture as rich curiosity pulled me from the ritual space to a nearby table filled with food. I wanted to taste everything, even things I don't like. Sweet was sweeter. Bitter was more bitter. Every taste was intense and full. Moments later, my ears were filled with the rhythm of drums and the haunting sound of a lone violin playing in the ceremonial crucible. I was fascinated in a way I've never been. It was as though it had been centuries since I'd heard these sounds. I danced. I chanted with the other participants. And even now, as I write "I," I know it wasn't me. I was being ridden by an ancestor who had not been in a body for a long time. She looked out of my eyes, and everything in view seemed to glow. The simplest sights—a leaf, a plate—were a feast for the eyes.

This experience was meant to last a few hours, and then, with guidance, we were to send our ancestors back to the place from whence they came. When it was time, I couldn't do it. I simply couldn't end the experience, so I let her stay. For more than a year, I had times of pure bliss as she shared my life and times of great sorrow that had no explanation. Tears flowed often, and I couldn't anticipate what would cause them. I was very aware that I felt like an outsider. Or, more correctly, *she* felt like an outsider.

Then, without any fanfare, she was gone. I never formally released her; I just didn't feel her like I had before. Perhaps she went back to where she came from, but I wondered if maybe she just integrated more deeply into my being until there was no more separation between her and me.

Fast forward to 2016. My father was diagnosed with cancer. We were blessed by the time we shared, which was the most difficult year of his life. He showed such bravery and positivity. When it became clear that there would be no cure, we had those conversations you have at the end of life: conversations about joys and regrets. One afternoon, when it was just him and me, quietly sharing our hearts, my father said, "I feel really bad that I never took your mom to Italy. I told her I would, but I didn't make the time." Tender tears rolled down his face. I'll never forget that conversation.

Without any hesitation, I did what any daughter would do. "I'll take her there, Dad! If you can figure out how to get out of Heaven for a few days, you should join us!" I joked, and he smiled in a melancholy way.

When I made that promise to my father, I could feel something inside of me spring to life. I was driven, perhaps by my great-grandmother or by the knowledge that the trip would help my mother heal from her loss.

Whatever it was that moved me, I felt both the magnitude of the task ahead and the determination to find my way. I also felt Cristina's presence once again.

Going to my ancestral homeland would have been much easier if I could've settled for a generic trip to Italy, but I couldn't. I knew I needed to take my great-grandmother home to the place she left behind. This would be a "coming-full-circle," and nothing else would be good enough. A string of small miracles was necessary to make it all happen because I had no idea from where, specifically, she came. All I had was a photograph of an oil painting my grandmother had created years before of a town square with a fountain graced by four lions and a church bell tower on the hilltop. On the painting was the word "Compobasso."

That photo was in an album from a 1977 family reunion my mother and grandmother attended. I'd looked at it many times but never noticed that my grandmother wrote the words "Grandma and Grandpa were born here" on the page next to the photo in the album. She was, of course, referring to her parents. When I saw those words, I instantly jumped online and looked up "Compobasso." It turns out, Compobasso is a province in the region of Molise, in southern Italy. I felt like leaping out of my skin with joy at this first discovery. The ancestors in my bones awakened.

There are 84 municipalities in the province of Compobasso, and I began the disciplined work of looking up each one to see if I could find any reference to my great-grandparents. While doing that, I came across one small random entry in an Ancestry.com report. That entry turned out to be a master key! The writer said, "Domenico Fatticci lived in the Santa Croce neighborhood." No town, just a neighborhood. I took note of it and, at the time, could not imagine how important it would be later on.

I must have searched at least 70 of the municipalities and, frankly, I was about to give up when I opened the next website. There on the page was a picture of the Fontana dei Quattro Leoni—The Fountain of Four Lions—an exact duplicate of the fountain in my grandmother's painting. On the hill behind it was a church with a two-windowed bell tower, called Chiesa Parrocchiale di Santa Croce, The Church of the Holy Cross; my great-grandfather's neighborhood church. I had found what I was looking for in a little township called Vinchiaturo.

It was time to travel.

We landed in Rome and, after a few days of sight-seeing, headed out to our destination. That day I got sick. Really sick. Throwing-up-in-a-bag-on-the-drive sick. The spirit of my great-grandmother resting within me was scared of what she would find. I could hear her thoughts in my head. *Will anything be the same?* I wondered how much things had changed and whether she would find any sense of familiarity.

When we arrived, the streets were mostly empty and quiet. Vinchiaturo is a tiny town of only 3300 people. It was sunny and warm where we parked the car in the town square. And there it was, just like in the picture: four wrought-iron lions atop a sand-colored fountain with circular steps around it. I got out, still feeling ill, and made my way to a bench. So much was like the painting; the same buildings, pink, and golden yellow, and brick. I'd never been there before, but I felt as if I'd been there a million times. My heart was both over-joyed and strangely sad.

There are so many things I could share about this proud little village. Most memorable was the visit to the church. The priest at Santa Croce showed us the written records of my great-grandfather's baptism and another entry that marked the day he and my great-grandmother married. Even in another language, the handwriting was beautiful and clear enough to easily read the names and dates written over 100 years before. He offered a blessing for my mother at the altar where her grandparents were married, and we placed our hands on the stone baptismal font at which my great-great-grandparents held their infant son, Domenico. I wandered amongst the sanctuary's white and yellow arches, noticing every curve and corner, filled with wonder about what it was like in centuries past. Each step affirmed the last. This was, indeed, the place of my ancestors. "Why would they leave," my mother asked out loud. "I was thinking the same thing," I replied.

I wish I had given myself more time. We only planned one day to visit Vinchiaturo, and that was a big mistake. I underestimated what I would find there. Someday soon, I'll return to walk the streets and visit the cemetery, to look through the records in the town hall, and to see if I can track down anyone who might be related. I believe my great-grandmother stayed when I left. That thought brings me peace.

Visiting my ancestral homeland brought me an unexpected gift, a sense that I belong somewhere. My whole life, for no reason other than ancestral history, I've felt like an outsider. Trans-generational wounds are passed down to us, woven into the fabric of our being. Italians were not liked much when they immigrated to the US. They were considered untrustworthy and uneducated, and they kept mostly to themselves, interacting only with other Italians. When her father died in a mining accident, it was arranged that my great-grandmother would marry her first cousin. There was no money to care for or support her, so this was the best choice for the family. "We were not in love," my great-grandfather once confessed to my mom. They came to the US to escape poverty. She likely felt very alone in a strange land, an outsider from a foreign world.

My feelings of being an outsider ended when I left Vinchiaturo. I brought my great-grandmother home and, when I did, I found my own place of belonging. I know who I am and where my people come from, and I feel my roots connecting me to my ancestors.

THE TOOL

Travel is not often recognized as a healing tool, yet it is what I'm recommending for you, dear reader. There is nothing quite like walking through a town your ancestors inhabited and looking—through the eyes of your imagination—at what they might have experienced.

Here are some simple instructions to get you started:

Step one: Be as specific as you can about your ancestor's origins.

• Talk to relatives and family members to see if anyone has come across a reference to a city. It's surprising how many of us only know the country of residence.

• Dig out photo albums and look at pictures. What are your ancestors wearing? Are there any street signs or landmarks that might give you a clue about which village or town was their home? Do you have baptismal papers or other religious indicators? Take time to look carefully. You'll be surprised what pops up.

Explore your genealogical history. Look for birth and death information.

- Old obituaries often include the place of birth and other life details. If you don't have any genealogical information, be sure to look up your ancestors' names in Ancestry.com and other online sources. You may be surprised by what you find and to whom you are related.

- Record everything in a notebook or digital file. Little details can be the key to big discoveries.

Step two: Use the dates of important events like births, marriages, and deaths to do some historical research. What was going on in the land of your ancestors during their lifetimes? Was it commonplace to emigrate? If so, why? What was happening that would motivate someone to move to an entirely new country? It takes a lot of courage, or desperation, for people to leave behind everything and everyone familiar to them, pack up what little they could carry, and travel a great distance, facing struggles and challenges along the way.

- Consider things like poverty, plagues, and health issues.

- Explore earthquakes and natural disasters that may have occurred.

- Check to see if there were any conflicts or wars at the time.

- Reflect on issues of prejudice and persecution.

Step three: Consider hiring an expert. I didn't take this step; however, even after my trip to Italy, I am considering it. In most countries, you can hire someone—a student, a professional historian, or a genealogist—to take what you know and dig deeper. This is especially useful if you don't read or speak the language. An expert can make phone calls, read records, and track down documents that will help you to reconstruct your ancestral story. They may even locate a relative who will be as excited to meet you as you are to meet them.

Step four: Go there. Call up the same courage your ancestors used to bravely explore a new land. It can be a little scary to travel internationally, but you can use the experience to imagine how they might have felt when they left the homeland.

- Choose a date for your trip and give yourself plenty of time to explore.
- Talk to people while you're there. Eat the local food. Don't act like a tourist.
- Imagine you are bringing your ancestors home because, in a cellular and spiritual way, you are.

Phillip Carr-Gomm, an author in the fields of psychology and Druidry, is quoted as saying, "The songs of our ancestors are also the songs of our children." When you visit your ancestral homeland, you learn the heart-songs that heal ancestral wounds for you and those who come after you. I wish you well on your journey.

Dr. Ahriana Platten is an internationally acclaimed speaker and socio-cultural innovator who creates understanding and collaboration between leaders in business, spirituality, and wholistic living. She is a master ceremonialist and practical mystic who is widely appreciated for her authenticity and positivity.

Ahriana mentors highly motivated individuals and teams who seek to align right livelihood, intuitive purpose, and heart-centered living.

A former Ambassador for the Parliament of the World's Religions, Ahriana is a featured Wisdom Keeper in the acclaimed international film and docuseries, "Time of the Sixth Sun." She has traveled the world to explore its cultural differences and human similarities, speaking to religious and tribal leaders from 250 countries. Her weekly newspaper column, "In Good Faith," is seen by over 120,000 readers each week.

To subscribe to her newsletter and enjoy free meditations, videos, other classes, or to inquire about scheduling her to speak, visit www.Ahriana.com

Chapter 17

FINDING YOUR WAY THROUGH ANCESTRAL FIRE
How Love Heals

ROBIN IVY HAYWOOD

MY STORY

Do you want to change? *From the ashes, the Phoenix rises.* Oh, how I love that saying. Like many of you, my ancestors have had generations of living from lack and a victim mentality. Over time this takes its toll. I was tired of feeling like life kept tossing me empty oyster shells, so I committed to change. I deserve the whole oyster.

I decided no more victimization or co-dependency, and I set my sails straight north to free myself through ancestral fire. As you take this reading ride with me, I whole-heartedly encourage you to question where you can shift and what small or large changes you can make. I'm sure if you do some investigation, you'll find that victimization and co-dependent patterns run thick as thieves in your family. Are you ready to hear more? You are about to discover how I grew through ancestral fire.

I was a few months into my year-long shaman program, and still deeply asleep in so many ways. I longed for something more. At fifteen, I injured my knee and heard, *you're a healer*. And now here I was at 51, having a major system breakdown. I had that sinking feeling like a five-hundred-mile-an-hour flying object was headed straight at me. Little did I know the impact was going to be like 9/11. I recently moved from Kentucky to New Hampshire; my old life was gone and rapidly turning to dust. I thought I had good roots to carry me through, but I didn't. My roots had decayed like Rome.

WTF was happening to me? I finished my Masters Energy Healing training the fall of moving to New Hampshire. I was about to become an empty nester, and my husband and I had some massive healing work to do between us. I was beginning to expose the major divides we had. They were like Russia and the USA. My self-love was in the toilet, as was my positivity, love, and zest for life. I was in a cyclone of turmoil. Like many women, I placed almost all of my energy into raising my children, serving on community committees, supporting my husband's career, and my apparent gift of being co-dependent. I was learning such tremendous medicine. I opened to my own deeper healing gifts of light language and sounding. But with the move, unhealed PTSD, and the apparent larger healing work I was doing at a soul level, I was having trouble anchoring any emotion above fear. I was in a cycle of pain as well as a habitual pattern of being driven from the outside in.

I worked with all my tools, grasping at an exasperated pace to establish a new life in New Hampshire. I was on FIRE but in an unhealthy way! I consumed every tool and teaching I knew and kept learning more. More is better right? Uh, no! I knew I was on an ascension path yet didn't have the skillset to work my light body. I was deep in the cycle of death, surrendering to all I learned. I prayed, I cried, I got up and did what I could. I did yoga, had regular massage, took walks, and began connecting with nature again. I discovered a budding artistic side of myself which lifted my spirits some. I also discovered I loved to create sacred home spaces. Finding a real connection in New Hampshire was still missing. I longed for girlfriends.

I learned a lot about myself through these years, especially about the need to go within. Spirit was speaking. I just wasn't a very good listener yet. Then one day, my grandfather in spirit came in with a message.

Like a light beam, once again I found my grandfathers' picture on my office floor. He seemed to have a habit of sliding down the bright, cozy ancestor alter I created. Maybe he didn't like being next to my grandmother, or maybe a blast of wind blew him down? NOPE, it was neither. He had a message for me to deliver. As I slowly bent down to pick up his picture, I felt the grief tighten in my lungs. Tears began to surge, and the flood was released. I heard him say, "I am so sorry for hurting the family. Please tell your aunts and your mother I'm sorry, ask them to forgive me for all that I've done." My grandfather had molested my aunt, which had been a heavyweight on our collective family soul. The pain of this darkness, along with my abusive childhood, stunted my development. Another way to view this is it stunted my DNA. I learned later on that many things stunted my DNA, but that story is for another time.

Shortly after this experience with my grandfather, I took a group trip to dig crystals in Arkansas. Arkansas was where he was born. I knew this was a divine calling on many levels. Having recently fallen in love with crystals, I was crazy excited to excavate them myself. I also looked forward to feeling the land where my grandfather and ancestors lived.

The second I stepped foot off the plane in Little Rock I sensed a larger connection with my heritage. As I walked through the terminal toward baggage claim, I felt this shift and expansion. I then heard, "You are connecting with your Sirian heritage." Crazy right? Crazy, not crazy! Laughing silently, I thought, *thank you for the gift.*

A day before my trip completed, I heard the inner call to visit the gravesite where my grandfather was buried. My initial response was, *no way.* I didn't want to drive eight hours roundtrip to spend 30 minutes or an hour to visit his grave, but I did it anyway. I had to; it was more than just visiting his grave; it was about driving through the land.

The sun was bright in the sky as cascading light rays edged me on. I was almost there. Hickory Creek Cemetery. The birds were singing, there was a soft breeze, and the air felt refreshing. Walking on the sacred ground was humbling. What I was about to see surprised me. I saw row after row of gravestones with the last name Eden. Tingles came over me. I continued my walk up and down the rows, wondering what my ancestors were like. As I walked the rows, I finally found it. Samuel L. Eden. I sat silent for a moment then began to pray. I opened my heart to him, and the sacred violet flame began. I continued to pour the fire of violet to him and the rest of my ancestors who wished to receive. I felt them light up. As my time came to an end, I thanked God for the healing and left in peace.

Visiting Arkansas helped further my healing and developing root system. Spirit is always cheering us on. I'm happy my grandfather was persistent in reaching out to me. Since that time, my roots are more clear. The picture of my grandfather is now framed and in a new spot next to my grandmother. I imagine they like the changes.

THE TOOL

A free audio version of this tool and other inspiration can be found at haywakeup.co under free content.

HOW LOVE HEALS

Healing through Violet Fire

Step one: Find two songs you would like to dance to or get your body moving to.

Choose songs that inspire you. Maybe a song from a fantastic time in your life, or even a song that moves you to cry. Whatever it is, get your heart in it. Feel it! The idea here is to let the music move you.

Step two: Get up, move, and dance. If, for some reason, you are unable to dance, move your body any way you can or simply enjoy the music.

Step three: Turn the music off and find a comfy seat. You are about to connect to the energy of the violet flame. You can gently place your hand on your heart, or anywhere that feels comfortable. Relax and open. Begin to open to receive self-love. Open to receive all the love you possibly can.

Step four: Breathe deep, expansive breaths. Drop within and decide what you would like healed, released, and uplifted.

Step five: Say out loud, "I am the violet fire." Begin to build the violet fire within your body. Feel your heartbeat and the breath that pulses through you. Ask for your prayers and intentions to be answered. Say out loud what you wish to be uplifted, healed, and released. Feel the divine light pouring in. Sense the amethyst energies and violet fire move through your body. Feel the flame build and move through you at the right movement for you. Feel the release of energies you no longer need. Stay connected to your body and breathe as you feel this energy gentle uplifting you. If any emotions surface, allow them to move through you. Let's intensify the energy a little more now. All that is not of love is being returned to love. Feel yourself being balanced and calmed. Feel yourself relax and deepen within your body. Give yourself a few moments to sit and enjoy how you feel.

Step six: When this process feels complete to you, take some deep breaths in and out and say out loud, "This session is now complete." Finish by thanking yourself, your higher self, and the spiritual team that supported you. Thank your ancestors for receiving and the violet flame. Give gratitude for what you have just accomplished—trusting in the positive changes that have just taken place.

Step seven: Get up and stretch your body. You may want to play some music and dance again, or go outside and get some fresh air. I encourage you to take a few drinks of water after the session.

You'll want to drink some extra water over the next few days to help your system flush out the old and integrate the new. It would also be helpful to get outside and do some sort of movement.

Thank you for joining me on this journey! With Gratitude, Robin.

Robin Ivy Haywood is a natural-born healer, intuitive and empath. At age 15 she dislocated her knee and had an instant knowing she was a healer. Robin officially started her expanded healing awareness in 2010 when she began working at a holistic wellness center, and shortly after became a Reiki Master. She has studied many healing modalities over the years, but none are as potent as her deepening connection with her wisdom guides, teachers, angels, and highest aspects within.

Robin is creator of Haywakeup Mind, Body & Spirit Wellness. She is currently expanding her teachings and growing her business. She will soon be guiding sacred journeys, trips and offering more in-person and online retreats.

Helping clients clear karma is the first order of business when working with Robin. She also teaches individuals how to fine-tune their inner healer, deepen their source connection; as well as help them shift the belief structures they have been in. During sessions, Robin may perform angelic surgery, offer light language activations, clearings, soul healing, DNA restructuring, and sound healing.

Robin is an Ordained Shamanic Minister, a Shamanic Priestess, Energetic Healing Practitioner, Soul Activator, Wife, Mother, and Frequency Keeper. She loves deep soulful relationships, travel, good food, stones, andaras, crystals, connecting with earth elements and helping others create more enriching soul-filled lives.

Robin has many new things to accomplish now. You might say, she is just getting started. She has learned, we were never meant to be in a reincarnation cycle and she is ready to help those brave enough to leap beyond the illusion to reclaim the truth.

If you'd like to work with Robin, or discover more about her work and inspirations connect with her at www.haywakeup.co

Chapter 18

BUILDING A RELATIONSHIP WITH YOUR ANCESTORS

Connecting with the Power of your Ancient Bloodline to Heal Generational Trauma

CRYSTAL RASMUSSEN
GENERATIONAL HEALING® TEACHER
& SPIRITUAL GUIDE

MY STORY

"You are never alone. We are here with you." The voices of the ancestors echoed in my ears.

As I listened, I felt unconditional love wash over me, accompanied by a sense of peace, security, and safety.

Finally, after decades of feeling shut down and disconnected, I knew no matter what was happening in my life, no matter how alone I felt, my ancestors were walking with me. They were both leading the way for me to step forward courageously, and surrounding me, offering support, guidance, and wisdom. I took solace in knowing they were protecting me and helping me maneuver through each moment of life; the challenges, celebrations, and the mundane.

When I realized this truth, a whole new world revealed itself leading me to my purpose, a deeper connection with self, and powerful relationships with the unseen world; ultimately experiencing more trust, happiness, and freedom.

Throughout life, I'd always felt the ancestors with me, yet I discounted their presence. I failed to trust what I was hearing, receiving, and experiencing.

Like many individuals, I was taught to shut down my intuitive gifts out of fear, religious beliefs, and misunderstandings.

It started when I was a young girl walking down the long dirt road from the school bus. To my delight, my Grandma Bess, who had passed over from complications during surgery a few years earlier, was suddenly walking by my side.

"Hello Crystal," she said softly.

"Grandma!" I exclaimed, "I've missed you!"

I told her about my particular difficult day at school.

She offered love and insight into the disconnection I experienced, and we continued chatting the rest of the way home.

Excitedly, I rushed through the door, "Mom, you won't believe what happened! Grandma came to see me! She walked me home from the bus! She's still with us and is okay!"

But what happened changed how I interacted with the unseen world for decades.

Instead of happy, my mother was disgusted and aggravated, "Crystal, that's ridiculous. Stop it! Enough with your wild imagination and stories. You know better than to make things up. Go to your room!"

I shut down and withdrew immediately. Seeing and speaking with the dead wasn't acceptable. I was heartbroken and confused.

Did I make it all up? I wondered.

Regardless of how unacceptable connecting to the dead was by my community and family, I yearned for it. I secretly sought it out. Of course, without expressing my experiences out loud again.

I knew there was wisdom in the ancestors' words. I felt safer and had more clarity when they were near. From beyond the grave, my grandmothers helped me through leaving toxic codependent relationships, picking me up when I didn't feel like I had the strength to go on, and leading me to exactly the right teachers, people, locations, and opportunities. Over and over again.

When I listened, that is.

When I "heard" them or "knew" something, my usual thought was *it's my imagination,* and I would easily dismiss it believing I was making it up.

I didn't trust it was my ancestors communicating with me.

So, I struggled through life with fear controlling me.

I spent countless hours stuck in my anxious mind, filled with doubt, worries, and a huge desire to run from people, situations, and circumstances. Hiding, avoiding, and pushing people away was my go-to. As long as I didn't "move" or things didn't "change," then I thought I was okay.

The funny thing was, I desperately wanted change. I yearned for it with every ounce of my being but was terrified of it at the same time. I craved connection with the ancestors and unseen realms. I longed to have a deeper understanding of life and relationship with all beings.

It was obvious I wasn't living life at all. Instead, I was filled with pain, sadness, lack, and limitation. I was only existing and barely breathing, stuck in a world where I didn't feel like I belonged. Mind chatter, chaos, confusion, and fear took over so much that I barely made it through the day.

Just surviving wasn't enough anymore.

I wanted to live.

I wanted to experience life in all its glory and what it has to offer.

I wanted my life to have meaning, to live with purpose, to do something greater than I could've imagined, to be of service to others.

One day, in desperation, I cried, cursed, and screamed underneath the apple tree that a grandmother planted decades earlier. In the chaos of being a single mom, I was being tossed around by life like a rowboat out in the ocean in the middle of a raging storm.

In a moment of helplessness and defeat, I begged the universe to show me the way.

"I don't want to do this anymore!" I cried, looking up to the sky with tears streaming down my face.

"I don't want to be here! Don't make me continue living this way. I want to be happy and feel like I have a purpose. Please, help me!" I begged.

The ancestors heard my call that day.

And they saved me, literally.

I felt their power.

They showed up in full force. Immediately following my plea, a website dropped in on my computer, and I knew, without a doubt, they were speaking so loudly to me that I couldn't ignore them anymore. I had to listen. I needed to study with Deborah Skye King, the founder of Generational Healing®. Not knowing how I would afford it, make it work, or even what would come from it, for the first time in a very long time, I fully committed to something. I told myself no matter what, I was going to enroll.

And I did. With support and guidance from the unseen realms, miracles happened. I paid the deposit and enrolled as a student.

As I began studying with Deborah Skye, learning about conditioning and the unconscious, my life began making more sense. The intense fears I felt from driving in bad weather to traveling by myself or having conversations with people all seemed less overwhelming. I was able to leave unhealthy relationships behind, feel more confident, be a better mom and improve myself. I felt more grounded and actually in my body and learned the importance of it. *I had no idea I wasn't in my body!* And I learned how the unseen realms affected us each and every day, something I'd always felt but didn't really know how to explain or begin to understand. I was fascinated with the knowledge that was being shared and how different I was feeling.

On a retreat to Sedona with Deborah Skye, she invited me to connect to the earth. I grounded into the earth and opened my heart to what Gaia had to share. That's when I experienced through my mind's eye how a tribe lived there in the past. I witnessed the children playing in the creek, the warriors up high on the rocks, and the women tending to the plants and cooking.

This was beyond anything I'd experienced before! Connecting to the ancestors in such a way felt powerful, healing, and eye-opening. I felt alive and excited! I needed more!

When enrollment for her Apprenticeship Training opened up, I jumped on it. I had longed to awaken my spiritual gifts after I had shut them down as a young girl.

After completing the initial 13 Mystical Wisdom Teachings Initiations online, I was invited to attend a seven-day in-person certification training. I had no idea what it entailed, but I knew I had to be there. Something inside me told me it would be life-changing, and it was!

There I sat, the first day of the training, in a pink chair in the corner of the room in my teacher's home, feeling uncertain and anxious. I'm sure if anyone was watching me, they could see my entire body shaking with fear.

I listened intently to Deborah Skye as she explained what she was training us to do; connect to the ancestors and heal generational trauma. Both excitement and curiosity took over. *What was generational trauma,* I wondered? *How does something that someone I never knew affect me, my choices, and how I live my life today? How in the world am I even going to be able to hear other people's ancestors? I could barely hear my own most of the time!*

With each word she uttered, I hung on to the edge of my seat, taking it all in. Intrigue, curiosity, and exhilaration filled me up.

As she shared her wisdom and explained our ties to our ancestors, everything was finally beginning to make sense. I'd always heard of gifts and strengths being passed down from one generation to the next; of course, suffering and traumas would do the same! *But really?* I thought.

I didn't think that my childhood was that bad. My parents were good and decent. I didn't have any "trauma" per se that I could remember. So how was this going to work for me? How can this help me? And how can it help the ancestors that are already dead? My mind raced with questions, yet I had no idea how to form them into words.

I was fascinated. I could see patterns that continued in my own family, including physical ailments, avoidance, depression, worry, particular beliefs. Then I looked at other families. The struggles they faced also continued from one generation to the next; addiction, limitation, fear, lack, disempowerment, physical disease.

The first in the training to experience a Generational Healing® session, I laid down on a massage table while my teacher began working with me; well, actually, she began working with one of my ancestors through me. In my mind's eye, I was able to see a woman that stepped forward. My ancestor, this woman, showed me her life, her story, the pain that she lived with, her thoughts and feelings, and how it has affected me today in my present life.

I felt so much compassion for her and what she endured. My heart ached for her. I never knew this story, but I felt it in my being. My cells felt it.

Once the session was complete, I sat up feeling so much lighter. FREE. Colors were brighter, a weight was gone, and I could see clearly every area of my life and how this one story, this one trauma that my ancestor experienced, affected many areas of my life.

I had such enormous gratitude for her in how she had the courage to step forward, share her story to heal herself, but also to offer this powerful healing to me and her lineage. This was healing her, me, and my children. I was in awe.

The ideas I had about how my ancestors supported and affected me had been so limited.

My second healing session left me bawling. The ancestor that spoke was a gifted healer who was an outcast and living alone. He experienced doubt in who he was, what he could do, and in his healing abilities.

This crushed me to the core. These were the same feelings I was experiencing in my life. I finally understood the pain I had experienced when I was shut down as a young girl. This inherent pattern of doubt was passed down from generation to generation, stopping me, my ancestor, and my family from trusting.

Learning these patterns run deep within the generational lines made me realize how important healing generational trauma is and the power it has to affect humanity.

By the third day of my certification training, I was captivated.

Sitting in the corner, nervously twitching my hands, I was called to facilitate. The first one out of the whole group of students, and I was terrified! Feeling supported by my teacher and other women, I stood up and within moments shifted into a multidimensional framework where a male Ancestor stood across from me sharing his heartbreaking tale.

When the session was completed, I stood there with tears streaming down my face, heart wide open, and humbleness I've never experienced before. The gratitude the ancestor shared with me for the healing he had received was filled with pure unconditional love.

When the recipient sat up, she related so deeply to what the ancestor had shared. The feelings, the physical pains, the thoughts, they all made sense to her. They were things she had felt, thought, and experienced in her own life.

I looked at my teacher, declaring, "I just found my purpose! Wow. That was incredible. Thank you!"

Hearing the pain and suffering of those that walked the earth before us gifted me with more compassion for people I meet. I now saw the world differently. I saw how much we carry forward from our ancient bloodline; pain, emotion, and beliefs that we are not aware of consciously, yet they affect every single choice, thought, feeling, and how we live our life.

Generational Healing® confirmed for me the importance and impact our Ancestors have in our lives.

I walked away from that training with a new understanding of life and my purpose and respect and honor for our ancestors.

Connecting to your Ancestors is one of the most supportive and rewarding relationships you will have. We all have access to it. It is not reserved for a special few. It's wired within you, something you were born with.

Your ancestors are with you every day. They reside in your blood and bones. Their memories are stored in your cells.

They may have walked the earth long before you, but they still exist within you. They desire to communicate with you, share their wisdom, offer healing, and help break the cycles of inherent family trauma.

Knowing my Ancestors and their wisdom are always with me, keeps me grounded, moving forward, and offers me clarity.

Building a relationship with your Ancestors will change how you experience your own life.

THE TOOL

To download a complimentary recorded version of this meditation to support you in connecting with your ancestors visit www.crystalrasmussen.com/ancestorswithindownload

Create a space within your home where you can sit in daily communication with your ancestors. You may wish to create an ancestor altar with photos of those who have passed over. Include special items that you feel called to place there. Be sure to include a candle.

Sit down in front of the altar with your feet flat on the ground or sit in lotus position if that is more comfortable. Focus on your intention.

Light the candle and invite your ancestors in. Close your eyes, place your hands on your legs with the palms facing up.

Take three deep cleansing breaths. Feeling the breath come in through your nose, following it all the way down and back out through your mouth.

Relax your body. Calm your mind. Know that whatever you experience is perfect. There is no right or wrong way to connect to your Ancestors.

Imagine a beautiful liquid golden white light spiraling down in through the top of your head, gently and slowly moving down the skull, the eyes, the ears, nose, jaw, mouth, neck.

As this light touches each cell, your body relaxes, and you feel more at ease.

This light moves down through the shoulders, the arms, hands, and fingers.

Now down through your heart, swirling, cleansing, purifying, healing, and relaxing your heart, chest, and lungs.

Imagine the light moving down through your stomach, solar plexus, womb, sacral chakra, and down into your root chakra.

Now down through your pelvic floor, hips, thighs, legs, knees, shins, ankles, and feet.

Imagine this light spiraling down through the bottom of your feet, down through the floor of your building, through the foundation, and into the topsoil of the earth.

Down through the rocks, the magma and the layers of the earth. This light continues to spiral down, down, down, into the core of the earth, anchoring you deeply into the center of the earth.

Take a breath here. Allow any and all fears, doubts, misalignments, worries, distractions, anger, frustration, sadness, pain to easily flow down with this light into the earth to be transmuted.

Feel how the earth supports you. Feel how safe you are in this space. Feel how relaxed you are.

Now, allow the earth energy to flow back up through the bottom of your feet, up your legs, your stomach and into your heart.

As the earth energy reaches your heart, imagine that with each breath in, this light in your heart becomes brighter and grows larger and larger until it expands out beyond your physical body, creating a sacred container for you filled with light.

Now, imagine a path in front of you leading you to a serene location. Here, it's filled with trees, water, sun, flowers, and a bench. You walk toward the bench, sit down and invite your Ancestors forward. Let them know you would like to connect and communicate with them. Introduce yourself. Invite them into your space, allow yourself to feel your Ancestors around you. Ask them to give you a sign that they are there. Begin a conversation.

Once the dialogue has been completed, thank your ancestors.

Quietly walk back down the path, coming back to your body, moving your fingers and toes.

Take out a pen and paper and write down what showed up for you.

Revisit this space as often as you would like to communicate with your Ancestors. You can tell them anything you would like to, including what happened in your day, what you would like support and guidance in, or how the family is doing.

Crystal Rasmussen, a professionally trained and certified Generational Healing® Teacher and Spiritual Guide supports you in releasing pain and suffering from your ancient bloodline stored within your genetic lineage to heal you today through in-person and distance sessions.

Her Apprenticeship Training for Generational Healing® began with the 13 Mystical Wisdom Teachings. She has been teaching the 7-day Generational Healing® Certification Training in the US and Canada for the past six years. Crystal guides women who want to serve humanity, awaken their spiritual gifts, and release pain and trauma passed down from one generation to another to heal the world. You can learn more about the training, book a session or connect with her at her website www.crystalrasmussen.com

Chapter 19

LETTING GO

The Collective Consultation Approach to Communicating with Ancestors

ARIELLE, SPIRITUAL MEDIUM

Through the crack of least resistance, my non-physical counterpart would speak to me, and in stepping toward my greater desire, I would allow myself to hear.

MY STORY

There she was, standing in Costco, fifty feet away from me. She was responding to the inquiry of an older woman who was asking about her mask. In the center of it was a large red heart with what appeared to be waves of energy emitting out from it in a rainbow of colors. It was positioned perfectly so that every breath, every word spoken, was filtered through the heart. Certainly, it was interesting.

My gaze dropped down to the name tag on her shirt, "Arielle." It was her. When I looked back up at her face, I saw she was looking at me. Without interrupting her conversation, she made solid eye contact with me, giving me a single nod. And then my view of her was blocked by people walking between us.

I circled back to where I'd seen her, but she was gone. I hurried out to the parking lot, thinking her royal blue scrubs would be easy to spot. But she wasn't there, and I wasn't surprised.

I sat in the driver's seat, feeling the sun's warmth. My entire body was vibrating. *Why here? Why now, and after so long? I know things are weird now with COVID, but I'm in no danger walking through this store.* The thoughts danced around in my head as if they were coming to me rather than being offered by me. I felt waves of heat moving through my brain. I'd have clarity soon enough, and in the perfect timing it always is. My thoughts shifted to the last time I saw her in this way.

"Do Something!" I screamed, with every cell of my body, every vibration I emitted. But this scream was silent, not intended for physical ears. I had watched as they took her off the ventilator on the fifteenth day of its breathing for her. It was disconnected to move forward with the procedure, an act of desperation, and a shot in the dark. With the height of technology and world-class physicians, they could come up with nothing. They simply didn't have an explanation of what was happening to her or why.

I was in the strictest mode of observation as they worked on my three-year-old daughter. I knew they'd remove me if I even spoke. The twenty-one medical professionals gathered in the small pediatric ICU room, in my perspective, were no longer relevant.

I processed the sound of the flatline.

Day after day, doctors wrote orders, speaking to me with an air of confidence and authority—each one assuring me that theirs was the answer and not one of them correct. Look here, try there, but still nothing. Their limited vantage point rendered them insignificant, regardless of training or expertise.

"Do Something!" I screamed to a broader perspective than that of any person in the room.

As they prepared to use the defibrillator, already performing CPR, my answer came. A single heartbeat, independent of the chest compressions. A sweeter sound I have never heard. "Wait," the lead physician said softly, sternly, putting her arm out over my daughter to block the staff's movement. There was a moment of silence as we all stood frozen. But then another heartbeat came. Slowly, but surely they returned; those precious beats of my daughter's heart.

They reconnected the ventilator, and one by one, exited with nothing to say. The lead physician finally spoke to me, her confidence and authority now gone, "I won't make you one more promise. The truth is I don't have the answers."

She left me alone to be with my daughter. They decided they would take no further action, feeling her state too fragile to take any more chances for exploration.

I resumed my half-bent position, keeping my face in her view in case she might open her eyes. With my hands, I applied a firm pressure to her head, seeking to calm her nervous system. I stood there for perhaps two hours, my gaze affixed firmly on her beautiful face. I was long lost in the now rhythmic sound of her heart monitor and the *breathe in, breathe out* of the ventilator. Everything else just faded away.

Then I heard her voice, speaking softly in the hall. She was checking in with the nurse posted outside the door, as all who entered were required to do. I thought it rude that the nurse didn't bother to look up at her but instead stayed engrossed in her book. She entered the room.

Laying her clipboard aside, still peering down at it, she spoke to me. "I'm Arielle with holistics. I understand you've had quite a morning."

I shifted my eyes to look at her, careful not to move my head and risk unnecessary stimulation to my little girl.

"I'd like to do an energy healing session on your daughter. I won't touch her. Would that be okay with you?"

I spoke softly, "Do I have to move?"

"No, I'll work around you. You stay where you are."

She could have said nearly anything to me. If there was the slightest possibility of her helping my daughter, I would have agreed. I wasn't exactly sure what she meant by "an energy healing session," but I wasn't entirely sure of the meaning of the word "holistics" either.

She moved quietly about the room, and I paid her little attention, this woman who shared my name. As she began to move toward my daughter's bed, she stopped rather abruptly on the other side of it from where I stood. It was as if something had just occurred to her.

"Here, you do it." She held out her hand above my daughter's body in a demonstration, lowering it slowly. "Show me where her energy is."

Saying nothing, I did as she instructed, showing her where I could feel the slight resistance of my daughter's energetic barrier.

"I thought so," she said in response.

She described to me what to do as I worked on my daughter's energy. With diligence, I did everything as she instructed. She even told me what intention to hold. "You are clearing your daughter's energy of toxicities. Toxicity from the medications, toxicity from environments, relational toxicities." As she spoke the last item to me, I could feel the significance of it.

At some point, a nurse came in. She never did acknowledge the woman instructing me. She didn't speak to her; she didn't look at her. However, she struggled significantly to not gawk at me as I continued to work, and she tried desperately to pretend she wasn't trying to figure out what I was doing.

"Any time you feel inspired to do this, do it again, throughout her recovery, and thereafter. You know now that you can." These were Arielle's parting words to me. We really had spoken very little considering how long we were together. I thanked her, and she left.

The next day, and with no further medical intervention, my daughter was taken off the ventilator. After another 24 hours of observation, she was released from ICU and admitted to a general care ward, where she would spend another three days of uneventful observation. We left the hospital with nothing more than a feeding tube to demonstrate what we'd been through in the 21 days prior.

A few weeks later, once things had begun to calm down at home and my daughter regained her strength, I called the hospital. I wanted to thank *Arielle with holistics* and make sure she knew the profound impact she'd made; for my daughter, for me, for my other children. In a final spout of sheer frustration at my insistence, the hospital operator blurted out rudely, "Ma'am, there's no one who works here by that name, and we don't have a holistics department!"

This was the crack of my own least resistance.

Had I understood that it was my own non-physical counterpart, I would have been hesitant. I would have been so busy questioning my sanity, and everything I placed stock into by that point, I would have been too distracted to receive the giftings of it. And so she spoke to me in ambiguity. And as years have passed, I've evolved and allowed myself to receive and perceive more and more. As I've let go of resistance (the only thing blocking my path) I've begun to understand what was already there and in place all along; the support of The Collective. And it began with my own non-physical counterpart.

Although The Collective is inclusive of our ancestors, it is not exclusive to them. At the core of The Collective are non-physical beings who have no intention of becoming physically focused, whose sole purpose is to support and assist those who do become physical; to interpret with them, through the crack of their least resistance. "And we've been doing it for millennia with humankind, such as yourself," to quote them. "Which is why things came to you in the way that they did, including the advent of your own non-physical counterpart, the day of your daughter's event."

In the culmination of these events, I began to allow myself to receive a gift from two of my ancestors; a treasure. In their lifetimes, they created fearlessness, but they never did allow themselves to receive it, to perceive it. Although The Collective, including their ancestors, tried to wedge it in through the crack of least resistance to them, they simply could not let it in. And so today it is gifted unto me, that which they could not bring themselves to perceive. It is my birthright to receive it. I can say, "No, thank you," and disregard it, or I can relish it, expand upon it, and leave it as my legacy for those who follow me in my ancestral line. The choice is always ours.

Both of these individuals held tightly to their beliefs of fear, and in time they saw the evidence of it. The following is an excerpt from a session I did, interpreting The Collective, during which one of my ancestors came through. These are my mother's father's words, a man I never met during his physical lifetime.

"It's never intentional [not letting it in]. I didn't mean to block off my own well-being to the extent that I did. That is why I died, and it's why I died so young, and it's why I died so painfully. The stories you heard were true. Though mildly exaggerated, my suffering was not less than what was communicated to you. But it was all born of my own belief, the thoughts I just kept thinking. I would not stop rehashing those thoughts. And so what I manifested for myself, what I created for myself, was great suffering, and your mother watched it."

"At some point, she used the rationale of 'he deserved it, he was an evil man.' No one deserves to suffer. There's no such thing as an evil man. Grasshopper (playful nickname from my father), I like to play with you, too. [Makes reference to my session work and those I interpret being playful with me and my clients] It doesn't have to be all serious. You were just so serious in the moment the last time I came through because you were so shocked to hear from me."

"You were wondering if I loved you at all because you've never heard from me. You had to move your beliefs that I didn't love you enough to come through. You had to let go of your beliefs that I was a bad man, that I wasn't loving, that I wasn't caring, that I would never have assisted another, that I would only have caused pain, given the opportunity. You had to let all of that go incrementally. And the path of least resistance was you not thinking about me for a very long time."

"There's a reason you haven't gone through that box of pictures (from my mother's estate, the only physical remnants of my ancestors that I am aware of). It's us! *We* talked you into not going through that box because we wanted you not to think about us, so you could let go of your resistance and allow us to come through because we've been chomping at the bit to assist you. *Truly, your ancestors have waited your whole life for this moment!* And here we are, and we're exhilarated! We have waited long for this moment."

"The resistances (beliefs, perspectives, thoughts, opinions, and even negative expectations) are like pieces. And as they accumulate, the path of least resistance gets smaller and smaller, and there are fewer cracks for us to wedge the assistance and messages in through. It's all in your allowance and perception of it; your allowance in perceiving what's available to you."

"That stream that you saw turn into a flowing river is your path of least resistance. From a little trickling stream to a swiftly flowing river, and you were in witness of it."

"Allowing yourself to receive the gifts of the assistance of The Collective, and the gifts *to* The Collective, in your allowing yourself to receive us."

"The many have much to say. Each one of us speaks to you as the path of least resistance for the recipient, whoever that might be, allows it to be. As it is the path of least resistance for the message to come through that individual and in the way that it comes through that individual. That's how it is decided who will speak, delivering the vibrations (that which you interpret)."

THE TOOL

The two main things that block so many from perceiving and receiving from their ancestors are relational toxicity and down-pulling vibrations. Below you will find the link to my website. I have posted the exercise instructions for Energy Raking, taught to me that day by my own non-physical counterpart. This is a highly effective method for letting go of relational toxicity.

However, I find the most effective methodology for the letting go of the vibrational down-pulling, that which prevents our vibration from rising to the vibrational range to perceive The Collective, including your own ancestors, is quite literally nothing. By this, I am referring to meditation. I'm not suggesting a guided meditation for this purpose, but rather more of a *blank slate* type of meditation.

Both of these can be found under the Tools tab of my website:

www.TheCollectiveConsultation.com

Arielle - The Collective Consultation

www.TheCollectiveConsultation.com

My name is Arielle. I am the interpreter of The Collective™.

The Non-Physical Counterparts of:

• Physically living people

• People not currently living a physical lifetime, but who have

- My clients

In addition to:

- The Non-Physical Consciousness, which has not been, nor will ever be focused into and through a physical body.

All of these come together to form the whole of The Collective.

I am the only person who does what I do, interpreting the vibrational communications of The Collective into spoken language, in a one-on-one format of Consultation for individual clients.

That which I interpret is a broader perspective, one which:

- Sees clearly around the bend.

- Knows the crack of your least resistance in perceiving and receiving what is available to you.

- Knows your every desire and your path of least resistance to the culmination of them.

- Has been in assistance of you all along, knowing your every intimate detail, with only your beliefs, opinions, and expectations to serve as resistance in allowing it to get through.

People are often amazed at who they're really co-creating with. It is not uncommon for this to include celebrities, those we associate with creations of greatness. No longer focused through their physical bodies, they continue the co-creation of the physical realm through subtle assistance of us.

This knowing of that connection affords clients a greater ability to *hear* for themselves.

The information comes through in layers, allowing one to receive from it time and again, as they're inspired to review their Consultation, receiving the next layer of assistance. A single consultation is expected to assist one through no less than a year's fast-paced positive growth.

Arielle - The Collective™ Consultation

www.TheCollectiveConsultation.com

Chapter 20

ANCESTRAL HEALING THROUGH GENEALOGY

Find and Recognize Repetitive Familial Patterns

JEANNE RUCZHAK-ECKMAN

MY STORY

"You live as long as you are remembered," promises an old Russian Proverb. Within me, my ancestors continue to live. Your ancestors continue to live through you. My story is truly and simply a continuation of my ancestors' stories.

Stories are what make one's family tree interesting. Tracing my family tree began as a special connection with my maternal grandmother. She knew everything about everyone (in her family line), and I was her sponge. With her, I visited family members I would never have met. We visited the various local cemeteries where our ancestors were laid to rest. She loved everything dealing with her Irish heritage and was so proud that all four of her grandparents immigrated from Ireland.

Spending time with my maternal grandparents was always interesting! They had an old record player in the living room, and she always played her Irish music. My cousins, my sister, and I were weaned on Danny Boy and the Irish Rovers! And grasshoppers! Forget Shamrock Shakes. My grandmother made all us kids grasshoppers. It was some green drink with alcohol, and it was a special St. Patrick's Day treat at her place.

I soon documented everyone's birth and death dates, who they married, where they were buried, and other vital information. She got me back to our immigrant ancestors in her lines. I was fortunate to have known and corresponded with many elder family members on almost every branch of my family, some of whom were the family historians of their generation.

Even though I lived close enough to drive over and visit most of my family, I wrote them letters. The letters I sent were short.

Dear Aunt Helen,

I hope this finds you well. School is going well.

I have a question about your sister. You mentioned before that Ethel passed when you were young. How did she die? Why had she been away at a school instead of attending the local schoolhouse?

After the niceties were taken care of, I would ask no more than three questions. Sometimes, it might have only been a single question, depending on the topic and the recipient. Once they responded, I would write again with my next question. It was long and drawn out, but now I have these wonderful letters and pieces of family history in my relative's handwriting. There were some good things to growing up before email and the internet.

Storytime is not just for children. I always tried to ask a more personal question.

Dear Uncle R,

Thanks for answering some questions. I'd like to know more about your grandmother, Anna. What was she like? What is your favorite memory of her?

I asked my uncle (my grandmother's brother) about their grandparents once, and he gave me a detailed description of her. Nowhere else have I found that detailed of a physical description. Often, I would ask a question pertaining to a story I already had heard. This way, I can confirm details or make a note to confirm that information.

Stories come from all different sources, and even though a story may not be about your specific ancestor, it still may shed some light on a piece of their life. I was at church one day years ago speaking to some of the older parishioners, the ones who knew my great grandparents and grew up with my grandparents. One conversation led to another, and soon we were talking about immigration and the passage over to America.

"You know they came over in steerage, right?" asked my dear friend Irene.

"Steerage? I think I knew that but just not what it meant," I responded.

My friend then explained that, while it did vary from ship to ship, steerage was generally over-cramped with very little privacy and very minimal amenities. The steerage compartment was where third-class passengers spent the majority of their time, having very limited access usually to a deck.

"The trip across the ocean," my friend continued, "took anywhere from seven days to 17 days. This was just the trip across the ocean. Their journeys began in their villages, where they left family and friends. They then had to get to the port city. For my Polish, Ukrainian, and Russian ancestors, this was Brennen, Germany. Some people got there by train, some by horse carts, and some walked. Walked!"

In the above example, while we were not specifically talking about my great grandparents, the similarities are enough to get a feel as to how their immigration travels were when they came over in 1912-1914.

When I was 14, I had my first job. With that job, of course, came my first checkbook. I remember being so excited to write my first check. It was to the PA Dept. of Vital Records. My first paycheck paid for the death certificates of Daddy's paternal grandparents! Now, those same death certificates are found through Ancestry.com at no extra charge, other than the membership subscription. When I was not working, I spent my Saturdays at the local libraries researching local history connected to my family lines.

Compiling their stories has, I feel, breathed life back into them. It seemed natural for me to do this. Since walking this path of life and after having taken a course in Ancestry Healing, I realize that, while natural, it's a way to honor the ancestors.

Over the years, I learned to speak, and more importantly, listen, to the ancestors as well. I intuitively realized that some spoke to me more on significant dates, and I began to recognize patterns.

Occupations are a natural pattern, especially in past decades and centuries when there were not as many choices in life. Some patterns were health conditions, like diabetes and heart disease. Some patterns involved childbirth, like miscarriages and multiple births.

Daddy worked at Lukens Steel Mill in Coatesville, Pennsylvania. It went through many names over the years, but it will always be Lukens. His brother worked there. Their father worked there. His brothers worked there. My great-grandfather worked there. A slew of cousins and other uncles were there as well over the years. What a great pattern of employment, right? Understanding the pattern is also important. They may have all worked there because that was the only major employer in town. It may have been that each got an incentive for bringing in an employee. More than likely, it was a combination of those reasons.

My mom's paternal side was predominantly farmers. A few enjoyed the cottage industries, such as blacksmithing, but for the most part, they owned land and farmed it. My great-grandfather, Pierson, was a blacksmith. His father, Franklin, was born and raised on a farm and farmed the land himself then. His father, George, farmed the land until Franklin took over. George's mother had him out of wedlock in 1808. Her father, Charles (I believe he was a tavern owner), "put her out on a farm," according to George's granddaughter.

Through my research, I noticed that heart disease was often a contributing cause of death. It was most noticeable in my diabetic family members. When I was first diagnosed with diabetes, I was not surprised. After all, it ran on both sides of my family. Because of my family knowledge, though, I recognized the early symptoms, and I work with my doctors regularly for treatment, not just for diabetes but also for those conditions that often accompany the disease.

Miscarriages and multiple births show up in several places in the family, though they are most noticeable on my maternal grandmother's side. She was the oldest of ten children. Ten! Of those ten, there is a set of unnamed twins who did not survive (1913). There is a stillborn child (1916). There is a son who died shortly after birth later. Her mother, my great-grandmother, was one of eight children. Her eldest brother, a twin, died at just two years old. When I asked my grandmother about these sad events, I was told, "It's just part of life."

I had a miscarriage in 1995, and I was heartbroken. I remember my mom telling me it was "for the best." In tears, I went to visit my Baba (Daddy's mom; my maternal grandmother had passed while I was in college). I remember my grandparents sitting on the couch and my grandfather leaning over and quietly saying, "Anna, tell her. It's okay." She proceeded to tell me how hard it was for her to conceive, and then she lost a child between Daddy and his brother. She let me grieve for my lost child (Katherine) and then told me a most important thing. I had to forgive myself. I did nothing wrong.

Forgiveness. That was my first lesson in ancestral healing, though I certainly did not know it at the time.

Trauma experienced by an ancestor which *we* feel is called intergenerational trauma. We might experience it through unexplained panic attacks. It might be a phobia or a fear. If you are experiencing fear, a phobia, or unexplained panic attacks and can not relate it to a personal event, then ancestral healing might be the answer.

So, what is ancestral healing?

Ancestral healing is a process—a spiritual, ritualistic process—in which we work with our ancestors to recognize, understand, and heal the issue passed through the generations, consciously or unconsciously.

It's widely accepted that children and grandchildren of the Holocaust survivors suffer from depression and anxiety, and even nightmares. That grandchild knows nothing of the horrors of that time, yet genetically those wounds have been passed down.

Our ancestors have survived severe illnesses (like the Flu Pandemic of 1918), wars, the Great Depression of the 1930s, and the loss of loved ones. I have an uncle who, as an infant, died in 1918 with the flu. Many family members fought in various wars for our country. One uncle was killed in action (though he died back home in the States from wounds). My great-grandfather's brother fought in the US Civil War, was captured, and later released to live another forty-plus years. My grandparents told me how they lived during the Great Depression and how long it took to feel any relief.

My paternal grandparents got married in 1939. Things were still tight after the Great Depression. Gas was just ten cents a gallon, but that didn't matter since they could not afford a car yet.

Once we recognize these patterns, it's easier to understand our ancestors and make different choices. It's up to us to release old patterns. Let go of that which no longer serves you.

By letting go and releasing old patterns, we make room for better relationships with the living members of our family. We give ourselves permission to be healthy and not hold on to stereotypes or other expected behavior. The ancestors are our allies, our guides, and sometimes our conscience. We can honor our ancestors by fulfilling our life's purpose.

Letting go techniques include journaling, visualization, and meditation. Genealogy can help you find your "Ancestor Zero."

THE TOOL

Genealogy, or tracing your family tree, can help you find and recognize the patterns in your family. A family tree chart can include as little or as much information as you need or want. The first chart I used was from Everton's Genealogical Helper, and I still use a variation of it today. Google "genealogy research forms" to find many free variations. The family record sheet includes room for all the vitals (birth, marriage, death) and space to write some notes. Early on, I began to include the cause of death (COD) and contributing factors.

If you use a program like Family Tree Maker (FTM) or Brother's Keeper, or a service like Ancestry.com, a "family record sheet" will automatically be created, as will an "individual record." Always document your work as you proceed. This will save you time and money in the long run.

Social norms and standards change over time, like my fourth great-grandmother, Margaret, having George out of wedlock. In 1808, that was not an okay thing. Today, no one would think anything of it. A genealogy, be it printed or online, is not the place for dirty laundry. Some stories are not yours to tell. Others may need to be put into historical context.

Let's get started.

Several basic tips are included at Getting Started | Ancestral Passages (https://ancestralpassages.com/getting-started). The more information you can provide, the better footing I have to begin the process if you would like me to trace your family for you.

My two go-to tools are the Individual/Family Group Sheet and a Timeline. If you have a specific ancestor you would like to get to know better, I create a timeline. This timeline will include your ancestor's dated events—born, baptized, graduated, married, etc.—as well as relevant historical events. Relevant historical events could be a war, when an area got electricity, inventions like the telephone or television, and any major event that happened locally.

First, begin with yourself. Now include your parents and their information. Normally men are listed to the left and women to the right. Include the vitals: the birth date, marriage date, death date, if applicable. Be sure to include locations. Now a warning here. Decide on a way of writing dates and information now and then be consistent. For example, I write my dates European style, so St. Patrick's Day this year will be 17 March 2021. For the location, always include the county as well if you know it. For example, I am currently based out of Lancaster, Lancaster County, Pennsylvania. Consistency is a good thing. Also, the majority of genealogists do write out dates in European style.

Many genealogists suggest capitalizing all surnames. I do not do this in software programs, like FTM or Ancestry, but I do in written reports for clients. My story is truly and simply a continuation of my ancestors' stories. Women should be listed by their maiden name. So, while I hyphenate when writing, in my tree, my last name is simply Ruczhak. When a surname is found with various spellings, use the one your ancestor used most regularly, but be sure to include those alternate spellings.

My great grandfather's surname is Hruszczak. I have found four different spellings. One was on a census and the enumerator, I think, tried to spell it phonetically. The other two are how his children spell it. Most spell it Ruczhak (like mine), and one branch flipped the C and the Z.

Continue back on each line with as much as you can fill out yourself. I often keep a notepad next to me to jot down questions or things I need to confirm.

Branches have a way of taking over the tree. I include siblings but then will enter notes on the direct relative. I will research further if someone on that specific line has asked for information or if something catches my attention and my family is not talking at the moment.

When working on your research, be sure to check out local records. Many historical societies offer day passes to visit and use their resources. If you are not local, call ahead, find out what restrictions are enforced. Ask about parking availability and the cost of photocopies. Confirm if electronics, including your cellphone, are allowed if you must bring a notepad and pencil.

Another great resource is old newspapers. Libraries and historical societies often have local papers available. Most are on microfilm. Newspapers.com is another great resource.

Here is one final thought regarding ancestral healing. An ancestor does not necessarily have to be blood. He, or she, could be an adopted parent or a close family friend. Whoever your ancestor is, may his or her memory be eternal.

Jeanne Ruczhak-Eckman is a Seeker of Ancestors, yours and hers. She has been walking this life's passage alongside her ancestors since she can remember. As Resource Goddess, she can help you connect to your ancestors and guide you as you walk your Ancestral Passage.

Her genealogy website is https://ancestralpassages.com. The site offers resources for those who wish to trace their family on their own. Jeanne also offers this service, as well as other research projects focusing on a specific time or place your ancestor may have encountered.

Jeanne belongs to the National Genealogical Society and the Deyo Family Association of the Huguenot Historical Society. She has been a member of the Chester County Historical Society, the Lancaster County Historical Society, the Lancaster Mennonite Historical Society, and the Schuylkill County Historical Society over the years, depending on where her research takes her.

She is also currently the heart, soul, and Publishing Editor of Therapeutic Thymes Magazine. The magazine is dedicated to promoting a more natural, therapeutic, and sustainable way of life. Through Therapeutic Thymes, she has joined and supports the Herb Society of America (HAS), the Holistic Chamber of Commerce (HCC), and United Plant Savers (UpS). The magazine website is https://www.therapeuticthymes.com.

Chapter 21

TURNING CURSES INTO BLESSINGS

Discovering and Embracing the Gems Our Ancestors Are Giving Us

RIKA RIVKA MARKEL

MY STORY

I am not crazy.

I am not like my mother.

I can't believe my husband brought everybody together in my living room and sat me on a chair to interrogate me about my mental state.

Who does that? I am an adult, married with two children, not a five-year-old.

I was defending myself. Words were coming out of my mouth, but I was not in touch with what I was saying. At a certain point, I disconnected, I saw myself sitting there, crying, in desperation, saying over and over again:

"I am not my mother! I am not crazy! Why are you doing this to me?"

Later that day, when everyone was gone, questions went through my head: *Why did my father allow this to happen? He let them torture me. He just watched and didn't say anything. He knows I'm not like my mother. I am not crazy. Why didn't he speak up?*

That day, I decided I would never allow anyone to tell me that I am my mother. Just because she gave birth to me doesn't mean we have anything in common. I would prove to the world that whoever she is, or isn't, did not influence me. I am who I am because of MY choices, MY decisions, MY education, period.

That day, it became clear to me that men were not to be trusted. My father just proved that to me, and as much as I hated to admit it, my mother told me this over and over again: "Never trust a man, no matter what happens, the day that he betrays you will come."

From that day, I was on my own. It was me against the world. I took my life into my own hands. I was not a victim, and my past was not going to determine my life. My biological family was my biological family, and unfortunately for me, I did not win the lottery here. I was determined to raise my kids differently; genes would not interfere with that.

Events like this color one's life. They really leave a mark, and being only 26 at the time, I had no idea that this traumatic event and the meaning I gave it would influence my future for almost 30 years.

Just recently, I caught myself dancing to radio tunes while cleaning my kitchen. I saw my reflection in the window, and for a second, I thought I saw my mother. I made exactly the same moves as her, and it cracked me up. I started laughing out loud. Wow, I really DO look and act like her. Amazing.

To make this story even more interesting, that same day, I saw my 24-year-old, Michelle, number four of five, doing the same; dancing in the kitchen while preparing lunch.

Me: "Michelle, I was doing exactly the same an hour ago, dancing to the music in the kitchen. Can you believe that?"

Michelle: "Yes, Mom, I can. Now that you point it out, I am doing this, exactly like you."

Me: "Isn't that interesting? And I'll tell you more because my mother, your grandmother, did the same."

Michelle: "Really? Not sure I like that. I don't mind being like you, but Grandma? Not sure about that."

There it was.

Grandma never did anything to her. I felt guilty immediately. It had to be me. I put this idea in her head. I made her not want to be like my mom.

As insignificant as this 'dancing in the kitchen' incident appeared to be, I knew in my gut that I just received answers for a lot of my suffering over the last decades of my life.

One of the biggest mistakes I made is thinking that genes and DNA are only a physical thing. It's easy to make that mistake because, in school, we're taught how DNA works, how we get the dominant eye color, how we end up with similar birthmarks, and how some illnesses are bound to be transferred from one generation to another.

What I never thought about is that our mental body, emotional body, and energetic body is created with this same energy. The egg and sperm that created us became not only a physical entity, it also has a mind, a soul, and an energetic field.

On top of that, we're conditioned by the same people we got the DNA from, especially in the first five years of our lives. So, we end up with not only our parent's and grandparents' eyes, body shape, and medical issues, we also end up with the same beliefs, conscious and unconscious.

It is fascinating that we all use phrases like: "You have your grandfather's nose." Or, "You sound just like your mother."

We see all the resemblances, but do we also understand the depth of our words?

As always, knowledge and understanding are power. If I paid more attention to all the statements about me that people around me made regarding my family, that would have saved me a lot of trouble.

We are spiritual beings, having a human experience. The reason for us coming back to this realm, lifetime after lifetime, is to learn lessons that we're not able to learn when our soul is not incarnated.

Before entering a new lifetime on earth, a tribunal of masters, guides, and angels come together to help us pick out the circumstances that will serve us best to make the corrections we have to make.

For example, if we are to learn to have more patience, chances are we will end up in a family where everyone is slow. Or when we have to overcome anger, we're sent into a situation that will trigger our anger.

Up until now, I thought I did really well. I see the world through that lens, and I always ask myself: "What do I have to learn here?"

I understand now that I wasn't consistent. The situations I thought were not really relevant, like the story I told in the beginning: *I am not my mother*, I just buried it. It is true, I AM not my mother, but she IS my mother. I chose her. She is exactly what I need to help me correct whatever it is that I have to correct. I cannot ignore this. If I do, the same pattern will repeat itself, with a different color, a different taste, a different smell, but with the same goal and purpose, allowing me to learn what I need to learn, the good and the bad.

What I'm trying to say here is, if we're smart, and if we understand the laws of the universe, then we'll understand that there is a well of wisdom in all the conditions we believe regarding our ancestors, in this lifetime, and many lifetimes before.

Our parents and grandparents, particularly their strengths and weaknesses that trigger us, are precious gems.

In our society, we're not taught to connect with anything we cannot grasp with our five senses. If we cannot see, feel, hear, smell, or touch it, it does not exist.

I remember having conversations with my friends as a teenager. Talking about how there's so much more out there than meets the eye. They had no interest in my stories about the moon's influences on the water and the earth. I was amazed how people who live in a place where they witness the tides, sometimes miles out in the sea, under the moon's influence, didn't believe that this also affects us human beings. It was mind-boggling to me. I was convinced I knew that the laws of the universe were way beyond our scope of what we discovered so far.

It cannot be that farfetched to consider the following: what if every person in your life has a task to fulfill, something you agreed on before incarnating in this body? And what if the people pushing your buttons the most are the ones closest to you on a soul level? In other words, souls that love you the most.

This would absolutely explain why you sometimes feel drawn to what turns out to be the "wrong" partner, "wrong" friend, or for that matter, the "wrong" mother and father. Other examples would be the girlfriend in high school that runs off with that one boy you have a crush on, and she knows it. Even the prince on the white horse, where everything whispers inside of you, *he is the one*, and he turns out to have not only your mother's bad traits but also your father's, as well as all the other people on the planet that trigger you. Or children that remind you of your mother-in-law.

I can go on and on here; you get my point.

Another law in the universe states that you cannot see in someone else what you don't see in you, meaning whatever is pushing your buttons is subject to inner work.

Running away is not smart; I can testify to that.

The sooner you understand that principle and take it seriously, the sooner you will get to a fulfilled and abundant life on all levels.

There is another big benefit to taking care of the things that bother you in other people, and that is, doing the inner work. Once you conquer whatever it is that they trigger in you, they are liberated too. Then there is no reason for them anymore to be the way they are, at least not in your presence. If they still have other things to deal with, they will move on. If the only reason for their "bad" behavior was for you to change, they are free now to let go too. Isn't that amazing?

I don't think that I'm capable of being mindful of this all the time, but I do try, and I believe this is one hundred percent true. I have proof. I saw this unfold in front of my eyes on many occasions.

Wouldn't it be amazing if we learned this law when we're children? It would save so much suffering and pain. I tried to teach my children this way of thinking, and I know they understand it. It's hard to get this through to the society that we live in, where most people just point the finger at everything outside of them. As long as you give others the power to influence your happiness, victim consciousness is winning.

Since our environment is judgmental, it takes courage to be on this spiritual path, knowing the whole world is just mirroring exactly what is going on inside of you. The opposite is difficult too. When people around you ask you when you get upset with someone, "What does this say about you?" Even though they are trying to help you, you just get further and further into a spiral of guilt and shame. This is what happens in a lot of religious environments.

In this time and age, we do have a choice, and we do have free will. We can do ourselves a favor. Our parents, caretakers, or grandparents are the first people we are exposed to. They are our first opportunity to learn about who we are.

Instead of dismissing their threats, we can use them to get over our first set of lessons to learn in this lifetime.

The sooner we get this out of the way, the sooner we can start living the life we're meant to live, bringing the gifts to the world that only we can bring. As much as we have a correction to make in this lifetime, we are also on a mission. We bring something to the world that no one else can bring; it is our unique contribution to humanity and the universe.

I know everything is perfect the way it is, but I wish I got with the program sooner. By understanding my limitations and limiting unconscious beliefs and conditionings, and getting them out of the way, I don't have to waste more time and energy on my correction in my current lifetime.

At this point, I hope you only have some questions in mind: How do I figure out the gems that my ancestors left for me? How do I get that info as soon as possible? I am ready to move beyond this and live my life of purpose all the time!

THE TOOL

This exercise will help you find the unconscious conditionings from your ancestors holding you back from living a life of purpose.

You will need a pen, paper, and a quiet place to sit.

Write down three things you like about one of your ancestors (mother, father, grandmother, etc.).

Example: My mother is an amazing cook.

Then write three things that you dislike about this person.

Example: My mother is inconsistent.

Try to really connect with the traits that you admire and then the traits that you dislike. Give it serious thought.

When you are sure what these six things are, then exchange "My mother" with "I am" in every sentence.

Example: I am an amazing cook

Example: I am inconsistent

Now, without judgment, look at these traits and look inside yourself. Does it resonate?

Accepting this is true is the first step, the good and the bad.

The next step is to use this knowledge to change and allow yourself to grow while ending the lineage for different burdens passed on for generations.

You can find detailed guidance for this exercise with integrating and transformational guided meditations at www.ancestrygems.com

Rika Rivka Markel is a women's empowerment coach and Clearing Facilitator who will help you detach from your past and thrive. With 30 years of expertise in holistic tools, strategies, and mindset hacks, she'll help you take responsibility for your life and release the circle of blame and shame.

She started her spiritual journey more than 40 years ago while trying to figure out her place in this universe. She feels fortunate that at a very young age, she already understood that there was more to life than what meets the eye. Rika is fascinated with both the seen and the unseen world.

She believes that everything is possible, that whatever you see around you is a reflection of what is inside of you, and she recently discovered the value of the gifts of our ancestors.

Rika was born and raised in Belgium but moved to NY about ten years ago, where she lives with her two youngest daughters. She has five children and five grandchildren on both sides of the Atlantic.

She loves traveling, cooking and started painting soul paintings during the pandemic.

Rika is a nutritionist, and inspired by her children, became a vegan enthusiast.

You can find what she is up to on her website www.rivkamarkel.com

Chapter 22

CLEARING ANCESTRAL TRAUMA

Letting go of the Cycle of Pain and Suffering

JAMES KEALIIPIILANI KAWAINUI, NATIVE HAWAIIAN
HEALER, SPIRITUAL COUNSELOR, KAHU

MY STORY

My life was coming apart at the seams. I was 2,637 miles from home, in a city where I knew all of six people (seven if you counted the girlfriend who was about to dump me). I was depressed, alone, and unsure of my direction. I still had my return ticket to New Zealand. I could go back there. I had friends, family, and a life waiting for me. But that's not where my Kūpuna (my ancestors) wanted me to be. "You need to move to the Mainland because people there need you and are looking for you." *Was I out of my MIND?*

So when I heard, "You need to do a ceremony!" I knew I had to listen. I knew this was important.

It wasn't often that I got messages like this. I realized years ago when I walked away from my "other" life that my Kūpuna had been trying (and waiting) to talk to me. As I began to listen, my life started to shift in radical ways. With their guidance and direction, my life took a turn I could never have imagined. It was the reason I left New Zealand, went back home to Hawaii, and was now in Portland, Oregon.

I asked when and where the ceremony was to take place. "It needs to be by the ocean." Along with my answer was a clear vision of the stones, crystals, and ingredients I would need for the ceremony. *Got it.*

Early on a foggy October morning, I woke up and realized that this was the day. My Saturday had mysteriously cleared. All of my appointments either canceled or rescheduled. My thought was to get to the beach around sunrise. I could barely see beyond the headlights, the road eerily devoid of other vehicles. The fog opened up begrudgingly in front of me, only to close again behind me as I drove. I had a general direction in my head but didn't quite know where I was going.

Every time I questioned myself or worried I was lost, my Aumakua, in the form of a hawk or an owl, appeared out of the darkness, perched on a power line or tree branch just at the edges of my headlights. Our Aumakua, to a Hawaiian, is akin to a person's spirit animal. *Just keep driving!*

Miracles of miracles, I got to the beach as the sun was coming up. I was in Seaside, a popular destination for Portlanders. The morning was clear and bright. I got out of the car and walked up to the sand dunes. *Is it here?* "NO! Keep driving!" Knowing it was useless to argue or question, I got back in the car and drove. *Cannon Beach?* "No!" *Rockaway?* "Nope!" *Lincoln City?* "Not even close." I kept driving southwards, stopping every few miles, and slowly made my way down the coast. Each stop being met with, "Not here. Keep going!" I had lost track of time. Seriously hungry, I stopped for lunch in Newport (having driven over 250 miles at this point). I got back in the car and kept going.

By now, it was late afternoon and raining like nobody's business. I had no idea where I was and about to give up when I caught a tiny hand-painted sign out of the corner of my eye. If I hadn't been paying attention, I would have missed it. *To Makai.* Makai in Hawaiian means "to the ocean." *What are the odds?*

Immediately past the sign was a state park. No cars in the parking lot. "This is the place. Stop now!" *Really? Here? In the rain?* I'm not thrilled, but I know it is useless to grumble. I park, get out of the car, put on my raincoat, and walk out to the beach.

I find a place to sit on the sand and gather myself. I pull out the offerings I was instructed to bring and place them in front of me. As I do, I say a prayer of gratitude and thanks and call out to my Kūpuna to ask for their guidance as I journey to seek answers. I dig a hole and bury everything. I turn on my iPod to a track with Native American drums that I use when I journey and go within.

Spirit journeys have been performed by indigenous cultures all over the world since time untold. They are done for many reasons, one of which is to help one understand the path that one must take on their journey of life, to receive answers to questions and guidance on things that may be happening in our lives. A spirit journey is a route that is taken to the spirit world. This could be in the form of an entry into a cave or through unfamiliar terrain as you move away from the earthly realm and into the world of Spirit. The spirit journey is often accompanied by the pulsating, irregular, and highly monotonous beating of drums or rattles, which help to create an altered state of consciousness. The darkness of the spirit tunnel leads to the entrance to the "other world," where the spirit seeker emerges.

I arrive at the entrance of a small, darkened cave. There is a reddish glowing light against the far wall. Twenty or so people are in the cave standing in shadowy silhouettes, their faces hidden. I realize the soft murmuring I'm hearing is the sound of their voices, although, in this moment, I cannot understand what they're saying. I feel no fear. I stand in silence and still myself, becoming as fully present as possible to what's in front of me.

The silhouettes part suddenly, and there in the center of the cave is a little boy of about five or six years old. He stands out in stark relief to everyone around him. There is a realization that the little boy is me. The voices are now recognizable. There is an instantaneous knowing that I am standing before generations of my Kūpuna. "We always wanted you to have our knowledge. We share that freely with you always. It is here for you whenever you need it. It is a part of you. Know that as Truth."

"What we don't want is for you to carry our pain and suffering. It does not belong to you. It never did. Whatever happened in our lifetimes was never your responsibility. We apologize for the pain it has caused you in your life. What happened to us in our lives is our burden to bear, not yours. We ask that you let all of it go and give it back to us."

"Know that we love you and are here to support you. We see the work you are doing. You are never alone, and we are always with you. All you need to do is to reach out and ask for guidance and feel our connection. Our knowledge is yours to access and share, but our pain is our own. Honor us by releasing it."

A wave of energy washes through me, like a breeze blowing gently across my body. There is a different awareness inside of me, and I'm not entirely sure in that moment what it means. The child, along with my Kūpuna, begin to dissolve, the cave slowly flickering out of my vision. I feel myself slowly returning. The drums have stopped beating in my headphones. I realize my butt is wet from sitting on the sand, and I'm cold. It's still raining. I am back in this world, again. I stand up slowly and walk back to my car on shaky legs, not totally in my body yet. The message, so powerful, still resonating through me as gradually I begin to grasp what my Kūpuna were saying to me. Their presence feels different now, stronger than it was before.

This was over ten years ago. Every day I pray in gratitude for the connection and relationship with my Kūpuna.

What I learned from this experience is that **we all have the ability to let go of the pain and embrace the amazing gifts that are waiting for us to tap into. Whatever happened to our ancestors, the pain they went through, passed down to us from generation to generation, is not ours to carry.**

Traumatic events affect us so deeply that they can literally change the vibration and frequency of our cellular structure, down to the atomic level and the DNA. We not only inherit our physical appearance and our body's cellular structure, we can also inherit the behavioral traits, ways of being, and conditioned mindsets of our ancestors. We have family patterns that we consciously or unconsciously replay repeatedly, never realizing that they may not be ours.

Have you ever caught yourself mimicking or replaying events in your life and then have an insight or sudden awareness that you've watched or seen someone else in your family act or behave in the very same way? You may be replaying family patterns, consciously or unconsciously, that go back multiple generations without even being aware of them.

I worked with a woman a few years ago who came to me because of a recurring knee issue. Having been to numerous doctors and specialists and not being able to find answers or get relief, she felt she was out of options and was considering surgery. During our session, as we looked into the "pain" to see what was happening. She shared with me that not only did *she* have problems with her knee, her mom, sister, daughter, and grandmother also *suffered from the same issue!* It turned out that just about every female member of her family she knew of struggled with pain in the same knee at some point in their life.

As we went deeper, we discovered through the memory held in her body that a grandmother four generations earlier was injured in an accident, and her leg had been amputated at the knee. She did survive but was in pain for the remainder of her life.

Once my client's awareness of the accident came into focus, *she realized that the pain was not hers.* In that moment, her body let go of her ancestral grandmother's trauma, and the pain literally vanished.

There is a way of recognizing and releasing the behaviors and actions of our ancestors so they no longer affect our quality and way of life, while continuing to honor the people who have come before us. I want to share one such way that I was shown by my Kūpuna that has helped many people that I have worked with over the years. There is a caveat, though. It requires a willingness to look deep inside of yourself and be brutally honest about how you've been living your life.

I promise there is hope and a way past the pain you've been carrying. It is time to look at it so you can give yourself permission to let it go. The transformation may shock and surprise you, but if you're ready, let's take that next step.

THE TOOL

LETTING GO OF THE CYCLE OF PAIN AND SUFFERING

For a link to the process and a copy of the meditation click here: www.jameskawainui.com/givingbackceremony

Most of us carry trauma and memories in our bodies passed on to us by our ancestors. There may come a time in your life when you become aware of negative repetitive patterns and behaviors in your life, and you choose to examine them at a deeper level. With reflection, it's important to note that there is a level of personal responsibility for everything that is happening and has happened to us in our lives. This can often be a very bitter pill to swallow for those who have suffered intense suffering and trauma.

I believe the Soul chooses the physical body it comes into as well as the people it will be in relationship with, such as parents, family members, or even partners. This is done as part of its process of growth and expansion.

Before we can look at what we may have inherited from our ancestors, we must first acknowledge that we came into embodiment for the lessons and understanding that allow us to grow as we travel the road towards increased self-awareness and enlightenment. With this understanding, we can then take the next step and choose how we want to live our life, independent of the old patterns and conditioning.

Have you ever watched your parents, grandparents, or other members of your family replay a particular pattern or behavior throughout their lives? You may have even heard stories about aunts, uncles, or great relations, some of them two or more generations back, who have been plagued by the same challenges. Alcoholism is a good example of this.

You may even be watching your children begin to go through the same challenges.

You know you are finally ready to take a hard look at whatever that is so you can make a conscious choice to stop living that pattern.

If this is you, then let's begin.

Find a quiet space or a place that you feel will support you as you go through this process. It could be in your meditation room or in front of your Puja (personal altar). It may be somewhere out in nature. The choice is entirely up to you. You can also light a candle as a way to help create sacred space.

Gently close your eyes and take a deep cleansing breath. Find a rhythm and pace that feels good as you consciously breathe in and out. As you do, bring your awareness into your body and feel your breath as a conscious physical act. This will help to center and ground your energy. Give yourself permission to go deeper as you feel your body begin to relax. When thoughts come into your mind, gently let them go. Give yourself time here to settle before you go on.

Invoke your ancestors through prayer and call them into a circle of light.

Here is a suggested prayer you can use (or you can create one yourself):

"I call out to Sky Father and Earth Mother and to the ancestors of the land. I ask for your help and support as I open this Sacred Circle. I call out to the four directions to help anchor this space. With gratitude and love, I invite my ancestors. Beloved family, thank you for being a part of my life. Thank you for the wisdom, the gifts, and the challenges that you freely share with me. I also give thanks and call to my guides, guardians, and angels to be present as we go through this honoring and this ceremony."

Feel the energy as it anchors around you and the presence of all who are in attendance.

In your mind's eye, see yourself in a circular room with dark paneled walls lit by candles in sconces on the wall around you. To your right is a small table, also circular, about waist high. There is a candle on the table, as well as four bundles about the size of small grapefruits, wrapped in plain, muslin cloth. You feel rather than see the presence of your ancestors in the room circled around you.

Four of your ancestors step forward to stand in front of you. They are nondescript, each wearing a plain cloak with the hood pulled over their head. Their faces are hidden from view. Who they are and how they look is not important. They stand as representatives of the generations that have come before you.

Silently, the first figure to your right steps forward, arms outstretched, head bowed. You reach for one of the bundles on the table and hand it to them. "I release the thought that I am not worthy back to you." They accept the bundle, touching it reverently to their forehead, and slowly step back, disappearing from view.

As they do so, the next figure steps forward. You reach for the next bundle on the table. "I release the pain I've carried for you." The second figure holds the bundle in front of them in silent prayer and acknowledgment and slowly steps back, fading out of sight.

The third figure steps forward. You reach again for a bundle on the table and, with gratitude and thanks, hand it to them. "I release back to you all the suffering and injustices." They bow before you, bundle held high in front of them as they slowly step back, turn around, and walk away.

The last figure steps forward. There is a hesitancy. It too reaches out as you hand the last bundle to them. "I release the feeling and thinking that I am not loved." It slowly and gently brings the bundle to the center of their chest, as if cradling a baby. You feel the deep love and connection as they begin to glow brightly, filling yourself and the room with the energy of Unconditional Love.

Become aware of the change going through your body both physically and energetically. There is a new sense of the presence of your ancestors around you. The darkened room is now full of light. There is a deep sense of connection and support. There is a knowing that your ancestors are there, as they have always been, to guide and support you. All you need to do is reach out and ask for their help. Their energy merges into you. You become One.

James Kawainui is a Native Hawaiian Healer and an expert in chronic pain, trauma release, and clearing of cellular memory on the physical, emotional, and spiritual levels. James works with people all over the world, who often come to him after having tried everything to overcome their pain. Through his connection with his Hawaiian ancestors (Kūpuna), James is able to read a person's energy flow and clear blockages from trauma, some of which have been passed down through generations. James's clients experience freedom, renewed hope, and a deeper connection with their body and soul on levels beyond what they imagined possible. James is also a trusted guide and mentor for his students, many of whom are corporate professionals and medical practitioners.

James contracted a rare and life-threatening form of polio at eight months of age, which he overcame through the love and healing touch of his grandmother. With his compassion and an understanding of pain at a deeply personal level, James has devoted his life to helping people live positive, productive, and pain-free lives.

Schedule your free 30-minute Healing session and consultation at https://jameskawainui.com/get-back-on-track/

You can find James at https://jameskawainui.com/

CHAPTER 23

ANCESTRAL POWER:

Claim Your Sacred Wisdom and Magic

JEN PICENO, SHAMANIC PRIESTESS, ENERGY MEDICINE PRACTITIONER, ORDM, RMT, LMT, THP

MY STORY

Imagine you're with me at my medicine wheel. The fire crackles and pops while swirls of smoke rise to our ancestors under the starlit sky. They let their presence be known with a gentle breeze that lightly caresses our skin. The cozy fire warms us from the inside out. The heartbeat of the drum draws you inward as my voice activates the elements within you. "To the spirit of earth: ground, nurture, and connect us to the strength of our ancestors. To the spirit of water: wash away the past and purify our true calling with clarity. To the spirit of air: blow in the winds of wisdom from our elders and guides. To the spirit of fire: burn away our fears and ignite our hearts with passion and purpose as we shed the past."

Swaying back and forth, you merge with the surface beneath you as Mama Earth kisses the chakras on the soles of your feet. She's reminding you that you are safe, loved, and protected. Beautiful remembrances begin to dance and awaken with joy.

Breathe deeply and receive the sacred scent of sage and sweetgrass as they're gifted to the flames as an offering to our ancestors. Reach your right hand out to take my hand and know that I will walk with you through whatever you are going through as you awaken the spiritual warrior within. You're called to this sacred path of inner wisdom to reclaim ancestral power, magic, and limitless possibilities.

The words within this chapter are blessed for your highest potential. Take this small but powerful wisdom with you into your heart—we're all connected. Go ahead, claim that knowledge now. Place your hands upon your chest and feel into it with your big, beautiful heart. You're my sisters and brothers. This sacred story is intended to guide you back home to yourself and your tribe.

I've studied tons of traditions and gobbled up delicious wisdom. Ancestors and guides are with us everywhere. Everything and everyone is connected: from the smallest grain of sand to the largest planet in our solar system. We're teaching each other even in moments of stubbornness, fear, anger, and grief. We're students of life on a journey back to our divine calling.

I solve problems, heal, and guide those seeking answers by traveling the three planes of consciousness: the upper, middle, and lower worlds. Yep! I'm a professional traveler flying between time and space on a shamanic adventure. I channel the divine and have been shape-shifting for over thirty years with spirit animals at my side. Archetypal worlds are the collective unconscious. Everything is connected, remember?

I'm fully plugged into the spirit world while embodied in each experience. I dance in tribal ceremonies, perform rituals, guard sacred sites, heal the land, fly with archangels, run, swim, and fly with spirit animals, and receive wisdom from our elders. Cool right? Without hesitation, I discover the sacredness in everything, expanding and enhancing psychic abilities and trusting divine clues along the way.

I've rooted myself in ancestral work and the mystery of it all. I love it! Everything is intertwined with eclectic, worldly wisdom and delivered with purpose-driven intention. I embrace the world through its traditions, spiritual practices, food, and dance. We're born with ancestral wisdom and lifetimes of experiences in our blood and bones. Eventually, it calls us home.

My connection with the ancestors is potent medicine that heals in ways too powerful for words to express. I've swallowed big doses to heal myself and witnessed lost, damaged, hopeless, stuck, and confused people align with crystal clear answers as they journey within.

Unfortunately, most focus on their pain, and it becomes a barrier that often feels too heavy to bear. So, they quit moving forward and stay stuck in their tiny box of confinement. I've been stuck before too. All of us on the healer's journey have been there wallowing in the emotional mess at one time or another.

In any good story, there are trials and tribulations before the brave one steps into their authentic self as the hero or heroine. To walk fiercely in sacred purpose, ya gotta keep movin.'

March forward, and you'll discover fascinating secrets through whispers our ancestors share. This wisdom heals broken hearts, repairs damage from long ago, and cleans up lineage in all directions. I do this work for myself, clients, my son, unborn grandchildren, and their children's children. Break the cycle; heal your lineage. If you are reading this book, you've been called to action. You're ready!

Cycles and patterns poisoned my spirit from carrying the baggage of my ancestor's fears, oppression, and shame. Then, I dropped the bags. I blended everything into a soul-expanding remedy, slurped down big gulps of handcrafted medicine, and poof! I felt their wisdom and strength come with a loving shove into sacred purpose. I felt lighter as their pain dissolved from my body and a deep knowing filled my heart.

This mystical path is filled with divine clues. Step into the field of interconnectedness with me, and you will soon realize we are here to experience life together. No one has to go at it alone. I've been at this for decades, and being the stubborn gal that I am, I mostly went at it alone. It's a longer, harder process filled with lots of detours. I don't suggest it, but I'm not complaining either. I had to experience things that way to cultivate practices that simplify this work for truth seekers craving more in life. Aligning people with their divine purpose and ancestral magic is a huge part of my mission here, and the hard way was my most valuable education.

Ancestral work is one of the best keys I've found in healing myself and others. We collect, hold, and carry a lot of shit from our family and even more wounds from multiple lifetimes. But that's not all. There's a magnificent flow of wisdom, peace, and power that's available to us. It's the most magical part.

Ancestral magic supports our psychic abilities simultaneously as we break patterns. It gives us the strength to release outdated agreements with courage, ease, and grace.

On the magical quest to self-mastery, we travel with heart-opening intentions that propel us forward with great purpose. This is the delicious feel-good medicine of the heart which also comes from our ancestors and lifetimes of experiences. Finding that medicine is certainly something to celebrate. And we do.

Show love and gratitude to them. Yes, even for stuff you want to get rid of. As we release traumatic bits and pieces through our lineage, we can say, "bon voyage" to the unhealthy parts with a wink and a smile. Hardships and challenges of the past transform into miraculous power for the greater good. As you heal your lineage, you'll receive ancient wisdom. Listen carefully and honor it all. Every salty tear you've cried matters. It's sacred water to anoint your healing process and remind you of who you are. You're a magnificent masterpiece, a work in process. You need each experience of all lifetimes throughout your lineage to ignite ancestral magic and power within you as you create the extraordinary life waiting for you.

Everything has a purpose which is sometimes hard to accept, I know. This concept is simple yet complex. It's helped me craft ancestral magic and wisdom into powerful practices and healing tools with countless generations of ancestor's love, wisdom, magic, and healing remedies. It's guided me to grow into the woman I am, knowing there's no such thing as mistakes when we're wise enough to learn from them.

By diving into sacredness with a leap of faith, my guides have led me back to foundational practices time and time again before expanding me into who I'm becoming. Those who have walked before us are great teachers. They remind us that we're connected to everything and that everything has an energetic imprint upon us—how we show up in the natural world matters.

With childlike eyes, I tune into the miraculous beauty and wonder of the natural world. I connect, listen, feel, and know, as my ancestors and spirit helpers lead me into a journey of enchantment. I receive the energy and send gratitude back out into the universe. It's a beautiful exchange between the worlds.

Most people lost this ability somewhere along the way. No worries, it's not hard to get back. I teach how to reconnect to the elements: earth, water, air, fire. Once reactivated, intuition grows stronger and we are more intune with everything. The elements are what we are made of; they open channels of communication and invite us to thrive. These initiations are powerful, and people's lives transform with passionate purpose.

The cycle of life is ever-expansive. Things I have taught for decades continue to take me deeper into the mysteries to claim ancient wisdom. Moving through life consciously in sacredness takes me further into higher states of divine purpose.

Recently I reactivated sacred rites from the Andean tradition. What a wild ride that was! I was wide awake for over a week buzzing with a power surge of energy from the lineage of the Munay-ki. "Munay" in Quechua means "love and will," "ki" is energy. An abundance of energy and love flooded my heart and into the essence of my divine self. Yep, it was amazing!

I live life in everyday ceremony, but this blew me wide open. The luminous energy was intense. Everything reactivated. I felt super-powered, like I had never experienced before. It was an explosion of high-vibrational sensations.

I was on the mountain tops of Peru. Zap! Flashes of ancient memories shot through me one after another. I was reunited with tribes, elders, and wisdom from multiple lifetimes. Downloads of divine wisdom, teachings, ceremonies, and pure sacredness were flowing abundantly through me with immaculate purpose. I saw this lifetime's divine blueprint. It was spiritually charged with mystical perfection.

Gatekeepers brought everything into perfect vision. Then, wisdom keepers said, *"You're being called into mystical action."* Oh shit! My responsibility as Priestess just got bigger. These were the ancient ones, my spirit guides. They were very specific about protecting the teachings I hold as they reactivated everything within my consciousness.

At first, I shared the excitement with a spiritual sister; I told her about the messages coming through. I even took her through the sacred rites step by step and shared what I typed up for the spiritual experience we were facilitating together.

Boom: my ancestors put an immediate stop to that. I saw the Peruvian mountain top grow taller and wider, then the elder's face appeared within the mountain; he *was* the mountain. A deep, strong voice vibrated throughout my physical body, *Protect the teachings.* My heart tightened, and my body became uncomfortable. Suddenly, a fierce, protective nature activated within me as bright flashes of white lighting anchored into my physical body and sent me to all the sacred sites around the world. *You've been here since the beginning of time.* I was shown each site and reminded of what I carry within my divine essence.

The sensations were off the charts. I vowed nothing would be released to anyone without divine counsel. Incredible power flooded through my veins. My senses were heightened, and I felt light as a feather.

Jaguar, my spirit animal, arrived, also the size of the mountain. Jaguar has always come to me as his normal big cat size, but this time he was as big as the mountain was wide. *Your teachings cannot be shared with anyone. Protect all teachings. Guard what you carry with great honor. Fear not, I'm guarding you.*

The gatekeeper said, *You are now protected under divine law.* Divine law? This was new. It shook me from the inside out. I was instructed to remove everything from a shared file, enough to fill an enormous binder full of my channeled messages. I was sleep-deprived, yet working like espresso was pumping through my veins. Everything happened at warp speed.

Jaguar was now staring at me face-to-face as I gazed into his gorgeous green eyes. He said, *Hold everything until instructed. You must protect the rites and the sacred collection of all teachings ever received. All that you carry must be protected. The ancient ones are sending more sacred wisdom to you now. You must be prepared. You must stand strong to hold such power. Trust no one until further instructed; more shall be revealed soon.*

Diligently, I removed the final pages of my work from the computer. As I came to completion, Jaguar instructed me with fierceness in his eyes, *Eat two heads of garlic to protect and purify the sacred knowledge planted within you.* I marched myself into the kitchen and devoured two full heads of roasted garlic like a starving wild animal. Weird, I know. It was delicious, but I smelled like a girl trying to ward off vampires for days.

That night while lying in bed with a big cup of lavender tea, my heartbeat grew stronger. Pachamama's heartbeat synced to my own. I could feel her within my chest. I knew exactly why I carry so many different lineages and traditions from around the globe.

Mary Magdalene came to me long before I emerged as Priestess and showed me visions of igniting sacred purpose into the masses of conscious-minded people ready to answer the call for a higher purpose. The vision has always been big and bold. I wept as the vision returned in perfect clarity.

Initiations and healing rites for spiritual warriors are designed to activate sacred purpose within the lives of many. Those who trust the process step into happiness, love, pleasure, playfulness, abundance, sacred wisdom, magic, and power so they can walk their path with confidence as change-makers here on Earth.

Are you ready?

THE TOOL

ANCESTRAL WISDOM & MAGIC RITUAL

Complimentary video of this ritual available at:
www.JenPiceno.com/resources

We're putting pure intentions into an object to support your ancestral healing journey.

For this ritual, you will need a few things within arm's reach: A candle and lighter, journal and pen, a pinch of cinnamon, a cup of tea, or my personal favorite, a mug of ceremonial grade cacao (purchase link and recipe on my resource page).

Take time to yourself when you won't be interrupted. Take a few deep breaths before beginning. Drop down and into your heart. When you are ready, say **"Ancestors, join me in this time and space. Walk with me to heal the past, so I may step into sacred purpose."** Feel their presence and honor them with gratitude.

In this ritual, the candle represents the mind, body, and spirit. The wax or base of the candle represents our physical body. The wick, our mind. The flame, our spirit, and the spirit world.

This candle is a physical object that invites our ancestors to guide us in this sacred process of healing mind, body, spirit. Hold your candle (unlit) between your hands and bring it to your heart. Say **"This candle lights the way back to my ancestral wisdom, magic, and power."** Place the candle in front of you and light the wick. Take your time to connect to the light, your ancestors, and your divine truth. Stay in this moment until ready to move on.

Hold your hands to your heart in prayer position, palm to palm. Activate the chakras in your hands. Allow the power to build between the two. Give your mind permission to drift, drop down into your heart, and tune into its rhythm. Stay here for a moment. Now, place your hands upon your chest, one on top of the other, feeling the warmth of your hands connecting with your divine self.

Love is channeling through you from the highest vibration of light. Feel yourself filling with golden light. Take a moment to sense any areas of heaviness within your physical body. The heaviness is the weight of the past. Scan your body and notice any place of pain, sadness, weakness, discomfort, oppression, scarcity, grief, fear, or anger. Visualize yourself handing it over to the ancestors. It helps to visualize it as a color, shape, or object so you can easily lift it out of your body and give it away. All you have to do is ask them to take it. Take your time. Once an area is clear, ask yourself, "Where can I let go next?" Continue to cleanse and clear your body so that there's room to hold the wisdom waiting for you.

Start writing as fast as you can. This is soul writing, and it's much different than journaling. Don't worry about punctuation or spelling.

Let the words of your divine essence pour onto the page. You may be surprised what comes through.

Now, take a pinch of cinnamon and drop it into the lit candle flame as an offering to the ancestors as you claim ancestral power. Say, **"Ancestors, I am ready to receive my wisdom, power, and magic now."** You may notice the flame spark. It's magical and so are you!

You've been ignited with ancestral power. The seeds have been planted within your heart space. Now, nurture them to grow. Take a sip of your drink. As it passes over your lips, hold the intention that these sacred sips are your healing remedy. You are divinely guided with the love and support of your ancestors. Complete this process by thanking them.

Please share your experience in my community Facebook group MYSTIC CIRCLE; join here. **www.facebook.com/groups/jenpiceno**

Receive meditations and spiritual healing practices here: **www.YouTube.com/JenPiceno**

Jen Piceno, Shamanic Priestess, ORDM, RMT, LMT, THP is an energy medicine practitioner, ordained priestess, and medicine woman with 30+ years of expertise in the healing arts. Through personalized ceremony, ancestral healing, and channeling divine wisdom, she'll help you bust through restrictions to solidify your purpose and begin the transformation you've been craving in any area of your life.

Get ready to align with everything you're meant to be in ways you've never experienced before.

Jen is the CEO of Gypsy Moon Inc. and a lifetime student of spiritual practices attained from cultural wisdom around the world.

She blends eastern and western modalities with light language, shamanic practices, and sacred ceremonies. Her work is infused with practices that activate the senses and alchemize challenges into purpose.

Jen is an Ordained Shamanic Priestess in the lineage of StarrFire OrbWeaver, Anyaa McAndrew, and the creatrix, Nicole Christine. Walking the Priestess path, she celebrates life in everyday ceremony, committed to making a difference.

As a Reiki Master, Jen was attuned in all degrees by Diane Steine, author of *Essential Reiki*, and holds a master's level in Usui Reiki. Jen is cross-trained in eclectic healing modalities and a master of the creative healing arts. Full credentials can be found on her website.

Jen offers shamanic healing, sacred ceremonies, personalized programs, spiritual development, and magical online courses to inspire soul growth.

She is available in person and in her virtual sacred space. Simply schedule a call by visiting: **https://www.JenPiceno.com**

You're invited to explore her free group on Facebook, where she shares Priestess wisdom and sacred sisterhood; check out her cool videos on YouTube; or grab some freebies on her resource page.

Get access to quick links here: **https://linktr.ee/JenPiceno**

Chapter 24

CONNECTING THROUGH HEART

Use Universal Love to Travel Time/Space,
Access Ancestors, and Shift Perspective

JONIANNE JEANNETTE, CMT

MY STORY

Back in 2014, I experienced a troubling attitude. The economic recession started its toll as early as 2006 for my practice paving the way of cumulative effect. My work in massage had become painful, both physically and emotionally. Mentally I was deeply affected; I became extremely disillusioned.

"It's not okay for me to be practicing a healing modality when I feel down like this," I spoke to my husband. "Every client coming across my table is a source of complaints, apathy, and victimization that they want me to make all better in a massage." Witnessing people's pain and suffering kept sparking the same in me. I lost my way. I didn't feel right in supporting people when I felt judgmental. In my head, I criticized their actions.

More importantly, I was devoid of caring whether I could bring comfort to their body, mind, or anything.

The innate observer in me kept me consciously aware that I needed help.

Everything felt like recycling of punishment. I also felt as if I was repeating some invisible pattern.

My dream was to create a public space again with a small shop to carry massage products. I was extremely frustrated that I spent two years in the new office without success. At this time, the economy was not picking up enough speed to invest in products or continued education. I felt discouraged.

How could I consider doing this feeling the way I was feeling? I was completely out of integrity with myself.

Networking nonetheless, I was introduced to a practitioner who taught me the ancient shamanic technique of journeying to your helping spirits. Instantly, I realized I was to pursue this path, not only for my healing but also to develop my practice.

Did you know the journey for self-healing always involves a heart-based question? Mine: I wondered why there were so much pain and suffering and why I was steeped in it. I was hurting. I didn't know how to help myself. What I saw in the world reflected to me things I saw in my own family. I no longer wanted to participate in living like this. Some part of me remembered better.

The practitioner said, "Let's begin the journey to meet with your spirit animal, who will guide you to the upper, middle, or lower world. I will play my drum while you lay back, cover your eyes, tune into your breath, and speak into this recorder everything you experience as you framed the question from your heart."

So, suspending reality and activating an open mind, speaking into the recorder:

"I am moving sideways. The world is tilting. Let me just hang on." It was all I could do to just hold on.

"Feeling the sand send up the heat. My hair's blowing across my face."

"I'm on a beach. Where am I?" I gazed around, seeing the ocean. I saw some trees, jungle-like, around the shore. I saw these huge flashes of light in the sky though there wasn't a cloud in sight. As I continued looking around, I noticed I was wearing old-style combat boots.

"Where am I? When am I? Who am I?"

I spoke out loud to the practitioner. Simultaneously, almost uncovering my eyes, I asked her, "Do you hear that? I'm so confused. I'm on a beach, but I also hear a chair on wheels rolling across a floor, plus there's a filing cabinet opening." I waited, trying to understand what was happening to me. My attention caught again on what I was experiencing.

"I can see a man on the shore has dark skin, short hair, wearing combat-type clothes and boots, gathering up a fishing net."

"He keeps glancing around as if he doesn't want to be seen by anybody."

"I'm looking in his net, expecting fish, but I see different objects." All the objects represented something important to this man.

"As I came closer, he swung the net up into a tree to disguise its location."

"I feel my attention drawn to a plant near the shore. It's spear-like with deep pink colorations on its tips."

Somehow, I knew this plant could alter whatever this man had done with this net. But I didn't yet understand why I was here with this man to answer why my family suffers so much pain and anger.

"He realizes I'm here with him; he is speaking to me."

I recognized him. I saw him around the house when I was two to three years old. He reminded me of my mom. They shared the same skin color, the same expressions.

I realized where I was. I realized when I was. I was on the island of Guam in wartime, and he was my grandpa Jesus.

How can this be? I wasn't born until 1970. My grandfather died in 1958. *Was I seeing his spirit before?* My heart hurt, but I opened it further to find answers. I was so out of love. Who knew it would be my deceased grandfather answering my question?!

"Longing to connect is NOT love. Stop fighting. Open up your heart. Family is connected. It's just how it is. You don't get your needs met there. It's just a way to be born. You make a family."

He continued, "Forgiveness. No expectations. Just be. Love is universal. Love is not individual."

With what I thought to be the last thing he had to say, I could barely hear over my outrage. *Them there's fighting words if I ever heard some. Asshole. I protested. How dare he say these things to me?* I revved. I'm in full fight mode now.

It's so familiar too, this power surge. This is the power of love that I didn't even know what to call at that time. As the interaction with my grandfather receded, I returned to the now with my conviction intact again, accepting his challenge of opening my heart.

I set out to understand how I had closed it. I started to develop an awareness of my giving heart, my capacity to love, and the awareness of my receiving heart.

After six months of journey work, it wasn't always easy to make time and space for the 80-mile round trip to see the shamanic practitioner, so I found ways to help myself. The answers kept coming as I was led into practicing mediumship with a nearby group, where my grandpa showed up every single time. The other mediums always felt the charge of his presence, accepting that while he felt dangerous, each of us would rise above through love to continue to communicate for healing.

As a bodyworker, I recognized my abilities to assist others' journey into their heart with my voice. By keeping my heart open and connected and asking Spirit to provide me the wisdom of what I was doing, I came to understand that by speaking to and thru universal love, I can access the truest power, the energy I call LOVE.

That love washes through us in waves and entrains the heart and the mind into the same wavelength, a consciousness connected to universal light and energy. These waves have names like alpha, beta, high beta, delta, theta, and gamma.

That practitioner used the drum and her heart's opening for me. The mediums used psychic energy and love to connect. I use my voice and my hands and heart, which is said to be my drum, to attune to this healing energy.

My journey with my grandfather wasn't over yet.

His final statement that day didn't bonk me over the head for a few more years.

I also had many conversations with my mom validating what I saw and heard as I spoke and spent time with my grandpa.

He was one of many children in his family. As a young man, he suffered through WWII, with Japan laying landmines all over the island that are still there today.

As a parent, he was a strict disciplinarian and arbitrary controlling authority.

When he wasn't practicing spiritualism, he forced everyone into Catholicism, including daily prayer at 5 a.m.

When my mom was young, he died from throat cancer. Many said he must've made expensive bargains in exchange for personal power.

Mom recalled the noise of the chair I heard that day was the janitor's closet at the hospital. The doctors were concerned he was contagious, so they placed him away from other patients. My mom explained the plant I saw was used to paralyze fish for capturing; it dissolved something in their skin. I was to mash it and dissolve his net to end his spiritual bargain for power.

I pursued my spiritual practice, including his directive to stop fighting and open my heart. For the first time, I made friends who also practiced healing modalities.

In our journeys together, we recognized the power of love through the collection of our spirits, choosing to follow divine guidance to develop this service for anyone. Our criteria for each practitioner included receiving sessions for ourselves.

In one of these sessions, we became aware of the presence of my grandfather, Jesus. While I practiced opening my heart, I spoke aloud that I acknowledged that much of my fighting spirit came in defense for me, my family, and these relationships fraught with problems, miscommunications, and unmet needs over the years.

I erected boundaries in my relationship with my grandpa, telling him what my rules of engagement were, and how he needed to respect that. But it never felt super right to me. I felt cold and like something better could be had.

He reminded me of his final statement. "I never really believed in love."

Oh, shoot, how did I not see that search from the beginning?

The healing team spoke to me, "Jonianne, you know the truest power. Isn't that what your grandpa spent his life seeking?"

With the highest honor, I opened my heart wide, letting the light pour through. I witnessed my grandfather's release and receipt of pure love.

He knew me better than I knew myself. He truly helps me all the time now, just not through poking and prodding but gentler guidance and wisdom.

This is why I created the access tool below for anyone in case they can't always make it to their practitioner or my table!

THE TOOL

Guided Imagery

Heart Light Expansion with Intention to Meet Your Ancestor

AUDIO of AAA GUIDED IMAGERY

https://directory.libsyn.com/shows/view/id/spirit-collective

Before beginning your self-care, gather these things: eye mask, pillows, blanket, headphones, recording app, 20-30 minutes. Try reading every step first before starting.

1: Anchor, Align, and Activate.

Sit comfortably, connect to the material world through your senses one at a time.

Breathe your spirit light in, then down to your tail bone.

Release your breath, reset.

Breathe your spirit light in, then down to your knees.

Release, reset.

Breathe your spirit light in, then down to your toes and soles.

Release, reset.

Breathe your spirit light in, then down to the planet's core of light.

Connect, release, reset.

Breathe planet earth's light in, then, up through your soles to your knees and thighs.

Release, let the light gather in your root chakra: I am one.

Breathe the light up to join your pelvic bowl.

Release, fill it up, let the light gather in your sacral chakra: I flow, I feel, I create.

Breathe the light up through your torso.

Release, fill in with the light in your solar chakra: I am powerful.

Breathe into your upper torso and heart chakra: I am love.

Release, extend the column of light through your heart space, co-mingle.

Breathe to expand the light.

As far as you can sense.

To where the earth meets the sky.

Let the sun, the moon, the stars light up your upper torso.

Breathe Spirit down into your heart.

Throat chakra: truth expresses, I listen.

Breathe in universal light. Enlighten your vision.

Third eye: I sense so I may see.

Breathe Spirit down into your heart.

Crown Chakra: I am All.

Let all co-mingle and expand.

Breathe past the field of your body, past the field of feelings, past the field of thoughts, past the field of your soul, into the field of potential.

Breathe in the field of love.

Breathe in the potential for All.

2: Your breath maintains the expansion.

3: Frequent the Frequency of Heart Space, the Energy called Love.
Uni-Verse: One Song, One Voice, One Love.

4: Seat yourself in Your Heart Chamber. (It may help to lay your hands over your chest.)

5: Express Your Intention to Connect. To family to receive a healing or a gift of knowledge to facilitate healing. To set the question framework, try using the W's: where, when, why, how, what, or who. You know the right question when you start to have feelings or maybe even tears as you express it.

6: Verbally record the entirety of your exchange. No detail is insignificant.

7: Resonate in a state of allowance. Trust in your willingness to receive. Relinquish the need to act, to do, to perform. Don't discount any of your experience and or believe you haven't received it; it doesn't always show up right away or when you expect, so practice frequently. Enjoy Spirit's provision. Give thanks, then return to now.

Jonianne Jeannette, CMT, holds certifications as an advanced apprentice with renowned energy medicine practitioner Cyndi Dale, as a quantum Akashic reader with Melissa Feicks, SEA-Spiritual Expansion Academy, as an *Irigenics*™ Ancestral Eye Reading consultant with Amy Gillespie, and a slew of bodywork training modalities, from clinical for posture and pain management to subtle energy systems.

She avidly pursues holistic healing to the nth degree whether she is collaborating with you or accessing Spirit for personal health and direction for heart-based living.

Jonni brings her love of relating with others and joy of sharing what she discovered about leading from one's heart to every encounter she witnesses. Her favorite engagement with and for others is self-empowerment. When you thrive, she thrives. Every training in her pursuit of healing revolves around the energy of love. She can be relentlessly passionate about it and tenacious about sourcing love in every molecule of your being. While she knows not everyone delivers their power the way she does, she really appreciates however other people shine their gifts and talents out to the world. She seeks to aid you in sensing this about you too.

She has set out to learn what really harmonizes her Spirit and seeks to share a way you can too. She never really knows how Spirit will lead her words or stories, forever remaining surprised and delighted how her experiences, when shared, lead to others making their own heart connections.

When Jonni chooses downtime, you'll find her binge-watching spirit or house shows, doing puzzles or her favorite video game Clockmaker, reading, and drinking sweet, creamy coffee while connecting to her beloved husband Larry, her kids, Jasmine and Lily, and her pet menagerie.

Reach Jonni at:

Jonni@jonnionthespot.com

www.jonnionthespot.com

www.spirit-collective.com

Ig: Spirit_collective_ or FB pages: JotsInc. Or Spirit-Collective

Chapter 25

OUR ANCESTORS THE WAYSHOWERS

Creating Flow by Making Life-Changing Decisions with Ease

Myrna Y. Triano, LMT, CST,
Integrated Energy Therapy® Master/Teacher

MY STORY

My story came from humble beginnings. My parents were born in Aibonito, Puerto Rico, surrounded by the Cayey Mountain Range. My dad, Felipe Rivera, was raised as a farmhand growing tobacco and cane sugar, along with raising chickens, cows, and pigs on his father's large farm. He worked alongside his twenty-one brothers and sisters.

My mother, Maria Luisa Cruz Lopez, was raised differently from that of my father. She also came from a large family, nine in total, but they worked on their farmland cohesively as a team. Each sibling used their skills to contribute to the family labor of farming and carpentry. In their garden, they grew fruits, vegetables, and herbs. Their clothes were washed by hand in a nearby creek, and they cooked over a wooden fire.

My mom's mother, Rosa Flores Lopez, was a tiny woman. Rosa had long, black hair with grey strands which she wore in a bun at the base of her neck. "Always do what you love," was her motto. Grandma Rosa was a great cook and midwife in her town. This little, amazing woman worked tirelessly on her farm providing for her nine children, educating them, and instilling in them her values and ethics they would carry with them throughout their life.

On April 5, 1988, a devastating house fire caused extreme smoke inhalation, and Rosa passed from this world to the next. I only knew Grandma Rosa for six years, but even in that short amount of time, as young as I was, she left a tremendous impression on me that made a substantial impact on my life. My grandmother continues to influence me from the other side as my guide.

Some people do not believe in card readers, intuitives, or mediums for various reasons. I was brought up a Catholic and then a member of The Church of Jesus Christ of Latter Days Saints. Both religions do not condone such things as card readings, but that did not stop my curiosity of learning more. *I have always seen things differently, even at a noticeably young age.* Five years ago, I gave in to the curiosity and decided to get a card reading. The reader I went to did not know who I was, but in that brief twenty-minute card reading, she knew me more than I could have imagined. This reading I had just for fun changed my life. In the first few minutes, the reader told me an older woman was saying, "Myrnita, Myrnita, do what you love, dance, be you, no matter what anyone says, it's normal. Be you!" I realized this older woman she spoke of was none other than my grandmother, Rosa. "You have my gifts," she said, "I am you; you are me!" My grandmother, Rosa Flora Lopez Cruz, is one of my ultimate ancestors who has guided me and continues to guide me in every aspect of my life.

My parents immigrated to the United States in search of a better life; my dad to escape his life from bondage, shame, and resentments; and my mom, whose dream was attending college. A few months after living in the U.S., my mother and my father were married in Brooklyn, New York, on February 2, 1963.

I was raised to speak in both English and Spanish, and at just six months old, I spoke my first words. I took my first steps at eight months, and by eighteen months, I was reciting commercials and their jingles while pointing out the billboards along the highways of New York. Instead of fantasy books, as a child, I was fascinated by encyclopedias. I found the writings of Nostradamus and Shakespeare captivating and enthusiastically read about UFOs. World History was my favorite subject—all the people who lived over thousands of years ago and the stories they had to tell. There is much we can learn from people in the past. At eight years old, I was like a sponge soaking up all the knowledge I could get my hands on. I would go to the library just to sit and read to collect all the information those many books contained. Not only did I venture to the library for myself, but also to aid my younger sisters with their schoolwork. My curiosity drew me to each section of the library, guiding me to the next topic I learned about.

I have always had this inner knowing, feeling guided to walk a certain way or another. I took a different route to school to later find out that there was a dangerous situation I would have encountered on the normal route (car accident, robbery, fire, etc.). I learned to trust these messages and follow their direction. They have never steered me wrong nor put me in harm's way, and for that, I'm grateful.

These messages have guided and shaped my life as I followed these extrasensory, gut feelings. Either a feeling or a whisper, I would listen. *Go this way. Do this instead of that.* After receiving a message, I would ask questions and then seek the answers to understand why I was guided that way.

There was a time in my life I believed everything I was taught. Growing up as a member of The Church of Jesus Christ of Latter-Day Saints, I followed the teachings without question. Then something changed, perhaps my inner rebel surfaced, and I began to question everything. The pivotal moment was when I became a missionary sister in Lima, Peru. I served this mission from 1983 to 1984. Our mission was to follow the guidelines of the gospel and teach those to others to convert them to the religion. As someone who was both a little too curious and rebellious, I was kicked out of Catholic School in third grade for asking too many questions. I was probably not the best person to be teaching a new religion to someone. You can imagine.

On that mission in Peru, converting others and introducing them to a new religion was more than a little challenging for me. I knew I was guided to knock on certain doors and not others. And I knew that following an eight-step protocol would not work every time and that simple teaching could be more efficient. We were given missionary companions, other sisters, to accompany us in our work. I had several sister transfers with the thought that each sister could help me get back on track to following the eight steps. Their effort was not successful. The best companion was from West Virginia, United States. We got along well and were able to go with the flow with each other. She understood my intuition, and because of the cohesiveness we had, we did manage to follow the eight-step program we were guided to do. Together we converted one woman from a small town in Huacho. This small town was such a humbling experience for both of us. They lived in huts and dirt floors, some of them not having shoes. I walked into the hut they called home wearing shoes and walked out barefooted. *They deserved those shoes more than I did.*

I only stayed in Peru for eight months and left my mission trip early. I became sick with an undiagnosed illness which caused me to vomit and expel blood from my bowels and urine for two months. After this, I was discharged as a missionary sister and left the religion to follow my own path, which led me to where I am today.

The path I took led me to work in the monotony an 8-to-5 job. I was successful, performed my duties, and often stayed late. The job paid the bills and allowed me to take care of myself and other responsibilities. As I continued in this typical five-day-a-week job, my passion began to fade. I felt as though I was not enough for the systems put into place and that I was a part of something that didn't work for me. Many others tend to face this challenge with their own careers. It's a normal thought about how life could be different and how you can regain that passion. Hint: You are evolving, do what you love. The repetitive work life made me ask myself, *what do I love?* I love to dance, have fun, know history, know geography, know telepathy, know guidance, visualize things, and feel things before they happen.

My grandmother Rosa always told me, "Be yourself, be who you are; that is enough." The world encouraged us that to be a lawyer, doctor, or teacher was enough. If it's who you are and what your passion takes you towards, I'm telling you that you're enough in anything you do which your heart desires.

The flow of life is constantly changing and evolving. Like a river that cuts through the land, it adapts, changing the landscape as it moves on. Life can change instantly; everything you have known, taken for granted, froze yet changed. My husband was in a severe hit-and-run accident. It was a simple fender-bender gone horribly wrong. A young woman, twenty years old, rear-ended my husband's Toyota Tundra. They went to the shoulder of the road to exchange insurance information when a third vehicle, a Dodge Ram pick-up truck, plowed into both vehicles, throwing the young woman into the oncoming traffic. Unfortunately, she did not survive. Tom, my husband, was also thrown. He saw his body rotate in the air and felt one shoe fly off during the impact. He landed onto the windshield face down and was then catapulted onto the chain-link fence, which caused him to tear his hamstring. This was the ultimate pivotal moment where my life as I knew it changed. The phone call announcing the accident is one I'll never forget. I felt abandonment, fear, and a menagerie of emotions that are simply indescribable.

My husband scathed death for a reason. Aside from the torn hamstring, he walked away with minor cuts and bruises. It's a miracle. I continued listening to my ancestors, guides, and past family members. I asked them to help me go deep and help others who've suffered from traumatic situations, but I had to help myself first. That's what I did. I was guided to do Reiki from a dear friend who was a reiki and crystal healer herself. Alongside her and my angel guides, I was healed from my past traumas. The accident gave me a choice. I could stay stuck in this fear, always being anxious about the dangers to come, or I could do something for others who have also experienced trauma. I chose to get counseling to heal myself mentally so that I could begin to assist others. I then chose to go back to school at 54 years old. I enrolled in massage school to help others with their physical ailments.

From there, I continued grief counseling while taking massage school classes and still attending that 9-5 job I was so desperate to leave. With barely enough room on the plate from more, I carried on while helping my daughter prepare for her next milestone of going to college. She said, "Mom, you got this; you know that you can do it, so do it!" And I did.

My soul tribe started to build, and I'm grateful to everyone who helped me learn to let the ego go and trust. After becoming a Reiki Master, I was guided to go deeper into another program, Integrated Energy Therapy®.

To honor my guides and my grandmother Rosa, I set the goal to complete the 12 DNA strands of trauma and receive my Master Practitioner and Teacher Certification. I graduated from massage school, then Craniosacral Therapy training with the Upledger Institute International. Craniosacral therapy allows me to see more than I ever have before. Only having the vision in my right eye, performing Craniosacral therapy opens my mind's eye, expanding my vision. I completed Integrated Energy Therapy to understand trapped trauma in the 12 DNA strands of memory. With Somato-Emotional Release, it helps rid the mind and body of residual effects of past trauma associated with negative experiences. Occasionally this trauma can last lifetimes, as it is passed down from one generation to the next. Healing your trauma helps to heal the trauma of those who came before. The body often retains physical forces and accompanying emotional energy triggered by physiological, emotional, or spiritual trauma. Now I know and can truly relate and create a safe space with all the tools handed to me early in life to value, facilitate, and guide you in your process to heal. There is no wonder everything happened the way it did. That was the way it was supposed to happen. It's how you have a positive outlook; search those roots, intuition, and guides to support you on your life path to become the best version of you.

"Make your mark in this world; you are valuable, you are a treasure."

THE TOOL

First, start by getting into a comfortable setting. It may be somewhere inside, like your home, car, a nook in the library, etc. Or it may be outside, in a park, on the beach, underneath a tree, etc. Anywhere you feel safe. Also, you may bring something with you, your favorite comforting piece. It may be a crystal, doll, truck, pillow, or that model you built that you were so proud of making and creating. It may be the very first image of what makes you happy, not anyone else's version of happy, yours (only you know this). It may even be an animal or pet. Now close your eyes. Sense yourself feeling limitless, beyond all labels (i.e., employee/employer, sibling, parent, etc.), beyond all systems (i.e., school, work, religions, etc.), and beyond the environment you were raised in. Go to that blissful place you have imagined in full screen. You might begin to see vivid imagery of colors you have never ever seen before, or maybe you have? If you are not visual, sense what you feel. Is there a tingling or warmth in your gut, belly, or heart? It is different for everyone. Open your senses as you let go of the worldly limits. Your body will start to meld, relax.

Place one hand on your chest and the other on your belly. Breathe. Take a deep breath through your nose for four seconds, hold for four seconds, then release out of your mouth for four seconds (Stinson 2018). 444 is an amazing angel number; see the works of Matt Beech, cited at the end, to learn more.

Once you get there, do you feel warmth or cold? Cold is higher vibrations from the realms. Do you feel their embrace? Do you smell that familiar scent that releases the tension on your jawline to smile as you are breathing? Some will see the light; some will see that beautiful waterfall garden with fantastic colors of butterflies. What you see is your world; you can create this; you are a creator. Stay with me until you're not thinking of anything but the place you are in this moment, present. You are a gift to yourself. Dive into it, cry it out, shed it out, scream it out you are safe, in this breathing.

You are you; you are love, you are amazing, you are safe, you are who you are always meant to be. You are releasing hindrance from your ancestor's trauma that they could not do. So now you are to go there and be the one that can speak for them, release it all. They only knew what they were taught.

"**YOU** are heard; **YOU** are a divine being of eternal light and unconditional love. **YOU** got this!"

Release the breathing come back, hug yourself, believe in yourself. Try to breathe every day. Start at ten minutes, then fifteen minutes. If you skip days, it's okay. It takes 21 days to create a habit you've never done before. It can take 14 days to notice a difference. This is a gradual change. Be gentle with yourself.

In time you will be awakened to conquer and reveal the best version of yourself.

References

The meaning of 444:

Beech, Matt. "Angel Number 444 Meaning: Decode the Message." *Matt Beech | Mystic*, mattbeech.com/repeating-numbers/444-meaning/.

Box Breathing:

Stinson, Adrienne. "Box Breathing: How to Do It, Benefits, and Tips." *Medical News Today*, MediLexicon International, 1 June 2018, www.medicalnewstoday.com/articles/321805.

Myrna Y. Triano is the Owner and Founder of TriAngelRivers, LLC – Gateway to Multidimensional Transformation. She is a Licensed Massage Therapist, Craniosacral Therapy Practitioner, Master Teacher, and Practitioner of Integrated Energy Therapy®.

Myrna is an old soul with wisdom and forward thinking. Her intuition has been present since her early childhood.

Myrna has suffered many ailments and conditions during her life thus far. From being blind in one eye, shingles, malaria, and gastrointestinal complications, she has undergone a long road to recovery. Through her healing process, Myrna began the path to help others with their own ailments. From this, TriAngel Rivers was born.

Myrna's versatile approach to healing is an expression of simple form. She is a soul activator and a light language communicator. Through her mental imagery, she scans your issues in your body, karmic and spiritual states.

Myrna's clients experience an energetic shift creating a glow and lightness in appearance. This is the visual of their true self being brought forth for expansion.

Myrna facilitates your process allowing change, growth, and healing. She is a motivator, innovator and is a bridge to your soul's mission.

To schedule your soul awakening, contact me at TriAngel Rivers:

Website: www.triangelrivers.com

Facebook: https://facebook.com/triangelrivers

Instagram: https://instagram.com/triangelrivers

OUR CAST OF AUTHORS, ARTISTS, AND ONLINE TOOLS

25 online tools and access points to reveal and heal the ancient memories you carry

Within these pages are more than 200 years of experience exploring the many ways we can work with our ancestral energies and gifts. Our 25 authors also provided the latest 2021 online tools for discovery, connection, and resolving ancestral patterns. It's our way of thanking you, and inviting you into our personal passion: discovering, embracing, and celebrating our ancestors.

It's my honor to present our cast of authors and artists on a more personal note, including their amazing on-line resources which they worked so hard to create for you, our reader. In order of their appearance:

Kevin Hutchins brings us his amazing artwork, Wakanda, which is an expression of the powers of the Great Spirit that moves through all life. You can see Kevin's artwork at https://www.chasingwolfcreations.com/

Chapter 1: Amy Gillespie Dougherty brings the gift of exploring your ancestral clues from within your own life, with her exercise that includes creating a personal timeline, family labyrinth and treasure map at www.amygillespie.com/resources

Chapter 2: Melissa J. Graves brings you an amazing tutorial of how to channel your ancestors, using crystals as the medium. https://euphoricsource.com/resources

Chapter 3: Asherah Allen uses her many years of training in spiritual traditions from around the world to guide you to weave your chakras with your ancestors' in order to enjoy deep connection, power, and healing. http://awakenedhearthealingarts.com/resources/

Chapter 4: Noah Smith unveils his incredible gift of channeling, which had been masked behind autism, in order to bring you the ancient whispering and messages of the ancestors. He is excited to be an author in this, his first book, though he has more planned in his future. https://www.sharonsweb.com/home/

Chapter 5: Sondra Lambert invites you and guides you in meditation to literally step onto the life-path of those who came before you, where they walked, and how they lived as you gather the soil of your ancestors to plant a sacred ancestral tree. https://www.galaxyhypnosis.com/sondra

Chapter 6: Lisa Newton takes you into an exercise of self-hypnosis to learn how to communicate with your ancestors, using the simplest tools of words and stones. https://earthaffirmations.com/

Chapter 7: Dr. Allison Brown uses her extensive experience in self-hypnosis and even deep-trance-channeling to guide you to release ancestral karma through spiritual hypnosis. http://drallisonbrown.com

Chapter 8: Jacqueline Kane guides you on how to reveal and become your authentic self as you release the unresolved emotional issues you've been carrying, that you didn't even know you had through her amazing soul activation meditation. http://www.jacquelinemkane.com/resources

Chapter 9: Deena Chester guides you through a past life regression exercise to access your ancestor's wisdom, in order to connect and embrace the power of your wisdom and talents. http://www.acceptyourpower.com/ancestorswithin/

Chapter 10: Carol Dutton empowers you to clearly recognize, visualize and write your ancestral story. She gives you the tools in her online link to make a profile that can become the cornerstone of your genealogy research and a sacred family keepsake. https://beingyouenergetically.com/resource/

Chapter 11: Tanya Harper-Colucci takes you on a deep shamanic journey so you can experience firsthand how to break the limiting patterns, by connecting with your ancestors.

https://www.sacredsoulguidance.com/resources

Chapter 12: Marcia Colver Reichert sings you into knowing your ancestors and to feel the incredible web of our lives and how we interact with their ancient experiences. Her online soundbath meditation gently helps you unravel and resolve their traumas.

https://marciacolver.com/ancestors-within-book/

Chapter 13: Michelle Troupe takes you on an incredible journey through the portal of ancestral healing in her heart space activation. The audio version gives you a deeper visualization experience of this activation at www.earthangelhealingllc.com/resources

Chapter 14: Phoenix Trueblood, walks you through how to reconnect your broken bonds and honor your ancestors while creating your own personal decree. http://www.PhoenixTrueblood.net

Chapter 15: Elizabeth R Kipp shares Ancestral Clearing® with you by guiding you to the deepest level of understanding and compassion for our ancestral lines and the ties that bind, inviting you resolve and heal the pattern for your entire lineage. https://elizabeth-kipp.com/resources/

Chapter 16: Dr. Ahriana Platten invites you to know the experience of traveling to your ancestral homeland, giving you the deep roots that support your beautiful and expansive life. Her chapter includes an invitation to subscribe to her monthly touch-point "Soul-full."

http://ahriana.com

Chapter 17: Robin Ivy Haywood walks you through an energetic rebalancing that will enhance your level of self-love to release and heal all energies that are less than that, which brings balance and healing to your ancestral lines. The link to her on-line audio of this exercise makes the experience even easier. https://www.haywakeup.co/freecontent/

Chapter 18: Crystal Rasmussen shares techniques to build a deep relationship with your Earth Ancestors and heal trauma that is passed down from one generation to another, supporting you in releasing pain and suffering from your ancient bloodline, that you inherently carry and experience from the moment of birth.

www.crystalrasmussen.com/ancestorswithindownload

Chapter 19: Arielle introduces you to Raking: An Energy Healing technique for removing relational toxicities, and allowing our ancestors to come through. She has also included a non-guided meditation to allow your vibration to rise so you can get in the vibrational range to receive from your ancestors. www.thecollectiveconsultation.com

Chapter 20: Jeanne Ruzchak-Eckmann takes you on her journey of doing ancestral research since grammar school. She then guides you on creating or enhancing your personal family tree to bring you to an amazing awareness of the ancestors within you. https://ancestralpassages.com/resources

Chapter 21: Rika Rivka Markel brings you an integrative meditation to help you heighten your awareness so you can access, discover and write about the hidden gems your ancestors are offering you. www.ancestrygems.com

Chapter 22: James Kealiipiilani Kawainui engages you in a deep visualization exercise in order to explore and experience what would happen when you connect to the wisdom of your ancestors and realize you don't have to carry their pain anymore. https://JamesKawainui.com

Chapter 23: Jen Piceno helps readers tap into ancestral power by sharing her Ancestral Wisdom & Magic Ritual. Get ready to align with everything you were meant to be in ways you've never experienced before. She guides readers into ancestral wisdom, magic, and power. www.JenPiceno.com/resources

Chapter 24: Jonianne Jeannette uses guided imagery to help you experience expansion, using the heart light of your spirit breath to connect through your heart and embrace the ancestors within you. www.jonnionthespot.com

Chapter 25: Myrna Rivera Triano teaches you a wholly unique experience of 444 moment breathing method to take you from stillness to awareness, then reset, recharge and repeat. This amazing tool can help you to change repeat patterns with mindful practice. https://triangelrivers.com/myrnas-blog/

CLOSING CHAPTER

Thank you for discovering, engaging, and embracing your ancestors by reading *The Ancestors Within: Reveal and Heal the Ancient Memories You Carry.*

Some of you bought this book because you had questions. You wanted to know more about your ancestors, who they were, where they lived, what they were about, and how they show up in your life.

Some of you had genealogy records going back hundreds of years. Some of you had DNA results in hand, telling you where your ancestors had lived during a certain time. Some of you were stuck in your ancestral research.

Some of you had no connection with, or even knowledge of your ancestors, only personal experiences, talents, and interests, along with the face that looks back from the mirror. And that's okay. That's part of your story. The next "chapter of you" is about to be written in the cosmos of time.

No matter what you had when you started this book, you have more now: techniques, clues, perceptions, even answers, or the tools to uncover them.

Twenty-five authors dug deep within themselves to find their best tool, the one that would help you ignite a deeper relationship with your ancestors and a deeper understanding of your life.

Each author had a sincere desire that readers would experience an "aha!" or a monumental shift in awareness, along with a new sensitivity and understanding of ancestral reflections and impacts in their current lives. We all tried to offer *the one story* you couldn't wait to share with friends and family.

Each of us would love to hear your feedback and experience using the tools we've offered. Please post your reviews and comments at https://www.facebook.com/groups/ancestorswithin

Your ancestors call you to your best life, your best experiences, and your best connection to them. Most of all, they are calling you to the person you were born to become.

Your story is an ever-changing novel of you.

YOUR ANCESTORS HAVE WAITED YOUR WHOLE LIFE

FOR THIS MOMENT!

AND THE NEXT!

MY PERSONAL ACKNOWLEDGEMENTS

My greatest gratitude to Daniel Dougherty, my amazing husband, who supports me through these last-minute creations and changes in plans. You're my guiding light and my anchor. I learn from you every day, and you make my life an adventure.

Huge and humble grace and thanks for my adopted parents, my brother, Tim, and my whole adopted family. When I was an infant, you took me in as your own, and I love you all so dearly.

To my birthmother, who watches over me from the heavens, as do all my ancestors. Thank you for bringing me into this life and for having the grace and wisdom to place me in another home until we could meet again. I'm so grateful for the 18 years we had together and for our continued connection from the *other side.*

To my birthfather for taking the chance in saying "yes" to meeting me as an adult after all those years: Having a relationship with you is the great surprise of my life. It's the little girl's dream I never imagined could come true. Thank you for tolerating all my questions about family and my unending requests to hear stories about you and your life.

To all of my biological family, for being willing to meet and get to know me, the lost relative most of you knew nothing about: You can't imagine the joy I feel in getting to know each of you. I respect how my appearance from nowhere must have been a shock, at best, and inconvenient at times, a kind of oddity that is difficult to explain. Bless you, one and all. Getting to know you is one of the greatest blessings of my life. Bucket list achieved.

Heartfelt gratitude to friends, family, and mentors who have supported and encouraged me throughout my life. Your support and insight help me in my quest to make the world a better place by spreading awareness of our connections through bloodline and experience. You've been cheering me on to write since my earliest years, and I wouldn't be here without your support and belief in me.

My Irigenics™ team: Those who have patiently been through the start-up of my business, social presence, and changes in direction: You are all amazing. It's my honor to work with you and learn from you.

Lynne Adams: The most amazing engagement editor and virtual assistant ever! https://theengagementeditor.com How you have taught me, tolerated me, inspired me, made me look better on my websites and social media than I ever could. You amaze me every time we connect. Thank you!

To my editor, Cheri Colburn, who's an amazing developmental editor with an incredible gift for matching the voice of her authors: Thank you for helping me comb through pages of my books, trimming them into thoughtful, engaging experiences for my readers. https://thegreenquill.com/

Tracie Bennett, thank you for making up for my lack of interest in punctuation and for your amazing work with dinosaurs.

Lisa Karasek, thank you so much for introducing me to Laura Di Franco, Brave Healer Productions, and this amazing adventure.

AN OVERFLOW OF GRATITUDE AND GRACE

I want to purposefully close this book with the energy of gratitude and grace in hopes that you will experience the same wave of emotion for the people and experiences that bless your life.

Being adopted, I grew up with a sense of grace in everything. I could have been placed into any number of households. The adoption agent could have picked up a different application and matched it to me. At any point, even before I drew my first breath, my life could have taken a completely different trajectory. But I was given a loving family and a good life: Every moment of my life has been filled with gratitude and grace.

My thanks go to God and the spirit of this vision to bring our world together to discover, engage, and embrace our ancestors. There has been such a tremendous Divine force and energy behind this book, and words can't express the deep pool of overwhelming gratitude I feel in my heart as these words, the words of twenty-five authors, come into print.

A huge, heartfelt thanks to Laura Di Franco for her amazing vision and guidance at Brave Healer Productions and dealing with my scattered messages and newbie mistakes in bringing this first collaborative book to publication.

To Lori Calvo, Dino Marino, and every member of the team at Brave Healer Productions, thank you for making this amazing book as beautiful as the words inside its chapters! You are the unsung heroes of this book, crafting and cleaning our words, pages, and covers.

Kevin Hutchins, thank you for granting us license to use your amazing spiritual artwork, "Wakanda," on our cover and for being on this journey with us. Your art from Chasing Wolf Creations is amazing, and I hope to see you as an author in one of our future books. Find Kevin's work at www.chasingwolfcreations.com

TO EACH AND EVERY ONE OF OUR AUTHORS, thank you for sharing your years of experience, study, and amazing gifts. You touch countless lives with all you do as a resource for transformation and ancestral connection. Thank you for saying yes to bringing your amazing talents, tools, and resources to our readers.

You are the power within these pages, and I dearly trust and am in awe of your work and your personal visions and tools for making ancestral connections. Your willingness to share your perspectives, along with your mission to leave our world a better place, inspire and uplift us all. Your willingness to participate in the journey of *The Ancestors Within* is now written in the super-conscious of our universe. Thank you!

Thank you to those who have reviewed and endorsed this book, who have supported our launch, and who propel us forward to the next book in this series. Special thanks to Tracee Dunblazier of COVR and Alison DeNicola of U.S. Games for taking time out of your busy schedule to review this book before our publication.

HUGE GRATITUDE TO YOU, OUR READER. You've taken a bold step to reach out and connect with the ancestors within you. I applaud you for not only seeking a personal relationship with your ancestors but actually taking this first step in exploring new tools to do so. By creating a wonderful world for yourself, you create a wonderful world for everyone around you—my deepest gratitude and thanks.

Share your personal experience of The Ancestors Within at https://www.facebook.com/groups/ancestorswithin

Have you tried the tools in this book? Have you worked with one of our amazing authors? Go to https://www.facebook.com/groups/ancestorswithin and become a member of The Ancestors Within Community on Facebook. We will soon be inviting you to learn more about the Ancestral Summit www.amygillespie.com/summit

Join the AUTHOR TEAM for the next
THE ANCESTORS WITHIN book!

Brave Healer Productions is now accepting applications to be part of the next book in "The Ancestors Within" series!

You're a teacher, healer, genealogist, scientist, life-skills coach, or Shaman, with a special voice and perspective for ancestral connections.

You currently bring your amazing gifts and talents for working with ancestry to our world through your business or non-profit, and are ready to bring your message and tools to our world in a bigger way!

Contributing a chapter to this collaborative project is much more than just having your name on a book.

It's about being a part of our community of ancestral trailblazers, working to change the world with innovative words, ideas, and tools.

As an author, you will share your story and teach an effective tool for discovering, connecting, engaging, or embracing ancestral connections as shared in your story. You will also have opportunities to do live training, podcast interviews, and business development activities as a part of the Brave Healer Productions family.

We can't wait to hear your story. Submit your application today! www.amygillespie.com/summit

YOUR ANCESTORS HAVE WAITED YOUR WHOLE LIFE
FOR THIS MOMENT...AND THE NEXT

ABOUT THE AUTHOR

Amy Gillespie Dougherty

Founder of Irigenics™ Ancestral Eye Reading

CLARA (Children's Lives Are the Responsibility of All).

Amy is a results-driven innovator, speaker, and bestselling author with more than twenty years' experience creating impactful self-discovery, awareness, and life-coaching programs. Amy's corporate experience in systems performance and disaster relief proved invaluable in creating survival skills programs for children and disadvantaged families in third-world countries. She received accolades from USAID and the U.S. Embassy for training programs she created in Mozambique through her non-profit, TIOS (now CLARA: Children's Lives Are the Responsibility of All).

Thriving as a trailblazer, Amy returned to the U.S. to create Irigenics™ Ancestral Eye Reading, developed as another survival skills program because the technique reduces self-destructive behaviors and suicide patterns in teens and young adults.

Amy believes in the power of the ancestral pulse within each of us and our ability to reach the best of our best. She has directly helped thousands of people understand the *rest of their story* by interpreting their ancestral and epigenetic patterns. She's given motivational speeches and interactive self-discovery workshops at Boys and Girls Club and the Department of Corrections. Amy does all of this with one goal in mind: To create new programs and systems that guide young adults to an earlier sense of life purpose, along with the ability to become the person they were born to be.

She has taught this innovative self-discovery approach to social workers and holistic practitioners to help them uncover their clients' true gifts and talents. She's inspired to continue teaching practitioners to recognize and assess ancestral information for their clients' best results. Moving the practitioner from being *one of the many* who offer traditional techniques to *the one* who uses this dynamic method to interpret ancestral patterns in their clients' lives.

If you want to become *THE ONE* to take your clients to the next level with this amazing training, click here: www.irigenics.com/training

OTHER BOOKS BY AUTHOR, AMY GILLESPIE DOUGHERTY

SIX YEARS IN MOZAMBIQUE: THINGS I HAVEN'T TOLD MOM

(by Amy Gillespie)

Six Years in Mozambique is the autobiographical account of Amy's six years creating survival skills training programs in Sub-Saharan Africa. As a woman of 39 years and no experience in aid work, HIV prevention, or even foreign languages, Amy forged forward to create life-saving skills programs in six orphan projects and schools in Mozambique. *Six Years* takes you on a breathless ride through the realities and grit of aid work in Africa, where using your common sense can effect a huge change in the lives of children.

THE LOST SCRIBE: FORGOTTEN CHANNEL OF THE ANCIENTS

(by Amy Gillespie)

The Lost Scribe is the first fiction book in the Maddie Clare Owens (MCO) series, a collection of novels Amy is co-writing with her husband Daniel Dougherty. This book embraces Amy's experiences working in Guatemala as part of her survival skills training programs, including a deeply channeled message from Melchiezedek about the workings of the Universe. *The Lost Scribe* seamlessly weaves together fiction and non-fiction, as Maddie Clare Owens finds herself thrown into a world of mysticism, corruption, and danger, not knowing whom to trust. Amy and Daniel look forward to the next MCO Book, which embraces the world of intricate ancestral synchronicities in our current lives.

THE ULTIMATE GUIDE TO SELF-HEALING, VOLUME 4

Chapter 6: Resolving Cellular Memory: Your Ancestors Have Waited Your Whole Life for THIS Moment.

By Amy Gillespie

Amy takes you on a journey into the deepest cellular memories of your life, your in-utero experiences, by having you meet your birth parents before you were conceived. Her audio tool will guide you through this walking visualization exercise to reset your internal dialogue by establishing a compassionate understanding of the first moments of the creation of you.

To learn more about her books, click here: https://amygillespie.com/

Made in the USA
Middletown, DE
11 August 2022

71176060R00144